Dear Harry, thank you
so much for your help
and fellowship.

John + Howard.
May. '83.

Repairing & Restoring
ANTIQUES

REPAIRING

AND

RESTORING

ANTIQUES

with an Introduction by

DENNIS YOUNG

First published in Great Britain in 1974 as
Encyclopedia of Antique Restoration and Maintenance
by Studio Vista

First published under this title in 1979 by
Ward Lock Ltd.

This edition published by Peerage Books
59 Grosvenor Street
London W1

by arrangement with Cameron Books Ltd
2A Roman Way
London N7 8XG

© 1974 Carter Nash Cameron Ltd

ISBN 0 907408 65 6

Printed in Czechoslovakia

50498

Introduction

One of the great joys in collecting rare and beautiful things is to cherish them by making sure that they are preserved and maintained in good condition. The greater one's knowledge of the materials and methods used to produce them, the better one is able to look after one's possessions. This is where this book is of particular and outstanding value. Each section has been written with the help of a specialist or group of experts, covering not only the best ways of looking after and repairing particular objects, but also explaining from what and how they were made. The book tells you how to maintain your antiques (this may mean no more than careful cleaning and dusting, but there are correct methods for doing even this!), and also what *you* can do if something more radical than cleaning is required.

The purchase of a very badly damaged antique should be considered very carefully. You may find that the price seems extremely low, but this could easily work out to be considerably more expensive than buying a perfect example, because of the high cost of getting it repaired and restored by a specialist. If, however, you feel you have the time and skill to do it yourself, this could be a worthwhile proposition.

If you decide to go ahead with the cleaning or restoring of a valuable antique object, you must take your own ability into account. It cannot be stressed too often that, if in doubt about cleaning or repairing a valuable object, consult an expert in that particular field and accept his guidance. He may be able to undertake the necessary work himself or suggest a suitable specialist craftsman. All major museums have their own conservation departments to attend to the works of art in their care, and many antique dealers employ specialist craftsmen.

To back up the information given in this book, further books should be consulted for more comprehensive historical or technical details. Visit museums, art galleries and other collections to study actual pieces similar to your own. This is really the only way to get to know and appreciate actual craftsmanship. Watching an expert restorer at work, if he will allow you to, or attending classes or courses on the restoration and care of antiques can be of great value. Watching and working under instruction is without doubt the best way to broaden and deepen your knowledge of techniques and the skill in applying them. Again, there are many clubs and societies which you can join, either covering antiques in general or specialising in one particular aspect of antique restoration, e.g. chair caning, upholstery, mounting and framing pictures etc.

During recent years, the shortage of craftsmen skilled in the art of restoration has become increasingly apparent, and as a result various specialist training schemes are coming into being. In Britain, the most important of these is being undertaken at West Dean College, Chichester, Sussex. Organised in conjunction with the British Antique Dealers' Association, the college at present runs three twelve-month courses for professionals, on furniture, clocks and tapestry. In addition, short residential courses of two to five days are held for amateurs. These cover a wide range of crafts—wood carving, basic china mending and restoration, caring for antique furniture etc.

Although my own collection of antiques is somewhat that of a magpie, furniture has always been my first love, linked with my work as a furniture and interior designer. Furniture has always been designed to meet the requirements of the particular period for which it was made, relating to the way of life, the styles and fashions of the time. When renovating furniture, you should always try to maintain the original qualities and features of the piece. To illustrate what I mean, let me quote two examples.

Mahogany chests-of-drawers made in the early 19th century were often fitted with wooden drawer knobs, and I feel that these should not be replaced with brass handles (often done to give an 18th century look to a piece). The Victorians, however, were guilty of removing brass handles found on earlier chests-of-drawers and fitting wooden knobs to make them look more modern. With such a piece you would be justified in making a change.

The second example concerns upholstered chairs. These have often been re-covered many times throughout their life. When covering chairs yourself always try to come as close to the original style of material as possible. Occasionally you find that a number of covers have been tacked on over the original. Although this will almost certainly be in too poor a condition to leave on, it will be a guide in choosing material for the new cover. Where there is no clue as to what the original cover was like, a visit to a museum, or consulting illustrated books on the subject, should help you to make the correct choice.

A word of warning before you start either cleaning or

repairing anything. Work very carefully, taking your time. If it is a matter of cleaning, test your method first on a small area which is not normally visible. If it is a matter of making a repair, try out the technique first on odd pieces of similar material. My words of caution stem from a lesson I learnt many years ago. I found an early 19th century oil painting of a tea clipper in full sail in a junk shop and bought it for five shillings. It was covered with dirt and grime. In my haste to clean it, using turps substitute on the middle of the picture, I removed a considerable area of the finely detailed rigging! A costly mistake, as I discovered years later when I came to sell the picture. So, I stress, 'better safe than sorry'.

This warning can be carried further with the insurance of any antiques you may own. With the ever-increasing value of all antiques, it you have not already insured your works of art, or it is some years since they were valued, some action should be taken. It is difficult to place a purely monetary value upon a treasured personal possession, but at least there is some compensation if loss or damage does occur. A point to bear in mind in this connection is, that after careful restoration, an antique piece will probably be worth considerably more, but poor workmanship can reduce its value. Keeping a photographic record of your silver, jewellery, antique furniture etc., can be of great assistance to the police in tracing stolen goods, as well as acting as a reference for yourself for the restoration of pieces if they become badly damaged in some way.

I hope this book helps you to realise what you can do for yourself in this fascinating field, given time and patience, and also extends your understanding of the problems facing the professional restorer in what he has to undertake. Let me finish by wishing you good luck and many hours of pleasure in preserving and bringing back to somewhere near their former glory, a few of the treasures of our forefathers. They are part of our heritage, linking the past with the present, and we can hand on to future generations, through our love and care, irreplaceable examples of craftsmanship and beauty.

DENNIS YOUNG

About This Book

This book is designed to provide specific guidance on how to care for and restore a wide range of antiques. It gives full instructions for the processes you can carry out yourself, and also indicates the more elaborate restoring techniques which require professional skill and costly equipment.

The main section of the book is alphabetically arranged under materials, e.g. mother-of-pearl, papier mâché, tortoiseshell, and categories of antiques, e.g. clocks, furniture, mirrors, etc. Information on materials and tools with a general application in restoring has been placed in two appendices at the end of the book. The main section has been provided with a comprehensive system of cross-references represented by asterisks in the text which will always direct the reader to an entry listed under the word following the asterisk. Cross references are always indicated upon their first appearance in any entry: subsequent mentions are unmarked.

Some examples should help clarify the system. Suppose that you have a cracked, chipped or broken wine glass. You should turn to the entry **Glass** in the main section of the book. There, below a general description and history of glass, you will find sub-sections on aspects of its care and repair: Cleaning and general care; Removing stains; Grinding out chips and glass cutting; Repair. In the section on cleaning, the use of *ammonia is recommended: you are thus referred to the entry in Appendix I, which deals with all the most important abrasives, adhesives, chemicals, compounds and cleaners mentioned in the main text. The ammonia entry mentions its other uses, the fact that it is generally sold as a 10% solution in water, and gives an indication of the precautions to be observed while using it. Similarly, the section on glass repair recommends *epoxy resin adhesives. Reference to this entry in Appendix I reveals the conditions under which these adhesives should be used, the other materials for which they are suitable, and a widely available proprietory brand.

For a more complicated example, imagine you have an upholstered chair in poor repair requiring attention to its structure, and upholstery. Clearly you will need to remedy structural problems before going on to deal with the upholstery of the chair. Information on *structural* repairs to furniture, e.g. mending the chair leg, will be found under the entry **Furniture: chair and table legs.** When you have repaired the leg and you need to re-polish the wood, the text will refer you to **Wood: finishes.** For re-covering the chair, instructions will be found under **Furniture: upholstery.** If you seek guidance on caring for the fabric of the newly upholstered seat, you should consult the entry on **Textiles,** or possibly **Carpets and Tapestries,** if the seat was, for example, covered in needlepoint.

This book tells you the best ways of storing and maintaining your antiques, protecting them against deterioration and damage. Knowledgeable care protects not only their beauty but also their value. Two points to bear in mind when consulting this book are:

(i) If you are in any doubt at all as to how to treat an object, don't attempt it without expert help and guidance.

(ii) If you know, or suspect that something is valuable, take it to an expert for assessment and valuation.

While we have indicated wherever possible that certain acids, alkalis, synthetic resins etc. are very dangerous, few chemicals are completely harmless and it is a good idea to take certain basic precautions when using them. Always wear rubber gloves and protect your skin, and in particular your eyes. Avoid breathing in any vapours or fumes which may be given off, working in a well-ventilated room. It is a good general rule not to smoke whenever handling chemicals or plastics of any sort.

Contents

ALABASTER

The name alabaster is applied to two different materials: a hard, marble-like, translucent, lime carbonate which was much used by the Egyptians, as well as in the Middle East and China; and a lime sulphate, a smooth translucent, fine-grained material which is softer than the lime carbonate sort and slightly soluble in water. It was used extensively in Europe during the late Middle Ages, and has been ever since.

Alabaster is less durable than marble, which it somewhat resembles. It is much more easily carved, and has therefore often been popular for sculpture. It can be white or yellowish, brown or pink, and it is sometimes veined or cloudy due to impurities. It has been found in France, Germany, England and Italy. The purest colours are found in the Near East. It will take a high polish, but it is very soft and easily scratched or bruised. It is most suitable for small sculpture and for work that can be protected from the weather.

It was very popular in the Middle Ages for retables, tomb effigies, small statuettes for placing on the altar and other church ornaments, especially as its surface would take paint without an underlying ground of gesso.

Alabaster declined as a medium for sculpture generally during the Renaissance, but returned to popularity in the 18th century for clock pedestals and similar ornaments in conjunction with ormolu mounts. It was also occasionally used for table tops (which have rarely survived intact), chimney pieces and other large decorative works. It has been used by modern sculptors, but its rather precious effect with its smooth, polished surface has generally limited its popularity to small ornamental objects, such as vases, lamp stands and ashtrays.

As alabaster is porous and may, when extremely soft, be almost soluble, water should never be used to clean it. Instead, use *white spirit, applied with a cloth or a soft brush. Never use acids to clean alabaster as they act upon it and will eventually dissolve it. If white spirit fails to remove stains, try *petrol, *alcohol, *acetone or *benzene. Petrol is suitable for fatty matter, alcohol for resinous matter, and acetone and benzene for materials of an organic nature. Paint solvent can also be tried. Whatever you use, always experiment first with a small, inconspicuous area. If the article has painted decoration, be careful not to damage it with paint strippers.

When you have removed the stain, clean the area with a little white spirit.

Alabaster ashtrays should be regarded as decorative rather than practical objects, as they quickly become stained.

Alabaster may be polished with wax furniture polish in sparing amounts.

If breaks have already been mended with glue, the joints will probably have become unsightly and dark brown with time. The old glue should be removed by applying little pads of cottonwool, which has been soaked in hot water and squeezed out, to the joint, and leaving them there for some time. This treatment will soften the glue, and the pieces will come apart. The surface of the break should then be wiped clean of glue with swabs of cottonwool moistened with hot water. The corrosive effect of water is not so serious here as upon the surface of the object, but it is advisable to keep the clean alabaster as dry as possible. If stains from the glue remain, gently swab them with cottonwool soaked in warm water containing about 20% *ammonia. If the stain is obstinate, leave the ammonia swab on it for up to an hour. Always work on a small area at a time, and test the result by letting the area dry out and polishing it to the same extent as the unstained part. This is important, because it may look lighter before polishing than it does afterwards.

The correct glue to use is *polyvinyl acetate emulsion. The surfaces should be thoroughly clean and dry before applying a thin layer of adhesive. During the setting time, the pieces should be firmly clamped together with strips of self-adhesive tape placed at right angles to the join.

Missing pieces can be replaced with melted *microcrystalline wax coloured with a little powder pigment. They can either be modelled with heated tools, or made with the help of a mould, provided a prototype exists. Veining can be painted in with acrylic colours after the filler has set.

AMBER

Amber is often thought of as semi-precious stone, but it is in fact a fossilised resin found in long-buried forests of fir trees. It is usually yellow, orange or gold, but it can also be brown and almost black.

It is made into necklaces, pendants, pipes, etc. Strings of amber beads were particularly popular in the 1890s. Artificial amber is made from copal resin, camphor and turpentine. It can be distinguished from real amber by its solubility in ether. Pressed amber is made by fusing small pieces together.

Amber can be cleaned with soap and water. If it is much discoloured or ingrained with dirt, rub it carefully with a little *French chalk on a damp cloth. *Don't* use spirits or other organic solvents such as alcohol or acetone, as they will soften and dissolve the resin. After cleaning, buff and finish with *microcrystalline wax.

Split or broken amber can be joined with a *celluloid cement or with an *epoxy resin adhesive. Before applying the adhesive, thoroughly clean, de-grease and abrade the surfaces to be joined.

BAMBOO

Bamboo furniture was very popular in the late Victorian period, so any surviving pieces are likely to be rather rickety because bamboo is not a very strong material. It was chiefly made into hall stands and tables.

A Victorian bamboo hall stand.

Bamboo can be washed with soap and water or salt water, and dried. It can be polished with a silicone furniture cream, *linseed oil, or a good wax polish.

Any major repairs will probably involve careful dowelling and glueing, because bamboo seldom breaks cleanly but tends to split into fibrous splinters. Insert a wooden dowel or rod through the middle of the bamboo to provide strengthening and help for sticking the splinters down again. As bamboo is closed off at each ring in its structure, you will have to bore through these rings in order to push the dowel through. This can be done with a heated poker or a steel rod with which you can burn the rings away inside. (Wear oven gloves or grip the poker in a pair of pliers.) Don't heat too much, or you may burn the wood.

If the bamboo is much frayed, you may have to cut some of it away. As grafting pieces of bamboo together is fairly messy and unsatisfactory, try to bridge gaps with some *plastic wood or *epoxy putty of a suitable colour. Then give the bamboo a coat of wax polish, which will bring up and preserve a good shine. If you want a waterproof finish, clean off any old wax or polish with a solvent and then spray on a coat of *polyurethane lacquer.

BAROMETERS

A barometer is an instrument measuring atmospheric pressure. It consists of a column of mercury enclosed in a glass tube which is sealed at the top and open and exposed to air pressure at the bottom. Variations in air pressure move the mercury up and down the tube. The instrument is used to forecast the weather. Aneroid barometers, which work on a different principle, did not become widely available until c1850.

Mercury barometers were first developed in the 1640s. By 1700 they had become pieces of furniture in their own right and often had handsome wooden cases.

Early scales were of silvered brass with engraved letters and numerals. They may become tarnished or worn. If so, they need to be professionally resilvered and engraved.

Later scales were made of ivory with letters and numerals hand-stamped or engraved on the ivory. Ivory scales can be cleaned by lightly washing with warm, soapy

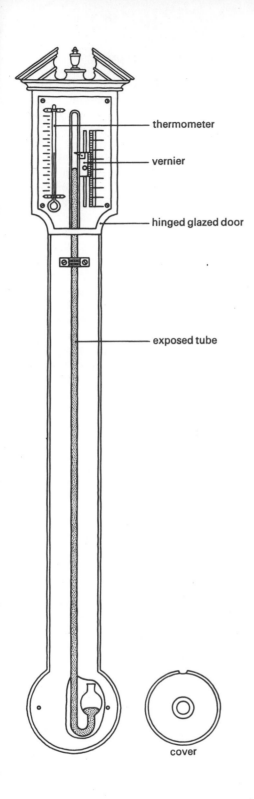

thermometer

vernier

hinged glazed door

exposed tube

cover

Stick barometer with cover removed to show bulb-type cistern.

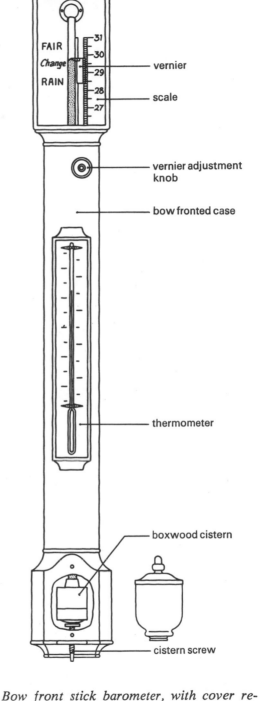

FAIR

Change

RAIN

31
30
29
28
27

vernier

scale

vernier adjustment knob

bow fronted case

thermometer

boxwood cistern

cistern screw

Bow front stick barometer, with cover removed to show boxwood cistern. The cistern screw is tightened to raise the column of mercury to the top of the tube when the instrument is moved, and is not for adjustment.

17

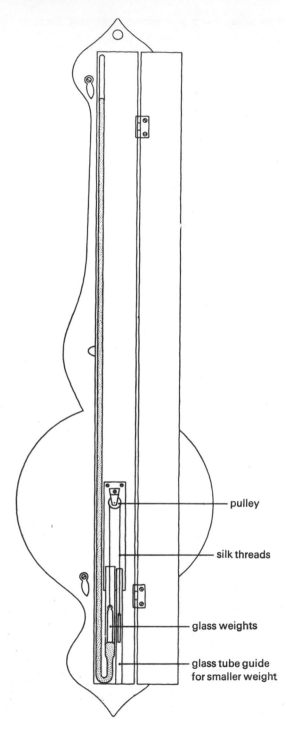

Mercury wheel barometer, with door at back opened to show bent or siphon tube.

— pulley

— silk threads

— glass weights

— glass tube guide for smaller weight

Scales may also be made of porcelain. These may be cleaned by washing with warm water and soft soap or washing-up liquid. Letters and numerals on porcelain scales can be repainted if you have a steady hand.

There are two main types of mercury barometer: stick or marine barometers, and wheel or banjo barometers, made of brass, ivory or wood. (*See* the entry for the appropriate material for advice on cleaning and repairs.)

Stick marine barometers

These have a direct-reading tube on an ivory scale. The case may be made of brass, ivory or wood. If the scale is really badly damaged, cracked or chipped, a complete new scale can be fitted. A broken tube can be replaced, but this has to be done by an expert restorer: every barometer of this type has to have a tube specially made for it since no two are identical. If both the case and the tube require attention, the case should always be dealt with *before* any work is undertaken on the tube.

Wheel or banjo barometers

These have a revolving pointer on a dial to indicate the reading. The dials are usually of silvered brass. Sometimes a thermometer is incorporated which can be replaced by a new one if it breaks or is missing. New mercury tubes are obtainable and can be fitted at home. Note that any work on the case should be done beforehand.

Once a barometer is in good working order, very little should go wrong with its mechanism. If it does stick or become erratic in its movement, it probably means that dust has got into the tube between the glass weights and the mercury. To treat, remove the barometer from the wall, taking care to keep it upright. Lay it face down, gently, always keeping it at a 45° angle. This is particularly important, as it prevents air bubbles getting into the mercury. A good tip to ensure the barometer remains at an angle is to balance it on, for example, a pile of books. Barometer workers use specially made baize-covered blocks.

Open the back of the barometer (usually a long, thin hinged door). Place an index finger on the silk thread holding the long glass weight in the end of the tube While

water; don't use a detergent. Go over letters and numerals carefully with a black wax crayon in order to re-black them.

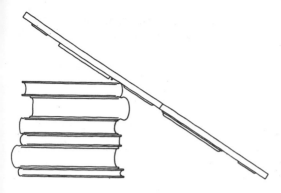

A pile of books can be used to support the barometer at the correct angle.

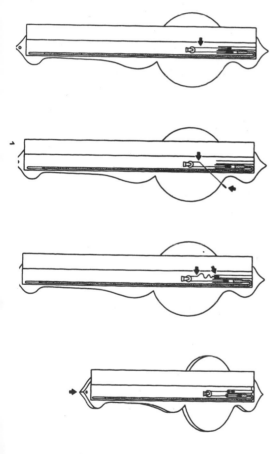

(a) *Place index finger on silk thread (1), and with the other hand remove weight (2).*
(b) *Keeping finger on thread, polish weight with cloth.*
(c) *Keeping thread taut, replace weight.*
(d) *Bring barometer slowly upright, so that weight slides into place.*

working, keep a finger on the silk thread. With the other hand, gently extract the weight. Polish with a clean cloth to remove the dust and replace it. If there are two tubes, repeat this process for the second weight. Close the back.

Bring the barometer slowly upright so that the weight slides gently back into position, and rehang.

Note that the procedure for removing a barometer from the wall and keeping it at an angle of 45° should be followed every time it has to be moved, for whatever reason. This rule applies to all types of barometer except the aneroid barometer.

It is a fairly simple matter to replace a cracked or broken glass face. This should be carried out by a professional restorer, as the new glass has to be ground into the bezel to fit properly and securely.

Aneroid barometer

This type of barometer measures air pressure by its action on a series of partially evacuated chambers within the barometer, rather than by the height of a column of mercury. It is set to give a reading correct at sea level, and must be adjusted in order to be used at any altitude above sea level. If this type of barometer malfunctions, it is usually because of one of two reasons. One, the vacuum seal may have perished. If this

Detail of a 19th century aneroid barometer from Queen Victoria's yacht, the S.S. Victoria & Albert.

has happened there is nothing that you can do yourself, but a completely new part can be fitted. Alternatively, the centre spindle of the barometer has been knocked and has bent. It can be straightened, but should not be attempted at home as the mechanism is very delicate.

BASKETWORK
Basketwork, *canework, and *wickerwork all respond to the same cleaning treatment and to the same basic method for repairing unravelled pieces.

To clean, simply wash thoroughly with soap and warm water using a nail brush or soft rag, then rinse with clear water and dry well. If possible, place the piece of furniture in the sun where it will bleach a slightly lighter colour. Another way to bleach is to wash with a very diluted domestic bleach after cleaning and allow to stand for about half an hour before rinsing with clear water.

When basketwork or canework has become unravelled, thread back into position and stick with a strong waterproof adhesive. Leave for a day. The pieces may need binding together until the glue has set hard. You should then polish the furniture with a good silicone wax polish using a cloth and soft bristle brush.

To protect basketwork, etc., from grime and reduce the chances of splitting and breaking, protect with a clean *polyurethane lacquer.

BONE
It is difficult to distinguish bone from ivory. Some guidelines for identification are as follows. Bone cannot be deeply carved because its centre is coarse-grained and has a sponge-like structure. Bone does not polish to the same smooth sheen as ivory. Bone objects tend to be more utilitarian, for example, lace bobbins, needles, pieces for games and handles. Both bone and ivory, however, are made of the same constituents, and so the treatment for the cleaning and repair is the same. *See* Ivory.

BOOKS
The first books printed in movable type appeared in Germany in the 15th century. Bindings were usually leather, although valuable books were also put between wooden, ivory and silver covers. Cloth bindings came into general use in the 19th century.

Books are liable to be attacked by insects. Silver fish like damp conditions and eat moulds, old glues, pastes and size. Fire brat thrive on warm conditions and a similar diet. Book lice eat fungi and leather bindings. Woodworm will eat any part of a book. Cleanliness will prevent all these insects thriving. Always dust books, particularly secondhand ones, before putting them on the shelves, behind glass. Shelves can be sprayed with insecticide or painted with an insecticide lacquer. Check your shelving for woodworm.

A page may have to be removed from a book for treatment. To do this, put a wet string against the page near the hinge; after a minute the page can be torn out easily. After treatment paste the page back with *flour paste, backing the join with a strip of mulberry paper or acid-free tissue paper. Make sure to align the page with the other pages. There is also a non-shiny self-adhesive tape which does a better job than the ordinary self-adhesive tapes, which tend to harden and darken. (For cleaning and restoration of pages *see* paper.)

Leather bindings
These are subject to chemical decay caused by the absorption of sulphuric acid from the atmosphere. This decay can first be detected by cracks along the top inside hinges of the book. In decay's most advanced stages the leather will disintegrate into a reddish-brown powder. Modern leather bindings are usually treated with *potassium lactate before binding. Such bindings should never be washed because this will remove the protection.

Leather bindings can be cleaned as follows. If the binding is extremely dirty, wash it with soap and water. Leave the book standing open and allow the binding to dry naturally. Dressing can then be put on the binding which will consolidate superficial powdery decay and retard the effects of wear and tear. *British Museum Leather Dressing is very good. Rub it into the leather, leave for two days, and then polish.

Vellum bindings
These can be sponged clean with a little water and dried at room temperature.

Victorian leather bindings and decorated cloth bindings.

*British Museum Leather Dressing can then be used, but sparingly, as vellum will not absorb much. The binding can be polished several hours later.. A good tip for cleaning and restoring the creamy colour of vellum is to use a piece of clean, soft cloth dipped in milk.

Cloth bindings

The sheen and colour of a cloth binding, can be restored by using one of the proprietary cloth cleaning fluids now obtainable. A point to remember when using one of these is that it should always be applied to the binding with a soft cloth. Applying it directly to the cloth binding and then attempting to polish it only marks the binding.

A professional bookbinder can renew a complete binding, replace a broken spine, resew or restick pages and trim them if they are irregularly torn.

BOULLE

Boulle work is a type of decoration for furniture and wooden objects, boxes, desks, clocks, etc. It was invented by a Frenchman, André Charles Boulle, furniture-maker to Louis XV of France.

It consists of an inlay of tortoiseshell, brass, ebony or sometimes silver. The surface of the wood is engraved with patterns in brass and the lines of the engraving are emphasised with black pigment. The area not decorated with brass is covered with tortoiseshell, which, like the brass, is stuck to the wood with glue. The brass is sometimes also attached by pins with engraved heads to disguise them.

When cleaning boulle work it is advisable not to use solvents, because these may dissolve the glue holding the inlay in place. Instead, wipe the surface gently with a piece of cotton wool wrung out in a mild, detergent solution. Don't let it get too wet or the water will loosen the inlay. Dry thoroughly and polish with a little *microcrystalline wax.

It is very difficult to replace missing pieces. If the object is at all valuable, this is a job for an expert. However, if the inlay is bent or has lifted away from its background, it can be straightened or stuck back. Handle with great care. Scrape away any old glue from the back of the inlay and from the groove it occupied. Glue it back in place with an *epoxy resin adhesive.

The technique for boulle work such as on this box lid was perfected during the 18th century.

19th century cameos. The subject for these pieces of jewellery was nearly always classical.

CAMEOS

Cameos were very popular in 19th-century jewellery and were used for brooches, bracelets, necklaces and rings. The most common material was mollusc shell, which was carved and imported from Italy and mounted and set in London and Birmingham. They were also made from a wide range of gemstones such as amethyst, emerald, garnet, agate, onyx and jasper. Designs may be carved in relief, or etched in to the surface (intaglio). There were also Wedgwood cameos, glass cameos and imitation cameos. The more expensive cameos were mounted in gold, and cheap ones had gilt or rolled gold frames.

Cameos look dull and lifeless when dirty. They can be cleaned by scrubbing gently with an old toothbrush dipped in hot, soapy water. Rinse thoroughly and dry with a soft cloth.

For cleaning the mounts, *see* gold. Repairing should be done by an expert.

CANEWORK

The use of caning for chair seats and backs was introduced into England soon after 1660. Split rattan canes were interlaced to form an open mesh, which was very resilient. The earliest canework was of large mesh. By the end of the 17th century the mesh was finer and closer. In the middle of the 18th century, canework was used in some chairs in the Chinese style. It had gone out almost completely by the early 19th century, but was revived to remain intermittently popular through the Victorian era up until the 1930s. If you have a Charles II chair with an upholstered seat, or an old bentwood, Thonet-type, chair with a plywood seat, look at the underside of the seat to see if it was originally caned. If so, then it is possible to re-cane the seat, as you should always try to match the repair to the original character of the piece.

Buy some seating cane from a handicraft suppliers. Soak the cane in cold water for several hours to make it pliable. Meanwhile, remove all the old cane and clean out the cane holes. Then find the central holes at the front and back of the seat. Draw a strand of cane down through the back central hole for half its length and then up through the next hole to the left. Take both ends of the strand to the corresponding

A. Starting from the centre hole, thread the cane back and forth to the side of the seat, using one peg to keep the cane tight, and another to plug each hole as you proceed.

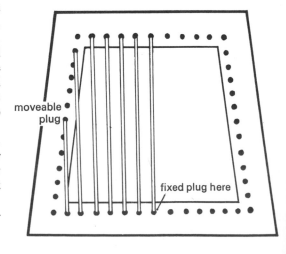

moveable plug

fixed plug here

front holes. Next, wedge one end of the cane in the front, central hole with a tapered dowel, or improvised plug, while continuing to thread the other end along the underside, up through the next hole, and across to the other end of the seat.

Keep the cane strands parallel while working with them, and leave slightly slack, for the cane will tighten as the work proceeds. The smooth side of the cane *must always* be on top.

B. Securing end of cane on underside of seat.

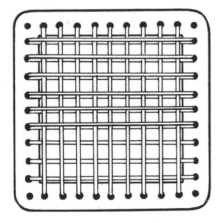

C. Thread the cane on top of stage A, at right angles to it.

Make the end of the completed, or new, strand secure by winding it twice round the cane running between the holes on the underside, and pulling it tight. When the left hand of the seat is covered, unpeg the end of the first strand, and complete the right side. Then thread the cane from side to side of the seat, on top of the front-to-back strands and at right angles to them. Thread another sideways set, but this time weave the cane under and over the intersecting strands.

To complete the mesh, weave diagonally *under* the sideways pairs and *over* the front-to-back pairs, starting from the corners. Take two diagonal strands from the corner

hole to get the correct spacing, but only one strand from the other holes. Then weave diagonally in the other direction *over* the sideways pairs and *under* the front-to-back pairs.

D. Complete mesh by weaving diagonally, under and over the existing strands.

Your mesh is now complete. To provide a decorative border strip, run a piece of cane between the corner hole, binding it at each hole with a loop of one of the underside strands.

If only a few canes are broken, a repair can often be made by removing them, replacing with new ones of matching width, and staining to tone in with old cane before weaving and pegging them in (*see* Furniture: staining).

Existing canework can often be improved in appearance and tightened up by scrubbing gently with lukewarm water and a nail brush. Leave to dry out in the open air.

A completed cane seat.

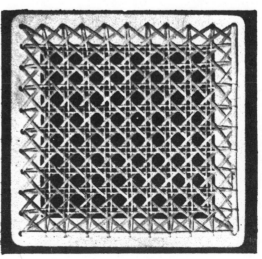

CARPETS AND TAPESTRIES

Although small pieces of tapestry weaving have been found in Egyptian tombs, tapestries were mainly produced and used as hangings from the 13th to the 19th century. They were woven on a vertical or horizontal loom, which held the vertical warp threads, onto which the weft threads were woven, thus forming the pattern. A pile carpet is made by tying knots onto the warp threads, cutting the ends short, and then laying the weft threads to hold the knots into position. Both carpets and tapestries are usually made of wool, but silk, cotton and metallic threads are also used.

Carpets and rugs obviously receive the worst treatment of all textiles, being worn underfoot, dented by furniture, and having the dirt constantly settling down on them. It is important to keep them clean, as dirt will cause the fibres to rot and to wear thin.

Treatment for carpets and tapestries is the same. The surface dust and dirt should first be vacuumed off. If the fabric is at all delicate, use the nylon monofilament square (described in textiles) as protection. If it is still dirty after vacuuming, particularly if there are grease marks, it can be washed, provided that tests are first made on the fastness of the colour. This is done by wetting a section and then pressing it with a piece of clean white blotting paper to check that there is no sign of the colour on it.

When washing, do not leave an article to soak for longer than ten minutes without checking that the dye is not running. Always dry a carpet or tapestry flat, and lay it on an absorbent backing to ensure that it does not stay sodden for longer than necessary.

Small rugs can be washed in the bath with lukewarm water and *Lissapol N. If the weaving is at all fragile, the rug should be supported on a piece of nylon net, so that no undue strain is placed on it when it is lifted out of the water.

A large carpet can be washed outside on a polythene sheet. Spray water and detergent onto the carpet, rub lightly with a soft-bristled brush, then carefully spray away all traces of soap and leave to dry. This can really only be done on a fine windy day.

Do not wash a carpet or tapestry interwoven with metallic thread. The thread will be very fragile compared to the wool,

and, if broken, the design will be spoilt and, of course, irreplaceable.

If a tapestry is to be hung, it should be lined. Take care that the lining is pre-shrunk, and that it is larger than the piece itself. Brown linen is a suitable material for the lining; it should be washed and shrunk to prevent it shrinking in the atmosphere and pulling the tapestry. It should be attached with lock stitch like a curtain lining, but fixed at the bottom as well. This will stop the dirt becoming lodged between the tapestry and the lining. The best way to attach a tapestry to the wall is with strips of Velcro.

In order to protect carpets, castors and the legs of heavy furniture should be placed in special cups, or coasters, of plastic or glass, which distribute the weight over a larger area. Carpets should always have an underlay to protect them from wear. They should be sent for expert mending if there are any signs of fraying or holes.

A mid-19th century needlework carpet.

CERAMICS

The term 'ceramics' is generally used to describe products in which the chief raw ingredient is clay, mixed with feldspar, quartz or lime. After mixing, these materials are worked into a paste which is then shaped, either by hand or on a potter's wheel, and afterwards fired.

A most important part of the potter's art is the use of glazes which prevent seepage of liquids in the softer wares, impart a pleasing finish and provide a medium for all kinds of decorative effects. A glaze is a thin layer of glass formed over the clay body during the firing,

Ceramics can also be decorated by carving, stamping and inlaying designs in the clay before firing, and by the more sophisticated use of moulds and applied work of all kinds. By far the most popular of all ornamental techniques has been that of painting.

As production processes improved, various types of ceramics emerged, each differing in their composition, the quality of their raw materials, and the temperature at which they were fired. The three main categories are earthenware, stoneware and porcelain.

Earthenware is by far the oldest, simplest and most common of all ceramics. It is the ordinary pottery of all ages, and it is still widely used for many purposes today. Made of clay, it has a porous, natural coloured body, with or without a coating of glaze. It is fired at around 700°C, or in the case of very soft wares even lower. Production of a finer type of earthenware developed rapidly in the first half of the 18th century in England, when a white, porous body covered with a white glaze was achieved.

Stoneware is midway between earthenware and porcelain. The peculiar nature of some clays or the addition of fluxes as correctives causes the paste partially to vitrify, becoming close grained and almost non-porous and forming an extremely durable material. In China it preceded porcelain, but in the West it was discovered independently some time after. Böttger's red stoneware at Meissen in the early 18th century was made in imitation of the Chinese ware imported into Europe at that time. In England, it was used by John Dwight of Fulham in the late 17th century, and then in Staffordshire by the Elers brothers and Wedgwood in the 18th century. Today, stoneware is principally used for utility objects.

Porcelain is a Chinese invention. A hard, white, fine-grained, translucent material, capable of the most delicate modelling, it is the most refined of all ceramic materials. True porcelain, known as hard-paste, is made out of petuntse and kaolin or china clay. It is fired twice, before and after glazing. No similar hard-paste porcelain was made in Europe until the oriental secret was discovered at Meissen in the early 18th century. However, various artificial porcelains, known as soft-paste, which in many countries remained in use over a long period, had already been developed. Soft-paste porcelain is made of vitreous substances, clay and marl, and is also fired before and after glazing. It is softer, not so translucent nor so resistant to heat as hard-paste, and when chipped it has a granular surface rather than the compact body of hard-paste. Bone porcelain is a compromise between the two, and is made of china clay and feldspar together with calcium phosphate from bone ash. It is harder and less permeable than soft-paste, but it has the same soft type of glaze. Whiter than soft-paste,, it is not as white as hard-paste. It was first used at Bow in the middle of the 18th century, and is the standard English porcelain today.

Before beginning any treatment, examine the article carefully, noting any unfired decoration or gilding which could be removed accidentally. Check for imperfections in the glaze and note whether any cracks are complete or partial.

To clean hard-paste porcelain and other non-porous materials, wash with warm water and soft soap or washing-up liquid. Don't use very hot water, as it may cause crazing, and avoid detergents—many of their ingredients can seriously damage some glazes, especially on earthenware and lustre ware. Guard against accidental chipping by using plastic containers. An old, clean toothbrush is useful for scrubbing broken edges which are the most important surfaces in the cleaning. Finish off by rinsing the piece in clean water and drying well, preferably with a silk rag, which leaves no fluff.

If the article has a metal mount, do not

immerse it in water as this will encourage rust stains. Both the porcelain and the metal should be treated separately, the porcelain part being cleaned with a rag moistened in warm, soapy water.

Earthenware and faience should not be completely immersed in water but cleaned gently with a damp rag.

Parian ware may be cleaned with a weak *ammonia solution or a mild chrome polish applied with a stiff brush.

Terracotta pieces should be cleaned with the minimum of liquid, so dust carefully with a soft brush before brushing with a little *ammonium acetate.

Articles that have become stained are usually those which have been used over a long period in a cracked condition. Stains caused by tea, coffee or gravy grease are most common.

Many stains on hard-paste porcelain and other non-porous materials can be removed with a little damp common salt or *bicarbonate of soda. Fruit and ink stains should be covered with damp salt, and left for about two hours and then finally rinsed in warm water.

*Hydrogen peroxide is useful for bleaching out very stubborn stains, but the object must be soaked in *distilled water for a couple of hours beforehand to prevent the stains from being drawn inwards. It is advisable here to test on a small piece first to prevent damage to the glaze. Try a solution of one part 100 vols hydrogen of peroxide to approximately three parts water, and add a drop of ammonia. Soak cottonwool swabs in the solution and place them on the discoloured areas with tweezers, leaving them in position for about two hours. Don't leave them for too long or you may damage the glaze, making the surface look like very fine sandpaper. Repeat the process for as long as necessary, and rinse off afterwards. If, however, you are treating a faulty unimportant piece, you can save a lot of time by using the peroxide undiluted, but don't risk it on anything really valuable. Do not use household bleach, as this may cause later discolouration or crazing of the glaze. Caustic alkalis should also be avoided.

Stains under closed cracks may prove difficult. It is sometimes possible to open a crack by inserting a fine razor blade, but

take great care that the crack does not develop into a break.

Stains in earthenware and other porous materials can often be drawn out by applying a *magnesium silicate pack. First soak the piece in distilled water. When it has absorbed all the water it can, coat it with magnesium silicate, mixed with distilled water to the consistency of a thick paste, to a depth of about 1 cm. Leave it to evaporate for about 24 hours, when the dissolved stains will be drawn out of the ceramic into the paste. When the paste begins to crackle, it should be removed. Repeat if necessary until all the stains have been drawn out, or until those left appear obstinate. In this case, try using a solvent such as *acetone, *methylated, *surgical or *white spirit, or *carbon tetrachloride on a cottonwool swab. Use these solvents with care, as they are inflammable and will produce fumes if used in a confined space.

Rust stains can usually be removed by applying rust remover on a swab of cottonwool, and brass stains with a 30% ammonia solution. The piece should be soaked beforehand in distilled water. Keep an eye on the action of the solvent so that it is not left for too long, then clean it off thoroughly with acetone.

Cabinet pieces

These are pieces of solely decorative value and they are usually kept on a shelf or mantelpiece or in a china cabinet. Although they don't get much wear and tear, they may be damaged by an accident or you may buy a slightly damaged piece that is well worth restoring.

If you still have the broken pieces, the repair is comparatively simple, as the pieces can be glued back on and any chips filled in (see ceramic repairs).

When the broken parts are missing, a mould can be taken if a duplicate exists (see ceramic moulding). But be careful not to give a statuette two right legs or two left hands, and avoid exact duplication of finger poses. Use the mould to provide a basic shape, and alter the positions slightly when the composition is only partly set. Flexible moulds are best for complicated poses because they are easily removed.

You may have to replace the missing

pieces by modelling freehand, so get some practice first. The new hand or limb must not only look convincing in proportion and bone structure, but it must resemble its counterpart, so you must adapt your modelling to the style of the original. In early Staffordshire pottery, for example, this may mean that the modelling will seem rather coarse, without much shape to it, but it is often difficult to achieve the original simplicity with conviction. Remember that painting and surface-coating will fill and blot out much of the detail (as well as emphasise the faults), and also increase the size slightly, so modelling details may have to be over-emphasised and the replica should be made a fraction smaller.

If you don't know what the missing piece was like, consult all the reference books you can and see if you can find a comparable piece in a museum. If this proves unsuccessful, use your imagination: a musician, for example, will usually be carrying a musical instrument, a shepherdess, a crook.

It is often easier to model the missing part away from the site. If you are replacing a hand or a limb, take exact measurements of its counterpart first. It is advisable to build up the piece over a core of bent brass wire, keeping the loop at the top and embedding the two ends at the bottom in plasticine so that both hands are free for modelling. Don't let the core extend too far if you are making a hand, as its presence among the fingers will cause difficulties. Cover the wire with a fairly stiff *filler, roughly in the shape required. Use fine modelling tools, dipped in *French chalk or *methylated spirit to prevent them from sticking, to carve and shape the piece. Leave it to set. Before it is completely dry, fill in any depressions and gently smooth out any bumps with a finger. When quite hard, fine it down with a razor blade, files and abrasive paper. Then emphasise any small details such as finger nails with fine engraving tools. If a thumb or finger gets broken off, it can be replaced with a little adhesive.

Having cleaned and smoothed the edges of the repair site, drill a dowel hole and put

Cabinet pieces: a Meissen group of two dancers with a guitar player, flanked by two Copenhagen figures of a girl and boy representing Spring and Winter.

a little filler in it. Cut the wire ends to the correct length and insert them in the hole, bringing the two pieces accurately together with a thin layer of adhesive between them. When repairing a hollow piece by this method, there is obviously no need to drill a hole; the wire ends should be wrapped in a little filler and inserted into the broken end of the main piece.

If you are working *in situ* on the broken article, the same method of using a piece of brass wire as scaffolding is advisable. In building up, carry the filler smoothly onto the body of the article to prevent a ridge forming. The chief disadvantage of this method is that you can't move the part so freely and it is more difficult to sandpaper it smooth, particularly if the part is close to the main body.

A limb can be built up in much the same way as a teacup handle (*see* ceramic spouts). The wire core should roughly correspond to the size of the bone. Take careful measurements of the width and length of the counterpart limb, and bend the wire accordingly. Roughen the wire with a file and taper it down at the end. Don't let the core extend beyond the palm of the hand when making an arm, as you don't want it protruding among the fingers. Insert the wire into a hole bored in the broken site and fix it with filler, supporting it until it has set. Build up the limb in two or three layers, as for a cup handle, modelling the final layer as closely as possible to the final shape and keeping a constant check on its size. Fill in any small air holes on the surface and extend the material over the broken edge to avoid a ridge. When hard, smooth with files and abrasive paper until the surface has no rough or pitted edges.

It is possible to make many delicate pieces such as ribbons and dog leads. Mix the filler to a fairly stiff consistency; roll it out into a thin layer on a piece of glass (the cleanest and easiest working board) and cut appropriately. Always ensure that the filler and the original surface merge gently into one another, and that adequate support is given during the setting stage.

Damaged porcelain skirts or aprons can be mended quite easily. Choose a lace as near as possible to the original design, cut it to the required shape, and dip it in a liquid filler. As it begins to set, stand it on edge, pleating it with damp fingers and copying the folds of the original material. Trim with scissors when almost dry and glue into place, overlapping the existing lace on both sides.

Bouquets of flowers and boscages behind statuettes are frequently damaged. In most cases, some parts will be left behind so that it is possible to copy the flowers and leaves.

When making the smallest flowers, the filler, mixed to a doughy consistency, should be rolled out as finely as possible and a small collar with shaped edges cut out with a small sharp knife or scalpel. Then roll this into a circular cluster, using your smallest modelling tools to open out the petals if desired.

For the larger flowers, the petals and centres are best made separately. Make a tiny central sphere first, and put a little ring of modelling clay around it over which the individual petals can be curled to give them a life-like appearance. Roll out the filler and mark out the shapes with a fine graver before cutting and moulding each petal. Ease each petal off your glass plate with a palette knife, and transfer it with the point of a pin to its position around the centre which, once the pieces are pressed into position with a small dentist's tool, becomes a round, flat disc.

Almost any flower can be made in this way if you cut characteristic petal shapes. If a petal or leaf is to be repeated often, you can save time by making a cutter out of a strip of brass or copper foil, bent to the appropriate shape. This can be made by making a pattern out of plywood with a fretsaw. Nail this to your work-bench and then, using a small hammer, hammer the metal strip around it until it takes on exactly the same shape. Use the cutter as you would a pastry cutter.

When you are making leaves, remember to add the veining, either by building up a very thin line of filler or by using a fine graving tool. They should all be similar but not identical.

When the flower or leaf is dry enough to be handled without distortion, transfer it to its prepared position and glue it in place. It is often possible to add an extra leaf, or to put in a small amount of filler disguised as part of the decoration to hold the modelled part in place.

If the boscage is missing, in part or in

its entirety, new branches can be made with sturdy brass wires, shaped as required. Stick one piece of wire together at a time, as you may need to support each at a different angle. When all the cross pieces are set in position, cover them with filler, roughly fashioned into branches. Allow it to harden before adding the flowers and leaves, bearing in mind the general formation of the tree. Remember that if the piece is to be seen in the round, leaves and flowers should also be added to the back. Allow it all to dry before carefully smoothing with fine abrasive paper, taking care not to damage your hours of labour.

If you have been working away from the piece, check the effect of the branch or the tree in its position before actually glueing it on. It is easier to get a better composition if you work *in situ,* but, on the other hand, it will be more difficult, because of the figure in front.

Dowelling

Today, with modern *epoxy resins, the technique of dowelling is rarely necessary, but it can be employed if you feel that a joint needs extra strength. It consists of boring equal-sized holes in both halves of the break. These are then filled with *filler, into which a metal peg is inserted before it sets. Thus the dowel is completely hidden from the outside. This method is also useful when the broken-off piece does not unite firmly with the base, so that undue stress would be placed on the adhesive, or when the break is such that it is difficult to maintain the correct balance during the setting period. However it can only be used when the ceramic body is thick enough and deep enough. A margin of china should always be left around the hole equal to, or greater than, the diameter of the hole. Clean the edges to be stuck together, and dry.

A dowel should be made of non-corroding wire, preferably stainless steel or half-hard brass or bronze, and its thickness must depend on the size of the hole. The surface of the dowel should be notched with a small file to give the filler an anchorage, and flattened or grooved slightly on one side. This indentation will allow air which might otherwise be trapped beneath the dowel to escape, eventually pushing it out

of its seating position. Be careful not to make the dowel too short; it should be embedded in the part and in the whole to a depth of at least three times its own diameter to ensure that holds firmly. If the piece is awkwardly shaped or especially vulnerable, it should be longer.

Wire dowel, with notched sides.

Dowel holes should be bored as nearly as possible along the axis line of the broken member. Mark the site and drill your hole in one piece with either a hand drill or a power drill (a secondhand dentist's drill is ideal). The dowel should fit the size of the hole as nearly as possible because the expansion of too much of the surrounding filler could cause the article to crack. The following figures give, as a rough guide, the nearest sizes of holes for the commoner gauges.

11 G. wire fits loosely $\frac{1}{8}''$ diameter hole.
13 G. wire fits exactly $\frac{3}{32}''$ diameter hole.
16 G. wire fits tightly $\frac{3}{16}''$ diameter hole.
18 G. wire fits tightly $\frac{3}{64}''$ diameter hole.
The 13 G. wire is generally the most useful. Measure the depth of the hole carefully with a pin, checking it against a finely graded ruler so that the length of the dowel can be accurately measured.

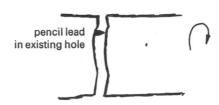

pencil lead in existing hole

Marking site for second hole.

It is most important that the two holes are exactly opposite one another, and even the most careful measurement may be out of line. Therefore, having drilled your hole in one piece, insert a soft pencil lead in it with the point just protruding. Place the two pieces carefully together in their correct eventual positions, and rotate them slightly so that the pencil marks the correct drilling site on the other piece. Then bore your second hole the same breadth and depth as the first.

Mix your filler, avoiding the sorts that are likely to shrink or expand in setting, and those that are mixed with water, as they need access to the air for the evaporation of the water. In most cases, unless you are dealing with a porous material, an *epoxy putty is best. Fill one of the holes (it is usually better to do the larger piece first) with filler and press the dowel firmly in, keeping the mark on the dowel level with the surface of the break. Clean off excess filler with a silk rag dipped in *methylated spirit. If the dowel shows a tendency to rise out of the hole, it means that air has been caught under the filler, but the groove or flattened side of the dowel will allow the air to escape in time.

Once one end of the dowel is firmly embedded, place the other piece of china over the other end in the correct position so as to secure the dowel. Tape the two broken pieces firmly and accurately together, using strips cut lengthwise rather than encircling the actual break. Support until dry.

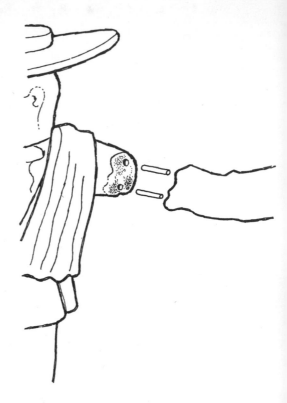

A dowelling joint for solid pieces.

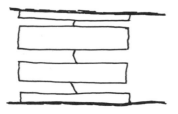

Taping the join.

When the filler has completely set, remove the tape and the piece without filler, and clean off the surfaces with a solvent. Fill the hole in this piece with filler as before. If the break is at an awkward angle, or if the two pieces do not fit together easily, apply a thin layer of adhesive to one of the broken surfaces. If the two pieces fit together perfectly, it is not always necessary to put adhesive between them, as this will only widen the join a fraction and make a line which will show. Press the two parts hard together, removing any surplus filler that oozes out. Tape the two pieces together and allow them to set, supporting as necessary. If you are using epoxy putty, the tape can be removed after between six and eight hours at room temperature. Excess adhesive can be pared off at this point with a razor blade or abrasive paper. Chipping of the

surface should be dealt with when the dowel is completely set in position.

Dowelling can be used to join modelled or moulded pieces to the whole in exactly the same way. It can also be used for hollow pieces, for which a heavier gauge wire is generally necessary because it is not a good idea to have too much surrounding filler. As with solid pieces, the dowel must be shaped to fit the cavity in both halves of the break, and the halfway point on the dowel should be carefully marked. Do not press the filler into the hole and then insert the dowel, as the filler will be pushed too far along the cavity, but wrap filler round half the length of the dowel until there is enough to fill the hole. Do not make the 'wrapping' too thick, or the filler will ride up in a collar around the dowel, which will then penetrate right through it; nor should it be too thin, or it will fail to adhere to the walls of the cavity. Push the dowel and its 'wrapping' firmly into place so that the halfway mark on the dowel is in line with the broken surface. Clean off excess filler

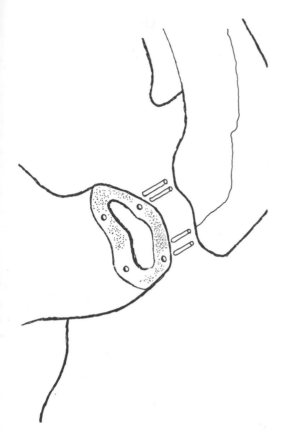

Dowelling joint for hollow pieces.

Wrapping dowel in adhesive sleeve.

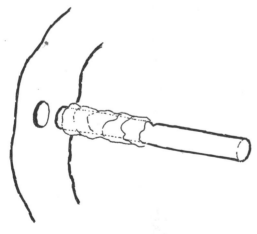

Moulding

Moulds can save much time and trouble. They can be used as a backing for the insertion of missing pieces (*see* ceramic repairs) or to facilitate the modelling of new parts, provided a duplicate exists or one part of the broken article is still intact. They are especially useful when a number of identical shapes have to be made. Pressed moulds should always take on the exact form of the prototype. Make sure that the impression is taken at a point corresponding exactly to the repair site. A mould should be made of a material that can be withdrawn easily without causing damage to itself or the original.

Flexible moulds which are easily removed, are the most suitable when restoring complicated pieces. There are a variety of materials available for making such flexible moulds, and among the most widely used of these is latex rubber emulsion.

However, this material does have disadvantages. Latex rubber cannot be used for making moulds on porcelain with metal mounts, or on a painted surface, as the ammonia contained in the emulsion will damage them. In such cases you can use silicone rubber, although this is less flexible than latex and more likely to tear.

When applying latex rubber emulsion you must take care to exclude air bubbles. On more intricate pieces you will need to apply several coats. To avoid distortion each coat has to be applied as soon as the previous coat begins to thicken as the membrane will fail to fill any depressions if it is allowed to dry out too much.

Because of the problems in using a latex rubber emulsion, it is probably better for the amateur restorer to use a *vinyl moulding material. This can be used on all types of ceramics, having none of the ammonia content of latex. It cures (i.e. sets) to a firm but flexible consistency and once a mould is made, it can be used again and again. When you no longer require a mould, it can be cut up with scissors, melted down and re-used. Always use a natural, pigment-free variety of vinyl moulding material to avoid any transfer of colour, either to the prototype or to the object cast from the mould.

and allow it to set. Use exactly the same method to embed the second half of the dowel, and then bring the two parts tightly together, with a layer of adhesive between them, if necessary. Tape in position and leave to set.

Two important points to remember when using vinyl moulding material: in its molten state it can cause serious burns, so it should be handled with caution, always wearing rubber gloves. Also, while melting it gives off powerful fumes which are aggravated if it is overheated. Work in a well-ventilated room, checking the melting temperature with a thermometer.

To make a wax mould, use modelling wax or *paraffin wax. Modelling wax should be warmed slightly to soften until just malleable, while paraffin wax will soften sufficiently by kneading in the hand. It is easier to use than modelling wax which sets harder. Roll out the wax into a layer half an inch thick, and cut an area somewhat larger than the missing section. Press it on the unbroken section or identical article so that it takes on the required shape, and leave it to harden completely before carefully loosening it off and placing it under the repair site, taping in position if necessary. It is easier to take internal moulds for repairing cups or bowls.

Now insert the broken pieces and feed in your freshly mixed filler. Use adhesive where necessary to stick together the pieces. The mould should be left in position until the adhesive or filler has set. It can then be removed, and any traces of wax wiped away with *white spirit.

*Plaster of Paris makes a stronger mould. However, you need to be careful when making internal moulds with it, especially if the article narrows at the top, to make sure that it will come out easily, as it lacks the malleability of a wax mould. Choose fresh, i.e. white, plaster of Paris. Remember that plaster should always be added to water (*not* the other way round), so place a small amount of water in a bowl and add the plaster to it, stirring gently to avoid mixing air in with the liquid. Mix to a stiff but pourable consistency. Coat the prototype surface with a layer of Vaseline and then slowly pour the plaster over the area to a thickness of a quarter of an inch. Leave to dry, and when it is set, place it over the repair site, securing it with tape.

Plasticine, beaten until there is no air trapped inside and rolled to a thickness of half an inch, is also suitable for making moulds in the same manner as wax or

plaster moulds, although it never sets really hard and can be pushed out of shape more easily than other materials. Always remember to moisten the prototype with water, to prevent it sticking, before applying the modelling clay. Any material which is likely to come into contact with adhesive or filler should be dusted with French chalk to protect it from the resin in the adhesive or filler. This should be done before the mould is attached to the object, so that none of the powder gets into the broken edges. Use a soft brush, as stiff bristles will mark the surface of the plasticine.

A dental plaster can also be used, and is recommended for its speed in setting and ease of handling. As it softens in hot water, it needs no parting agent, and can be removed from the prototype and placed over the repair site while still slightly plastic. It will cool quickly in about a minute to its original hard condition, and the filler can then be applied.

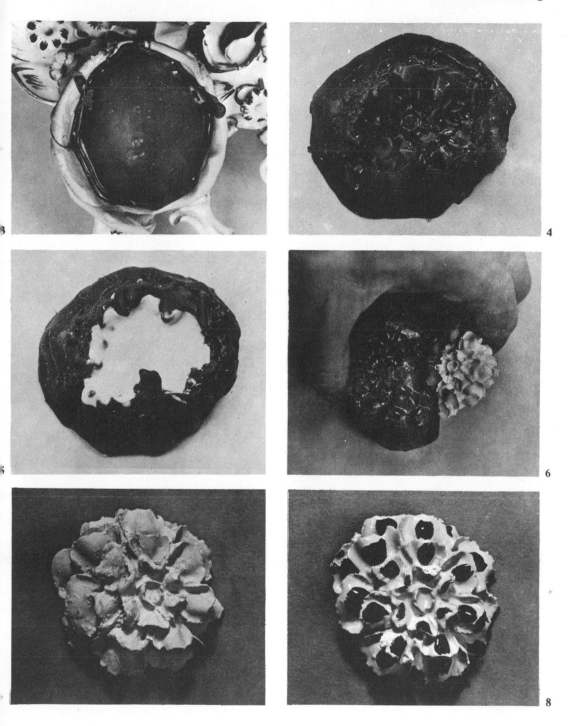

Making a flexible mould using vinyl moulding material: Having decided what you wish to take a mould from (1) build up a wall of plasticine around it (2), making a well into which you can pour the molten moulding material (3). When this has cured, remove the plasticine and *then the mould (4). Pour in your prepared filler (5) and leave to harden. As the mould is flexible, it is easily removed from the cast (6). The cast is then ready for retouching to match the original (7). When this has been done (8), the cast is ready to be glued into position.*

The removal of old glue. It is essential to remove all traces of old glue before starting on a new repair. Glue on non-porous articles can usually be removed by soaking the object in warm, soapy water. First make sure that there is no other repair elsewhere which you don't want to come to pieces; if there is, you will have to find a way of immersing only the part with the break, e.g. by suspending the article from a piece of wire, or nylon thread. A delicate piece such as a porcelain figure should be suspended in a nylon net in the water to prevent further damage as a result of pieces collapsing as the old glue dissolves. Don't use detergents, and don't boil the article, particularly if it is delicately coloured. As the glue softens, it may be possible to pull most of it off in a single strip with a fine pair of tweezers, or to lift it off with the point of a fine knife.

If soaking in warm, soapy water is not effective, try using a solvent such as *acetone, *methylated or *surgical spirit, *white spirit or *carbon tetrachloride. The most difficult glues to remove are: shellac resins, which can be broken down with a mixture of half ammonia and half methylated spirit or with a *methelene chloride paint stripper; and modern *epoxy resins, which methelene chloride should dislodge. Clean the article well, between applications of different solvents.

Be very careful when working with soft porous china and earthenware. Test on a small chip before applying any solvent. The article should be soaked for two hours in cold distilled water before beginning work, in order to prevent either the solvent or the old adhesive being drawn into the body. This is very important, especially if the old glue is a *shellac resin, because this will leave a permanent purple stain as the solvents chase it further into the porous body.

Apply the appropriate solvent freely with a swab of cottonwool. If the old repair is extensive and the piece is not too big, it may be easier to immerse the whole object in solvent.

If no solvent is successful, you will have to resort to using glass-paper or chipping away the residue with a razor blade or dentist's pick. Sometimes you can hear the difference between glue and body when you move over it with the point of a probe, even when it is not possible to see it. A watch-maker's glass or a magnifying glass may be useful for finding the glue when cleaning broken edges. Scraping must be done with great care, particularly on soft clays and porous materials whose surface comes away easily.

Take care not to damage the glaze on all surfaces, hard or soft.

The removal of rivets. Unsightly brass and iron rivets were often used in past restorations. These can be removed either by swabbing the area with warm water before gently extracting them with a small pair of pliers, or by clipping out the surrounding filler with a fine-pointed scalpel before slipping a knife under the rivet and carefully lifting it out. If this fails, the rivet can be carefully sawn or cut through with small cutting forceps (obtainable from dentists's suppliers), and each half gently eased back and forth until it comes out.

If the rivets have left a stain, remove it before proceeding further.

Cracks. If you hope to achieve an invisible repair, you must first make sure that your hands, tools, working surfaces and the article itself are absolutely clean. It is best to work in a warm room, and to warm the piece and the adhesive near a radiator or

Below: *A Chelsea swan, c1750, which had been originally repaired with ugly, old-fashioned rivets.* Right, above: *The rivets have been removed and the breaks re-glued and taped while the adhesive cures.* Right, below: *The swan restored to something very close to its former glory.*

over a stove. The warmth not only dries up any traces of moisture but also encourages the adhesive to flow more freely.

Before starting work, cracks should have been bleached or thoroughly cleansed of all traces of dirt and grease, including fingermarks, and the surfaces should be completely dry.

Insert a thin layer of suitable adhesive (*see* adhesives) into the crack with a palette knife or razor blade. This is easy with wide, lateral cracks, but more difficult with a narrow one. In this case, apply the adhesive to the surface of the crack, and then use a

hair-dryer to warm the adhesive and the object, moving it up and down the line of the crack. As the piece warms up, the adhesive will flow down into the crack. Alternatively, warm the piece and the adhesive, and then use a razor blade gently to open the crack sufficiently to insert the adhesive. When the adhesive is absorbed into the crack, remove the razor blade and press the two parts together. This can be dangerous, as the crack may extend into a break, so it should only be done with the greatest care. Surplus adhesive should be swabbed away with *methylated spirit or *acetone.

Strips of self-adhesive tape, applied at right angles to the line of the crack, are an effective means of clamping, particularly as this tape shrinks in drying, and in doing so pulls the two parts together. However, beware of unfired decoration or gilding which can be pulled off accidentally when the tape is removed. To prevent this, swab the adhesive tape with white spirit which will dissolve the glue and enable it to be peeled off easily, without harming the decoration or the adhesive used to bond. If there is any remaining excess adhesive, it can be taken off with a razor blade when it is hard.

Simple breaks. When repairing simple breaks, first clean and dry the separate parts and prepare a suitable support (*see* ceramic supports). Then mix the adhesive and with the tip of a palette knife or spatula, spread the thinnest possible layer of adhesive, as too much will only emphasise the break and prevent a close fit, pushing the pieces slightly apart. Such displacement may seem minute, but when dealing with multi-breaks, it can cause serious difficulties.

2. *Apply the epoxy resin adhesive carefully to both surfaces to be joined.*

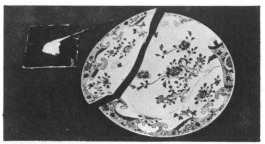

1. *Before mending a simple break like this, make sure the broken edges are clean and smooth.*

A clean break with both pieces fitting together perfectly only needs adhesive applied to one edge. It is usually easier to apply it to the broken piece rather than to the whole. When dealing with damaged edges, apply the adhesive to both edges, as the surplus is driven into the cavities. With porous materials such as earthenware, the surplus is driven into the cavities of the grain, so that instead of keeping the edges apart it binds them together.

Use a broken piece of pattern or a jagged edge in the break to judge how the pieces fit together, and press both parts hard together to expel as much of the adhesive as possible along the join. There is only one position in which the two pieces will join perfectly, and you must find it. Check that there are no ridges, using your fingertips or a probe rather than relying on your eyes, although a magnifying glass is helpful.

Remove excess adhesive with *methylated spirit or *acetone on a cottonwool swab, but don't use so much that it runs into the crack and loosens the join. Surplus adhesive along the actual crack should only be removed after it has set. Check that no adhesive has run onto gilt or lustre surfaces, as if it

sets it will remove gilt and lustre when it is taken off.

Once the edges have been joined, they must be held in place until the adhesive has set. Strips of self-adhesive tape should be applied evenly at right angles to the line of the break on both sides of the article. Leave the article in its support until the adhesive has partially set, that is, hard enough to hold the piece firmly in position, but still soluble with methylated spirit if a mistake has been made (3-6 hours for an epoxy resin). Then re-check the alignment and swab off excess adhesive. When the adhesive has completely hardened, any excess should be pared off with a small piece of folded

3. *Press the two surfaces together, making sure you achieve a tight fit.*

6. Once mended, the break in the plate should be virtually undetectable.

4. Use brown gummed paper for taping joins rather than self-adhesive tape which is harder to remove.

*glass-paper or *wet-and-dry paper, or a razor blade or scalpel, taking great care of the surrounding glazes.

You may find that a close join can only be achieved at one end of the break. This

5. Support the plate carefully while the adhesive cures. An old biscuit tin filled with sand is a great help for doing this.

will be because the article has 'sprung', caused by the release, on breakage, of the tensions set up during the original firing of the article. In this case, only apply the adhesive to the area where a perfect fit is obtainable, and use self-adhesive tape to hold the pieces together as before. When set, remove the tape and add more adhesive to the rest of the break, using the tape to help draw the two pieces gently together. This method will not always achieve a successful result, and in some cases it may be necessary to fill the gap with filler.

Multiple breaks. If the article is in many pieces, it is best to make a trial run of the assembly to see whether any part is missing and how the pieces fit together. Place the pieces together carefully, holding them in position with self-adhesive tape.

This will show you the order of the final assembly and whether all the pieces should be glued together at one time, or separately in different sessions. If the latter, the alignment of the separate pieces must be perfect, for you will be in serious trouble if one piece is badly positioned or excess adhesive has been left in the joints. Rounded, hollow vessels are often easier to mend in one session.

The general instructions for bonding a simple break should be followed. If one half of the article remains intact, or a duplicate exists, mending multiple breaks can be made easier by using a mould as a backing (*see* moulding). Tape the mould into position and then assemble and glue the broken pieces. The pliability of wax or rubber moulds will allow the edge to be eased in order to insert the last pieces around the rim. The mould will act as a support for mending a plate or flat dish, but it may have to be tilted, when mending a bowl or a cup, to prevent the replaced pieces from falling inwards or outwards, according to whether it is an inside or outside mould.

Chips and shell-breaks. The edges of plates, cups and bowls are particularly susceptible to chipping, which often leaves a grooved area like a scallop shell. As the little fragments are usually missing, the resulting gaps must be filled. Those with a ragged edge, those that penetrate deeply, or small, shallow chips running along the edge of a crack are easier to fill than wide open chips with a smooth surface. With these, grooves ground into the broken surface with a file or an abrasive wheel will give the *filler an anchorage.

Thoroughly clean the surface and moisten it a little, especially if your chosen filler is liable to shrink. Apply a thin layer of adhesive, and then build up the missing surface with a fairly stiff mixture of filler.

For porcelain, an *epoxy resin adhesive mixed with *titanium dioxide thins out at the edges and makes a smooth united surface better than any other. Press it into the cavity and allow its edges to flatten out towards the perimeter until it blends smoothly together with the original surface. This can be done all at once, or in successive layers, allowing each to harden before applying the next.

The layer method is preferable for porous materials. Apply an excess rather than allowing a concavity to develop. Wait at least an hour after applying the last layer before cleaning off any surplus, using a silk rag dipped in *methylated spirit. Allow the filler to harden completely, and then rub the surface with a small piece of *flour-paper to make it completely uniform. Another final application of filler may be necessary to fill

in blemishes, as the smallest inaccuracy will show, especially when a surface coating of paint is applied.

Holes. For the filling of holes, use your chosen *filler in a putty or dough-like consistency.

Clean the surfaces thoroughly, and then moisten the edges of the hole to be filled. Insert a little filler, using a small dentist's probe or the tip of a fine knife; the size of the hole will decide the size of the tool. Press the filler well down to prevent the formation of air cavities, and over-fill rather than under-fill. Smooth off until flush with the surrounding surfaces, removing any excess with a silk rag moistened with solvent, or with a razor blade. Allow the filler to harden before rubbing it smooth with a small bit of flour paper, taking care not to damage the surrounding glaze. Check the result with a fingertip.

If the article is made of a very porous material like thick earthenware, build up the repair in layers, using the appropriate filler. Allow each to dry before applying the next, as this reduces the amount of overall shrinkage.

If a large hole is being mended, some support may be needed. The site can be backed with self-adhesive tape or a piece of stout Indian muslin. Make sure that you use an easily soluble adhesive, and certainly not an epoxy resin, so that the backing can be removed without difficulty. Alternatively, you can use a mould, in which case the filler can be fed in at one end, and then rolled across the floor of the mould, thus gradually expelling the air in front instead of trapping it underneath. If you use a mould that curls over the top of the filler, it is wise to pierce it with a pin in one or two places to help the air to escape. It is not possible to insert a backing for narrow-necked vessels, so the filler must be built up from the outside, little by little; the repair will bulge a little on the inside, but it will not be seen.

Disrupted surfaces and flaking glazes. Unglazed earthenware is usually rather porous and will therefore tend to absorb soluble salts. Variations in humidity, will cause these to expand and crystallise, and so the surface will be disrupted. Salts may also get into glazed ceramics where the glaze is incomplete or imperfect, and when they expand, they will cause the glaze to flake off. Damage from frost can also cause the surface to be disrupted in these ways.

Any valuable article in this state should be sent to an expert. However if you wish to carry out your own treatment, the following should help you.

Before consolidation is attempted, the offending salts must be removed by soaking the article in de-ionised water. In order to prevent flakes of loosely attached glaze from blowing off, place it in only a small amount of water at first, slowly increasing it as the water is absorbed by the ceramic. This, process allows the air to escape gradually, instead of being suddenly forced out, which results in the loose flakes going with it. Badly flaking areas can be protected during immersion by stretching thin silk over and around the object.

Change the water daily until testing with silver nitrate shows that all the salt has been removed. The following test for salt is recommended. Pour about 10 ml of the water to be tested into a bottle, and add several drops of dilute *nitric acid. Put on the top of the bottle and shake it to mix the solution. The mixture should be clear when examined in good light. Add 5 drops of 2% silver nitrate and mix as before. Then allow time for any opalescence, which indicates the presence of salt, to appear.

When fragments are held to the article only by salt crystals, or there is loose painted decoration, it is necessary to consolidate the surface before washing out the salts. Brush on a 5% solution of *soluble nylon in ethyl *alcohol. This will form a protective film which does not exert any force on the surface as it dries, and is sufficiently permeable to permit the salts to escape.

Having washed out the salts, leave the article to dry thoroughly before consolidating it with a *polyvinyl acetate emulsion. The strength of the solution will depend upon the density of the article and the degree of penetration required. Either place the article in the solution, allowing slow absorption, or apply the solution with a brush. Press any loose flakes gently into position with a heated spatula.

Retouching

Painting. It is very important that the surfaces to be retouched are as perfect as possible, because the paint will reveal any mistakes rather than hide them. But it is also easy to spoil a good repair by retouching badly, either because the colours don't match or because of a clumsy merging of the paint with the original surface at the edge of the repair. The colour must match absolutely, and this may only be achieved after several coats and the careful thinning out of the paint at the edge of the repairs. If there are variations in tone in a single colour surface, it is important that these too are faithfully imitated, or the repaired area will look dead in comparison.

Although you can colour the filler, it is unlikely that you will be able to get a good enough colour match to be able to dispense with surface painting. However it is useful to be able to colour small chips and the filling of former rivet holes, as these small areas cannot support too many coats of paint without becoming obvious. Few topcoats will be necessary providing you have a well-matched filler. A coloured filler is also useful when the ceramic is a deep, intense colour, and particularly with coarse-grained pottery, where a break is inclined to reveal the brown earthenware beneath, however carefully mended. In order to obtain a coloured filler, add dry powder pigments when mixing the filler.

For surface painting, the paints should be easy to mix, permanent, and indifferent to hot and cold temperatures. Artists' dry powder pigments, providing they are well ground into the medium, are the best. Or, you can use watercolours in tubes, which are particularly suitable for plaster fillers or tempera (especially casein tempera). On top of both of these you must add a protective coating which should also simulate the original surface glaze. Avoid oil paints, as they tend to discolour. Enamel or car touch-up paints, made of cellulose lacquer, give a beautifully smooth surface and a porcelain-like glow, thus dispensing with the need for a separate surface glaze, but their colour range is limited and they dry far too quickly to allow time for careful colour mixing.

If the paint is to lie smoothly, it is most important that the surfaces involved, the paint-brushes and the paint are all free of dust, dirt, grease and loose hairs, because all of these will cause small irregularities which show up glaringly on the painted surface. Dust all surfaces with a soft brush and wipe clean with a silk rag moistened with *methylated spirit. Use good-quality watercolour brushes, making sure that you have a good selection of fine ones, and keeping separate brushes for different media. Keep these and the mixing palette scrupulously clean. (See brushes).

Whatever colour medium you choose, it is advisable to seal the surface of your filler, unless you have used an *epoxy putty, in which case it is not necessary. Sealing may be done by using an additive in the paint itself rather than coating the surface before applying the paint. Either add powdered size to the paint, or a little picture varnish or polyurethane varnish to the colourant, mixing it thoroughly with a few drops of *white spirit. Don't add the white spirit until just before painting, as it evaporates very quickly and in doing so thickens the paint.

If you want a matt finish for unglazed articles, a small amount of a matting agent made of a *hydrolised silica should be mixed with the colouring medium before application.

The texture of the paint should be very smooth, and thick enough to prevent it flowing off a rounded surface, but not so thick that it drags at the brush while you are working.

It is important to test the colour match by making a small brush stroke on the patch you are trying to match. If it is wrong, leave it there, adjust the colour of the paint, and try again. When you have obtained a good colour match, remove the test strokes with white spirit before they dry.

Apply the paint evenly over the surface and allow it to dry. If it is not quite smooth, rub it gently with *flour paper, and test the result with your fingertips. Apply successive coats, allowing each to dry so that it is not disturbed by the solvent in the following application. Add a little more white spirit when necessary, and rub each coat smooth with flour paper in preparation for the next one, until the exact matching colour is obtained.

The final coat must be applied very carefully; the paint should be brought up very lightly over the original surface in a feathering motion with reduced pressure on the brush, so that the new and old colours blend together without any hard or visible line between them. Allow at least a day for the object to dry out fully, storing it in a dust-free cupboard. Clean brushes, palette knife and palette immediately with *white spirit or *acetone.

You can also retouch by spraying with an *air-brush, a small pneumatic instrument which ejects the paint as a vapour rather than as a liquid. This is particularly useful for fading off the paint so that it merges imperceptibly with the original surface on pale-coloured ceramics on which there is no pattern or moulding. Fading off can be very difficult on a small area like a crack, as the paint will betray itself by its additional height and volume, however carefully its edges are softened with a brush. The air-brush avoids this, because it sprays the paint in the form of a wet mist without volume. By repeated movements over the crack, the mist becomes sufficiently thick to efface it, but without any perceptible edges.

Its disadvantage is that it shows up any irregularities even more clearly than paint applied with an ordinary brush, and it is less firm and invulnerable than brush-applied paint until the final coating of glaze is applied. It also produces a broader band of paint which can easily encroach accidentally on the original paint in the wrong places.

Before using the air-brush, begin by painting on a coat which has a fair amount of white in the mixture (whatever the final colour); apply with a brush and fade off at the edges. When dry, rub over with flour paper as usual, removing the paint from the high spots altogether, but leaving it in any depressions. Clean away the resulting dust with methylated spirit. Repeat if necessary until you have a smooth surface.

Then you can start using the air-brush to apply a more translucent or matching colour. Add enough solvent to the medium until you have the right consistency for an even spray. Always try the air-brush out on a practice piece first, as it may spit or dribble if it is partially blocked. Use back and forth movements in a series of parallel and slightly overlapping lines until the area is covered. Do not hold the air-brush too close, or you will get a concentration of paint. Once the surface becomes thoroughly liquid, allow it to dry, even if some of the under-surface is still visible. A second coat can be added when it is dry.

If the sprayed paint does extend too far (this will only be visible where the light catches it), remove it with a little mild chrome cleaner on a clean rag rather than using flour paper or solvent, as either of these will create just the kind of edge to the paint that you have been trying to avoid.

An air-brush is also useful for gradual shading if the brush is lifted further away from the surface in the course of spraying. Speckled effects can be achieved by holding the air-brush further away according to the density required. Beware of covering too wide an area, as in cleaning off the surface you are likely to defeat the aim of spraying.

Don't allow the paint to dry up in the air-brush. Between bouts of sprayings, spray some solvent through the brush to remove all traces of colour and medium. For a final cleaning, a little acetone should be sprayed through.

White. White porcelain is extremely difficult to match because true white seldom exists in porcelain, which is often covered with a creamy, blue, greenish or greyish glaze. Tubes of pure white paint such at Titanium White can be bought, but you will probably have to mix your whites to get the exact shade you need.

Apply a foundation coat of white paint. When it is dry, introduce a little of the required colour, usually a little yellow ochre, blue, green or grey, into the polyurethane or picture varnish to give it a transparent overtone. A little white can sometimes be added now, but it must not diminish the transparency, because the dazzling whiteness of the whole depends upon the shining undercoat penetrating through to the surface.

Colours. It is seldom possible to obtain the right shade direct from the tube or bottle, and so you will have to discover by experience how to match colours by mixing. Always mix your colours in daylight, as artificial light can alter certain shades, especially greens and blues. Remember that freshly mixed paint will look paler in the liquid state than when dry. Watercolours are the exception, since they may lose their brightness, especially on plaster. However, their colour is restored after glazing, so the colour on the palette, and not that on the plaster, should be considered correct.

If you want a dark colour eventually, mix some white in the first coat because this will coordinate the paint and give it body. Otherwise the mixture will have a transparent quality which is not desirable in the first coat whose main object is to hide the repaired surface. A whitish base also gives a certain luminosity which is important, as the colouring on porcelain is only rarely opaque, even in the darkish shades. Although the *filler may be white, it is not necessarily uniform in colour, also it meets the original surface in a definite line which a base coat of whitish paint will obscure.

Pattern. Complete the background painting first, and then you may need to replace the missing pattern. Unless you are extremely skilled at free-hand painting, you will do better to measure out your design, and draw it in lightly with a volatile pencil. Always use one colour at a time and allow it to dry before applying the next. Alternatively, you can make a series of stencils with tracing paper, one for each colour. Once you have done the tracing, cut out the pattern for one colour, place it in position, and paint the required colour over it. Let it dry before starting on the next. A watch-maker's glass is useful for fine details. Remember that it is important not only to replace the exact colours, but also the depth of the pattern, so that extra layers of paint must be added for raised patterns.

Crazing. Certain glazes develop small surface cracks which, if not faithfully imitated, would show up the repair, so these features too, must be reproduced in your repair.

This is also true of the crackle on some Chinese porcelain, although this was produced by the Chinese potter as a deliberate artistic embellishment.

Usually these cracks have no colour, and are only visible as a shadow in the transparency of the glaze. They are therefore extremely difficult to reproduce. However after some practice beforehand, they can sometimes be satisfactorily achieved with a lead pencil. If a glaze medium is then carefully applied, the markings will be partially removed but still sufficiently visible to give a shadowy effect.

Limbs and faces. Although Flesh Tint is a standard colour, it is very florid, and it is really better to mix your own. Flesh colour is usually made up of white and a little black, grey or blue, yellow ochre and red, the proportions varying according to the tone you are trying to match. Don't mix all these colours and apply them in a simultaneous coat, because this would result in a dead colour. To give the flesh its delicate, living quality, apply successive coats of white with traces of black, grey, blue or yellow. The top coat should be nearly transparent with a touch of red in it and no white at all, so that the white or cream undercoat shines through the surface transparency. Minute brushes and extremely thin layers are necessary, or the finer details of the modelling will be obscured.

When retouching the faces of antiques, remember to use brown eyes, because blue eyes are rare on porcelain figures before 1850.

Gilding. This is the last process in painting restoration before the final protective coat of glaze.

Gold paint of various shades can be bought and applied in the same way as any other paint. You can obtain any shade of gold, if you buy a yellow gold and a red gold, and mix them. An undercoat of Indian Red enriches the tone of any gold paint. American Treasure Gold, though expensive, is useful, as it can be rubbed on with the tip of the finger which gives a smoother and closer finish than a brush.

*Gold leaf is difficult to put on but a good result is easy to obtain. It is applied with size. Special *gold size can be bought, but polyurethane varnish is equally effective. It is painted on the article and allowed to grow tacky before the gold leaf is applied.

The gold leaf must adhere to the size only, so the surrounding surfaces must be dry and clean, as it sticks only too easily to any shiny surfaces if they are at all tacky. So the article should be cleaned carefully and dried with a silk rag. If enamel or lacquer paint has been used for retouching, allow at least three days before applying the gold leaf. Ensure that the mixing saucer, brushes and tools are scrupulously clean.

Polyurethane varnish is so transparent that it is difficult to see against the background, so mix a tiny trace of Ivory Black paint with it to make it visible. Apply the size as thinly as possible. If it is applied too thickly, the gold pattern or line will appear clumsy and will also be liable to crinkle, because the outside will dry while the deeper portion is still soft. Size may be removed with a small brush moistened in water or *methylated spirit.

Allow the size to grow tacky before applying the gold leaf. It is often easier and more economical to cut the transfer into the desired shape, but don't remove the backing until the leaf is firmly stuck in place as it will fly away very easily, fold over on itself or stick to your fingers. For this reason, avoid draughts, and do not breathe directly on it. Lay it in position, still backed with the tissue paper, gold side down, and rub along the back of the paper with your finger or a fairly stiff brush so that the leaf goes into any irregularities in the surface. When it has adhered, carefully peel off the paper.

Dust gently over the gold leaf with a soft brush, removing any loose particles. If any flakes off and settles on the painted surface, remove it with a brush or with the transfer paper; if it still sticks, use a sharpened piece of wood to push it away. A second application may be needed if the size has not been completely covered.

For places where the original gilding has become very worn, leave the size longer before applying the gold leaf, which will then only adhere patchily. This will avoid making the article look too new with a homogeneous coat of gold leaf.

Burnishing should only be done when the size and gold have dried completely. It can be done with special agate burnishers. If you don't have one, rub gently with a smooth tool such as a toothbrush handle over a sheet of clean celluloid until the surface matches the lustrous appearance of the original gilding.

A final top coat resembling the original glaze will protect the gold leaf from wear and is essential for pieces in constant use. However, the appearance of the gold is never so satisfactory as before the final coat, so on ornamental pieces it is often better to apply a double coat of gold leaf to an already glazed surface, and leave it without any protective coating.

Glazing. The glaze of the original has to be simulated. This is done after the painting and gilding. It is not necessary if polyurethane and dry pigments or enamel or lacquer paints have been used. It is done by applying a *polyurethane glaze or a good-quality clear lacquer coating with a very small brush, feathering it onto the original surface. It can also be applied with an airbrush, but it is not so stable. As many glazes are slightly coloured, add minute touches of colour to the glossy mixture until the right tint has been obtained. Polyurethane glaze should be left for three days before any polishing or rubbing is carried out. To increase the sheen, you can polish with a mild *chrome cleaner.

Lustre glazes are generally a combination of colour with an iridescent metallic film. They can be imitated by mixing bronze powders, which come in a variety of colours, with *amyl acetate, though these are far from perfect, as any contact with sulphur fumes or acids will cause oxidisation and bad discolouration. If they are used, they must be mixed extremely smoothly. It may, however, be better to use paint, because they are liable to tarnish.

After a repair has been decorated, take care not to damage the new decorations, as the new surface will not be hard like the original one, so that it can be scratched or partially removed by any sharp contact, even if a protective coating of glaze has been added. Always wash re-decorated articles gently by hand with warm water and a mild soap, and never use harsh detergents, abrasives or scalding water. Never leave them to soak or put them in a dishwasher. Dry with gentle patting rather than rubbing.

Spouts, knobs, handles and ears

Spouts. The spouts of tea or coffee pots are very vulnerable, but they are easy to repair. It is usually better to build up a new spout, even if you have the chipped pieces. If the pieces are missing and you don't know the original shape, examine similar articles or check in books or museums before deciding on the shape. Make a rough sketch to guide you.

Clean the spout carefully, removing any tannin stains (see ceramics). Mix a drier *filler than you would for flat ware, then smear a little adhesive on the broken edges as the drier filler will lack some of its adhesive quality. Roll the filler into a small, thin sausage and place it along the broken edge of the lip, drawing a little (not more than an eighth of an inch) back to overlap the surfaces of the spout. It is very important that the filler and body should meet closely, especially on the inside, and there should be no pit in the surface into which hot liquid might settle. Dust your fingers lightly with French chalk or kaolin and dip any tools in *methylated spirit to prevent them from sticking to the filler. Draw the filler upwards and outwards into the shape you have decided on. If you don't have enough filler, add a little more and smooth it out; if you have too much, trim off the excess with sharp scissors. Make the lip a little larger than the desired final size. Leave it to harden, well supported. A fulcrum support may dislodge the moist filler so it may be better to support the object with the spout uppermost in a sand-bed (see ceramic supports).

When the filler has completely dried, pare it down with a razor blade if necessary and then smooth it with *glass-paper or moistened *wet-and-dry paper. Make sure that both sides are identical. Be careful not to graze the original surface. Use a file to pare down the inside, and then finish it off with abrasive paper, wrapped around the file.

Knobs. Knobs on tea or coffee pots, or on sugar basins, are easily broken. If you have the broken knob, stick it on with adhesive, following the instructions under ceramic repairs.

However, the piece can easily be replaced if it has been broken beyond repair or is missing. You may find that you have a piece that will match, but that the broken surfaces do not fit together. In that case, file both surfaces level with glass-paper, smooth them, and then glue them together. If this reduces the stem or the shank too much, build it up with filler. If you want to make a replacement, you can build one up free-hand, as with a spout, making sure that you choose a shape suitable for the piece.

If the broken article is part of a set, a mould can be taken from a similar piece (see ceramic moulding). If the article is in constant use, you. might feel that extra strength is needed, which can be obtained by dowelling (see ceramic dowelling).

Handles and ears. Missing cup handles and the ears of vases are frequently a problem, but they can be replaced either with the aid of a mould or else by building them up free-hand.

If you have an identical or similar article, make a wax mould by pressing the slightly warmed handle of the duplicate into a slab of paraffin wax larger and wider than the actual handle and half an inch thick. The impression should be deep, more than half the diameter of the handle in size. Allow the wax to harden. Do likewise for the other side of the handle.

Take a piece of brass wire about a third or a quarter of the diameter of the handle, and cut it about half an inch longer than the handle to be made. With a small file, make a dozen notches along the wire to give the filler an anchor. Shape the wire to the contour of the duplicate handle, and lay it along one of the moulds, shortening it until the two ends will, in their final position, touch the centre of the two broken sites, which it is advisable to mark with a pencil.

Mix your filler, lift the wire, and pour a little beneath it. Tape the two moulds together and seal one end with a blob of wax, leaving the other end open. Pour in the filler through this hole, and leave until almost set but still malleable. Open the moulds with a sharp knife and remove the handle, checking it for any holes. Fill these in if necessary, smoothing the surface carefully with your finger and paring off any excess with a razor blade. Leave the handle to set until completely hard, using one half of the mould as a support. Smooth with sandpaper and trim the ends to fit the already cleaned sites. Glue into position and support until dry.

Provided you have a prototype, this method is much easier, especially if the handle or vase ear is elaborately shaped or has ornamental moulding on it.

The following method of building up, however, is probably stronger, but make sure that you have supports ready before beginning as it is time-consuming.

Mark the centres of the broken stubs and drill a small hole in each, providing they are deep enough. Bend a piece of notched brass wire into the desired shape, cut it to the required length, and place the ends in the holes, embedding them in filler.

Alternatively, if you can't drill holes because the sites aren't thick enough, put a blob of adhesive on the centre of the stubs and on both ends of the wire, and place the wire firmly in position, checking this not only from the sides but also from above, and maintaining it by the use of one or more plasticine columns (see ceramic supports). Make sure that the ends of the wire are well covered with adhesive; if it begins to run down, pull it back with a dentist's probe or similar tool. This will strengthen the joint. Don't try to smooth it, as a certain roughness here will give the filler an anchor. When the glue is completely dry or, if holes have been drilled, the filler is completely set, remove the plasticine supports and check your success by lifting the cup by the brass handle. If any adhesive or filler has flowed over the edge of the stubs, pare it off with a razor blade.

Dust your hands with French chalk or kaolin. Then make a fairly stiff mixture of filler and roll it into a thin sausage in your hands. Cut it to the required length and roll it in a few drops of water. Run wet fingers along the wire also. Place the filler along the wire, pinching it into position with moistened fingers. It is much better to build the handle up in two or three layers, allowing each to harden before applying the next, than to do it all at once, so do not make too thick a strip the first time. Don't attempt to smooth it at this stage, although large bumps can be removed with scissors or a razor blade.

When dry, moisten the surface with your fingers and apply the next layer. Gradually build up the handle to the shape and size required. If the filler shows any shrinkage, add another layer rather than change materials during the job.

When you have applied the top layer, smooth the surface with a damp finger, filling in any holes with moistened filler. Be careful not to use too much water, or you will find that a seemingly solid surface will, when dry, have small depressions. If you are using an *epoxy putty, it is unnecessary to moisten it or the wire with water. Make sure that the filler carries down evenly all round the stubs to avoid a ridge.

Allow to set until completely hard, recheck for any depressions or bumps, and fill in or file down accordingly. Then rub carefully with glass-paper so that the surface is completely smooth, as the smallest unevenness will show up when the article is painted.

Supports.

The glued edges of mended articles must stay exactly in position until the adhesive sets, or the perfect union that you have worked so hard for will be ruined. If self-adhesive tape has been used to clamp the join, the mended article may not need a lot of support.

The join should generally be kept horizontal, so supports are needed to maintain the balance required. These should be prepared in advance.

Nearly every repair needs a different kind of support, so you will need to use your ingenuity in construction. The following suggestions may be helpful.

A large, deep container of sand is very effective, as the mended article can be embedded in it at any angle. Take care not to get any sand into the adhesive. If there is any unfired decoration or gilding on the article, use flour rather than sand.

Plates and other flat articles can be stood vertically in a drawer by supporting the base in a box or a knob of plasticine, and closing the drawer as far as necessary to hold the piece steady. Clothes pegs can be used to clamp the rim edges of the repair.

Plasticine is invaluable for supporting a mended article at any angle. Rolled into a column, it can be useful as a bridging support where two glued sites must be kept in position simultaneously, as in a cup handle repair. Roll a small length of the material into a thick sausage, and flatten the two ends, sticking one onto the nearest body surface, and the other round the centre of the glued piece. Avoid getting any in the joints.

Fulcrum supports are useful when you want to hold a piece from underneath, as for the broken lower lips of spouts. One way of making them is to take a box or tin, or a block of wood, a little shorter than the repair to be supported, with a knob of plasticine pressed on the middle of the top. Take a narrow strip of wooden lath or a wooden skewer, longer than the box, and place it across the box, embedding it in the clay, so that one end rests beneath the repair. If you hang a small sand-bag, about the size of a tea-bag, on the other end of the wood, the weight of it will press the strip with the small knob of plasticine on the end sufficiently to keep the repaired piece in position.

A tall, hollow object, such as a vase or a coffee-pot, can be supported at an angle by three wooden skewers, or pencils, of different lengths. Their bases can be embedded in the sand-box, or in egg cups, and their tops, covered with a small knob of plasticine, will press against the sides of the article.

CHALK DRAWINGS

Chalk was a popular medium during the Renaissance, when it was usually black or red. Like pastel, chalk is made of a combination of chalk and pigment with a binding of gum.

Chalk drawings should be treated in the same way as *pastels.

CHANDELIERS

Special crystal chandelier cleaners are sold in a spray form. Liquid window-cleaning spray can also be used. Wipe each prism dry afterwards.

By far the best way of cleaning chandeliers is to dismantle them and wash them with warm, soapy water, as for all glass. Rinse in clear water and polish each prism with a fluff-free cloth.

If the wire pins or hooks that hold the chandelier together are very rusty, they should be replaced. You can buy pins of malleable brass or silver wire $\frac{3}{4}''$–$2''$ long at glass stockists or hardware shops. Do not try making your own out of household pins, because they are so tough that they may break the prism when you are trying to manipulate them.

Missing parts can be replaced from glass stockists, or an antique dealer may have some spare pieces that will match yours.

CHRONOMETERS

The term 'chronometer' is usually taken to mean a timepiece of great accuracy, fitted with a detent escapement, although it is now sometimes applied to a high-quality lever watch. It is often applied to ship's timepieces.

The movement of a marine or box chronometer is housed in a brass bowl, kept in place by a bezel which is screwed on and off. The bowl is mounted on gimbals (to keep it upright in a moving ship) inside a wooden carrying case. The case has a hinged lid with a glass top, and a further hinged wooden cover to protect the glass. (For advice on cleaning the bowl, case and glass, *see* entries for appropriate material.) The covers of most chronometers used on board ship used were removed when the instrument was placed inside the ship's fixed chronometer box. For this reason, many chronometers have holes in the woodwork of their cases where the hinges and catch were originally fitted. The restorer's usual practice is to conceal the hinge rebates with

A marine chronometer, made by Arnold & Dent, London, 1917.

A Regency chandelier c1810 with ormolu branches for ten candles. Height 3 ft. 10 in. Width: 2 ft.

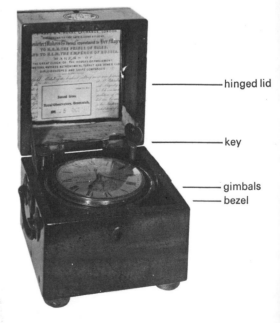

hinged lid

key

gimbals

bezel

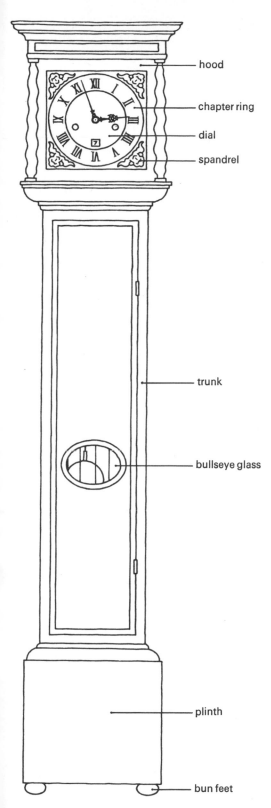

- hood
- chapter ring
- dial
- spandrel
- trunk
- bullseye glass
- plinth
- bun feet

Typical long-case clock, c1680c–1720.

a strip of wood to match the rest of the case, and the catch hole with a brass plug.

Except in a very few examples fitted with special winding mechanisms, winding is carried out by inverting the movement on its gimbals and inserting a key through a hole in the bottom of the brass bowl. This hole is covered by a sliding or pivoted plate to exclude dust.

To set the hands, the bezel must be unscrewed and the winding key applied to the square holding the minute hand. No attempt should be made to move the seconds hand, as this may cause damage to the escapement.

Smaller versions of the chronometer movement are fitted in watch-type cases, or as desk chronometers in wooden standing mounts. Pocket chronometer cases should be cleaned in the same way as *watch cases. But although they are designed to be worn and carried, they should be treated with the great care appropriate to the delicacy of their mechanism.

Only a qualified craftsman should be allowed to clean or adjust a chronometer movement, since the damage caused by careless handling is expensive to repair. Regulation is not possible except by adjusting the weights on the balance, and this should not be attempted at home.

CLOCKS

Domestic clocks have been used since the 15th century, although public, or turret, clocks had been introduced at least by 1300. The basic mechanics of clockwork remained unchanged until 1650–75, when both the pendulum and the balance spring were introduced, replacing the earlier unsprung circular balance or weighted horizontal bar (foliot), whose inertia alone provided the clock with a rough timekeeping element. The mechanism or movement of the clock was continuously improved throughout the 18th and 19th centuries, mainly by the development of new forms of escapement to link the train of wheels to the pendulum or sprung balance without interfering with their timekeeping properties.

Clocks can be categorised by the varied forms and materials of their cases and by the mechanical details of their movements (*see* clock cases, clock dials and hands, clock movements). The basic principles of

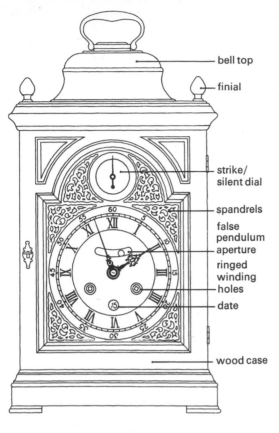

bell top

finial

strike/
silent dial

spandrels

false
pendulum
aperture

ringed
winding
holes

date

wood case

Typical bracket clock, c1740–c1820.

move with the oscillation of the pendulum, and, in extreme cases, may prevent it from going at all.

A clock should be wound at regular intervals: A thirty-hour movement should be wound at the same time every day; an eight-day movement at the same time every week. If a clock is weight-driven regular winding simply ensures that it is not forgotten and allowed to run down and stop. If it is spring-driven, particularly if it is of an early type with a verge escapement, the state of winding of the spring may affect its rate of timekeeping. If it is wound regularly, the average rate of going will be more nearly constant.

The movement should be cleaned and oiled at approximately five-year intervals. This is not an expensive process when compared with the value of the clock, and saves the considerable cost of the repairs which will be necessary if dust and thickened oil are allowed to accumulate to the point where the clock stops. If the clock does stop, don't try to restart it by putting more oil on the pivots, or by adding additional weights to a weight-driven clock. Either of these may set the clock going, but they will only accelerate the process of wear and destruction.

care and maintenance apply to all types. Neglect will destroy a clock's usefulness as a timekeeper and its value as an antique.

Place the clock in a position as far as possible free from dust (which will combine with the oil on the moving parts and form an abrasive mixture), damp (which will cause corrosion of the metal parts), and extremes of heat and cold. Although many clocks from the mid-18th century onwards were fitted with some form of temperature compensation on the pendulum or balance, this was not designed to cope with the rapid changes occasioned by modern heating methods, which may also cause the case to split or crack.

Accuracy depends to a large extent on the firmness of support; this applies particularly to long-case, or 'grandfather' clocks with a heavy pendulum and weights. These clocks should be placed on a level floor surface and fixed to the wall behind through the upper part of the back of the case. A loose fixing may cause the whole clock to

Transportation. Carriage clocks and other types with a balance rather than a pendulum were designed to be moved about and need no special treatment, although they should be guarded from jolts and vibration.

Pendulum clocks, however, may be damaged if they are moved carelessly. Before moving a long-case clock, remove the hood over the dial and movement. It normally slides forward, although the earliest examples were made to lift vertically. Occasionally it may be necessary to release a locking device which can be reached by opening the door in the trunk of the clock. When the movement is exposed, the pendulum can be removed by lifting the rod gently, releasing the block or pin from its retaining slot and drawing the rod downwards through the crutch (the linkage which connects the pendulum to the pallets within the movement). Lay the pendulum horizontally to avoid bending the rod. Reach through the trunk door and unhook the weight or weights. The movement can now

Verge escapement, developed c1300, used in modified forms to c1810.

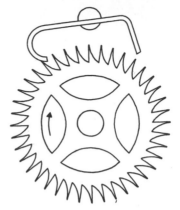

American version of anchor escapement, simplified for mass-production. From c1840.

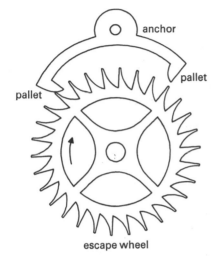

Anchor recoil escapement, invented c1670 and used, in various forms, to the present day.

Brocot deadbeat escapement. This mid 19th century French escapement is usually visibly, forward of the dial.

A modified anchor escapement: George Graham's recoilless deadbeat escapement, invented c1715.

French Tic-Tac drum escapement.

49

be lifted off its seat-board and the various parts of the clock packed separately for transportation. Note that some escapements (the dead-beat type) can be severely damaged if the driving weight is removed first and the pendulum allowed to swing with no power on the train. The pendulum of smaller, spring-driven clocks can be removed in a similar way. The crutch may now start oscillating rapidly and allow the train to run down. To prevent this tie a piece of thread from the crutch to the back plate. If the pendulum rod is fixed directly to the end of the axle on which the pallets are mounted (the pallet arbor), do not attempt to remove it, but tie or wedge it so that it is held firmly without being strained.

Setting a clock in beat. If the 'tick' of a pendulum clock is uneven, the clock is said to be out of beat. This indicates that the two pallets are not engaging the escape wheel to the same extent. Apart from producing an annoying sound, it may interfere with the clock's accuracy. It is usually caused by standing the clock on a sloping surface, and it can be cured by levelling with wedges placed firmly under the base. Alternatively, the crutch, through which the pendulum passes, can be bent carefully towards the louder tick until the beat is even. Only a very small amount of bending will normally be necessary. The upper end of the crutch must be held very firmly so that no pressure is exerted on the pallets or the escape wheel.

Regulating. The earliest clocks were regulated by relatively crude methods, such as moving small weights along the arms of a bar balance, or foliot, or, since the verge escapement is susceptible to changes in driving force, by changing the weights or the tension of the main spring.

Pendulum clocks are regulated simply by altering the effective length of the pendulum. Raising the weighted bob at the end of the pendulum rod brings the centre of oscillation closer to the point of suspension and makes the clock go faster. The commonest method of raising or lowering the bob is by turning a threaded nut which holds the bob on its rod.

In small clocks, the bob itself is often threaded and may be screwed up or down.

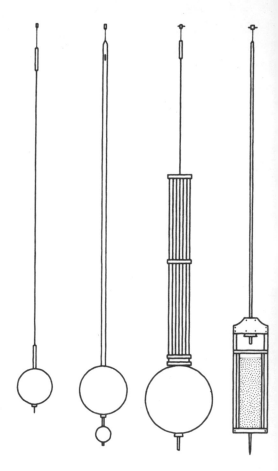

Normal seconds pendulum (far left) compared with 3 types of temperature compensated pendulum. From left to right: wood rod pendulum; gridiron pendulum; mercury compensated pendulum.

The Brocot suspension frequently found on small French clocks embodies a sliding section at the upper end of the pendulum rod and can be adjusted by a small winding square which passes through the upper part of the dial.

Precision clocks may have a tray attached to the upper part of the pendulum rod, on which small weights can be set. Weight may be added here which shifts the centre of oscillation upwards and increases the rate of the clock. This provides a very exact means of regulation.

Carriage clocks and others with balance springs normally have a regulating lever or index, as in a watch. Occasionally portable clocks have a chronometer escapement and a helical balance spring which cannot be regulated except by adjusting the balance itself; this should be left to an expert.

Locking plate or count wheel striking. This system dates from the earliest clocks of the Middle Ages, and remained in use to the present century, although it was superseded to a considerable degree by rack striking from the beginning of the 18th century.

The strike is unlocked by a pin on the minute hand arbor, acting on a lever or lifting piece, and the number of blows struck is determined by the position of the locking plate or count wheel. The circumference of the plate, which is driven by the striking train, is divided by slots, the intervals between each increasing proportionately from 1 to 12. When the striking train is released, a finger is lifted out of the slot. The plate revolves until the finger drops into the next slot. The bell hammer is actuated by pins or cams on one of the wheels of the striking train. The going and striking trains are connected by the unlocking pin only, so that they may easily become unsynchronised, for example, by the striking weight or spring running down, or by the hands being set forward too rapidly. The result will be that the strike will be at variance with the time shown on the dial.

To prevent this, when the hands are being re-set, allow the clock to run through its strike every time the minute hand passes the hour. If the strike has already got out of step, it can be corrected by moving the hour hand on its own to register the hour last struck, then setting the clock to time normally, again allowing time for each strike. Alternatively, the striking train can be let off by raising the lifting piece as many times as necessary to bring the strike into synchronisation.

In some types, particularly American 19th-century wall clocks, a wire rod connected to the striking work projects downwards inside the door of the case, and can be pushed up to let off the strike.

Locking plate striking is especially susceptible to damage if the hands are turned backwards past the hour, as the lifting piece, instead of riding over the pin on the arbor, will become trapped underneath it. Timepiece clocks, without striking, alarm or repeating work, are not damaged by turning the hands back, although if the hands are turned through several revolutions, the power delivered to the escapement may be reduced for long enough to stop the clock.

Rack striking. In this system, introduced at the end of the 17th century and quickly adopted for most good-quality domestic clocks, the number of blows struck is determined by the position of a stepped cam, or snail, mounted on the arbor of the hour hand, and directly related to the time shown on the dial. Since the striking train cannot get out of step with the going train, the hands can be set without difficulty, and the system allows the use of strike/silent devices to disengage the strike when not required. Rack striking work is less liable to damage if the hands are turned back, but the practice should still be avoided. If the strike is out of step with the time shown, the hour hand will have been fitted on the arbor in the wrong position: it should be removed and replaced correctly.

Clock cases

For the methods of cleaning and repair *see* the entries appropriate to the material of the case. Before undertaking any substantial work, remove the movement, first taking off the pendulum and weights if necessary (*see* clocks). The movement may be held in place by weight alone, as in long-case clocks, but in many types it will be necessary to extract several screws or bolts. Mark all their positions, as they may not be interchangeable. In many wall clocks, the movement is attached to the dial plate, and the two together can be unscrewed and removed from the front of the case. Carriage clock cases are normally held together by screws through the bottom plate into the brass corner pillars. It is advisable to dismantle the case before attempting any thorough cleaning, to prevent a residue of polish and dirt accumulating in the joints. Lay out the glass panels and other parts carefully to ensure correct reassembly.

Cases in need of extensive repair should be taken to a professional restorer, as amateur treatment may severely affect the value of a clock. In some instances any form of restoration may be unwise.

Clocks which have been mutilated in the past, e.g. long-cases which have been cut down to fit under low ceilings, can be restored to their original condition: An expert will be able to advise whether this is worthwhile.

Minor repairs to wooden cases, such as sealing cracks, or covering the inner surface of a cracked panel with paper or thin card to exclude dust, can be done at home. However, do not attempt it if the clock is very valuable.

Broken glass panels can be replaced quite easily if they are flat, although modern glass will not match the original in appearance. Shaped pieces, especially the glass domes of 19th-century skeleton clocks, are becoming more difficult to obtain.

Clock dials and hands.

Dials. Clock dials are made of a wide variety of materials. The most common are brass, plain, silvered or gilt, white enamel on a copper base, and painted iron. Different materials and finishes are frequently combined.

To clean a dial effectively, it will be necessary to remove the hands. These are normally held friction-tight on their spindles, or arbors, and can be drawn off by pulling carefully on the central boss of the hand. The minute hand is usually secured by a pin, which can be removed by a pair of fine pliers. Never force a hand off by levering directly against the dial surface: this may distort the hand and damage the dial.

The dial itself is usually fixed to the movement by dial feet which are pinned or screwed to the front movement plate. If the dial is embellished by separately applied sections, such as the ornamental corner pieces (spandrels) on many long-case clocks, these can also be removed and cleaned. Once the dial is removed, the motion work, the gearing connecting hour and minute hands, will be free. Make sure that the parts are not allowed to fall off. For methods of cleaning dials *see* entries for the appropriate material.

It is essential to establish the material of the dial exactly before attempting any treatment. Examine the dial as a whole, as it is not uncommon to find enamel dials to which a painted decoration has been added. Plain white enamel dials can safely be washed, or even boiled in detergent to extract dirt from the cracks. However, the pigments used on many painted dials, particularly on provincial English long-case and American shelf clocks, are water-soluble. These should be cleaned with an appropriate solvent.

Restoring damaged dials is difficult and cannot be recommended for an amateur. Cracked or chipped enamel dials may be repaired with one of the cold enamel compounds available from art materials suppliers, but they can never be restored to their original state. Painted dials can be retouched by an expert. Metal dials have often been worn by excessive polishing in the past. Some which now seem to be plain brass were probably originally silvered, but have been deliberately reduced to the base metal as the silvered coating wore thin. Resilvering is possible but it is hard to reproduce the antique texture, which varied over different periods and according to the area. Like regilding, it may produce a harsh, modern-looking appearance.

Hands. The present system of concentric hour and minute hands did not come into general use until the beginning of the 18th century. Minute hands are sometimes found on 17th-century clocks of exceptionally high quality: Many clocks, also, particularly the provincial English thirty-hour long-cases, were made with a single hour hand well into the 19th century. Dials designed for use with a single hour hand can easily be identified. The ring carrying the numerals I–XII (chapter ring) is divided on its inner circumference only, with the half-hour divisions marked by a fleur-de-lis or similar stylised device. After the minute hand was introduced, an outer circle of divisions was added to the chapter ring. If there is no outer ring of minute divisions, but a minute hand is present, it will have been added after the clock's original manufacture, probably in conjunction with a conversion of the escapement. If there is a minute ring but no minute hand, the clock has probably been modified to give a false impression of antiquity, although it is possible that the original dial has been damaged and replaced. Inexperienced collectors may be misled by the absence of a minute hand into thinking that the clock is incomplete, but this is not usually so.

The most common material for hands is

blued steel. (Blueing is an oxide coating on the surface of the steel.) If the surface is marked or rusted, it can be re-blued. Hands were sometimes blackened with lamp-black, particularly when the clock was expected to withstand damp conditions, for instance on board ship. This coating can be renewed by holding the hand in a candle flame until a thin layer of soot has accumulated, and then covering it with lacquer with a soft paint-brush.

Hands are often damaged or broken by careless attempts to remove them or to set the time by applying pressure to the tip. They can be repaired by a clockmaker. It is not a good idea to do it at home, as the operation is delicate. If the hands are beyond repair or are missing, new sets can be made, but the job should be done by an antiquarian clock restorer who will have a proper regard for the shape and material appropriate to the type and period of the clock.

Clock movements

The movement of a clock is its mechanism, as distinct from its case, dial, hands, etc.

Before taking a movement out of its case, remove the pendulum and weights, if any. The movement may be held in place by screws or brackets, or it may simply rest on a seat-board, as in most long-case clocks. The dial and hands should also be removed and set aside (see clock dials and hands).

Now examine the condition of the movement. If it is complete and undamaged it will need no attention except cleaning and oiling. If parts are missing or broken, or there are signs of wear, repairs will be necessary. Before undertaking cleaning and oiling or any repair, the movement will have to be stripped down to its separate parts. Note that most serious repair work should be carried out by an expert.

Dismantling. First ensure that all power is removed. The spring itself must be 'let down' in a spring-driven clock. Even though the clock has run down, there may be enough residual tension in the spring to cause damage and injury if it is released suddenly. In movements with a fusee, the conical pulley which equalises the variations of power provided by the spring in different states of winding, the stationary arbor, or

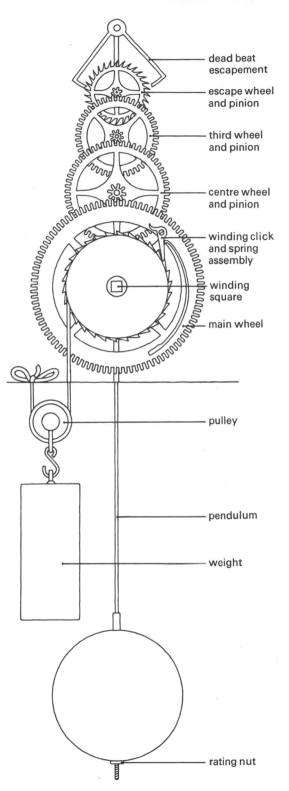

Arrangement of weight-driven 8 day long-case movement.

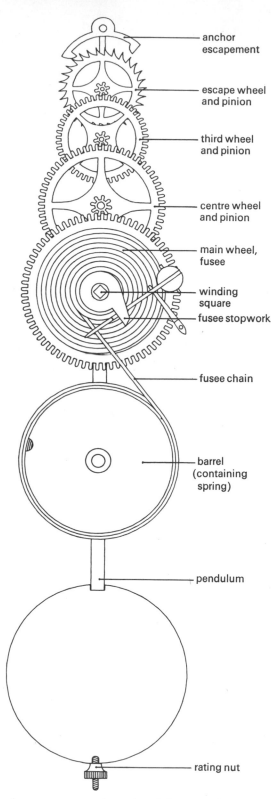

Arrangement of spring-driven wall clock movement.

anchor escapement

escape wheel and pinion

third wheel and pinion

centre wheel and pinion

main wheel, fusee

winding square

fusee stopwork

fusee chain

barrel (containing spring)

pendulum

rating nut

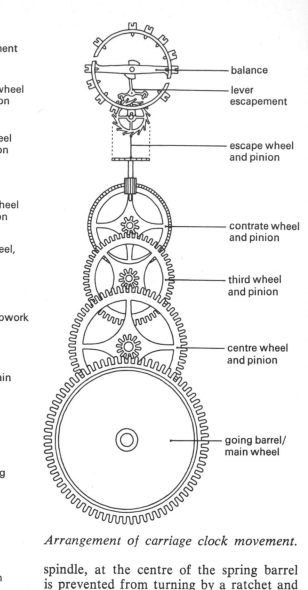

Arrangement of carriage clock movement.

balance

lever escapement

escape wheel and pinion

contrate wheel and pinion

third wheel and pinion

centre wheel and pinion

going barrel/ main wheel

spindle, at the centre of the spring barrel is prevented from turning by a ratchet and click attached to one of the movement plates; this also allows the minimum tension of the spring to be set up. Hold the squared end of the arbor firmly with a key or hand vice (not pliers, which will burr the corners and may slip), and release the click. The arbor can be allowed to turn slowly until the spring is completely unwound. If necessary, do this in stages, replacing the click between each turn. Whenever possible, allow the movement to run down normally before letting down the spring, so that the number of turns needed to set it up can be noted for reassembly.

Apply a similar technique to movements without a fusee, e.g., many American and

German clocks, in which the ratchet and click are mounted on the first wheel of the train.

Repeat the procedure for the springs of any striking or alarm work.

Most domestic clocks are constructed on the plated frame principle, in which the pivots of the train revolve in holes in two parallel plates which are separated and held rigid by pillars. The ends of the pillars are secured by screws or tapered pins. Some of the pivots may be mounted in separate cocks, or brackets, screwed to the plate. It may be advisable to make sketches of the complete movement or of individual sections to avoid problems when reassembling. Clocks of good workmanship usually carry filed or drilled marks at the junctions of pillars and plates, etc., to indicate the correct positions.

The wheels and pinions of striking work must be assembled in particular positions; they may also be marked to show which teeth should mesh together.

When drawing off the front plate, be certain not to tilt or twist it, as any deviation will bend, and may break, the train pivots. Cocks, click springs, etc., which are screwed to the plates, are also located by steady pins, and must be removed carefully to prevent damage. Note that the various screws are probably not interchangeable, and should be replaced in their own holes.

Place each part as you remove it on a clear surface. A series of trays or boxes is helpful to prevent confusing or losing the smaller pieces.

It is not advisable to take springs out of their barrels without the appropriate spring-winding tool: they can be hazardous to extract and almost impossible to replace.

Cleaning and oiling. The dirt in the movement is a mixture of atmospheric impurities, dust and thickened oil. The amount of it will depend on the conditions in which the clock has been kept and the length of time since it was last cleaned, which should not exceed about two years. Cleaning cannot be carried out without dismantling. Don't, for example, attempt to do it by rinsing the whole movement in a solvent.

Once the parts have been separated, remove the surface dirt by brushing with *paraffin or *benzene.

The parts should then be treated with a cleaning fluid. Clock material suppliers sell various proprietary fluids which should be used according to the instructions. A substitute can be made from household *ammonia with a few drops of liquid detergent added.

Wear rubber gloves and work in a ventilated area. Soak the parts, a few at a time, in the solution for 10–15 minutes. Rinse thoroughly in very hot water and dry in warm air. Repeat if necessary, then brush out any residue. Avoid steel wire brushes which may scratch the surface of the metal.

Finish brass pieces with metal polish and chamois leather, handling them afterwards with gloves or tissue paper to prevent fingermarks which may leave a corrosive trace. Steel parts will normally need no further attention, but they can be treated with a rust-removing compound.

Plates and frames. After cleaning, peg out the pivot holes to extract all traces of dirt and oil. Trim thin slips of pegwood to a point and rotate in the hole. Repeat, cutting now points, until the wood comes out clean. The traditional material for this is dogwood, but deal and other woods can be substituted.

The finish of plates varies in different types of clock. French ones tend to be highly polished, while the plates of many English movements are 'papered', that is, given a fine grain by rubbing in straight lines against a block covered with *emery paper.

Polished surfaces can be protected with lacquer, but this must be kept clear of screw and pivot holes.

Wheels. Use a stiff brush to clear the teeth, and thin strips of chamois leather to remove polish from the inside of the crossings or spokes. Handle the escape wheel with particular care, as it may be light and easily damaged.

Pinions. If the pinions are badly corroded or the dirt cannot be brushed out, cut a piece of wood to fit between the teeth and rub with *emery or another abrasive powder mixed with oil. Finish off with the finest grade of abrasive powder. Then wash in *benzene.

Lantern pinions, formed from lengths of steel wire fitted between two end collars, are often found in American clocks. They are laborious to clean thoroughly. Work strips of cloth charged with a little fine abrasive and oil gently to and fro between the pins. Note that the pins are fixed firmly into the collars, and are not meant to rotate individually.

Screws. Slots in screw heads are often damaged by careless handling or using the wrong-sized screwdriver. If the edges of the slot are burred or pitted they can be filed true, but may then need to be re-blued.

Fusee chains. These can be polished by charging a groove in a piece of softwood with very fine abrasive and pulling the chain through it end to end. The chain should be washed very thoroughly in *benzene afterwards.

Reassembly. Collect the parts so that they are easily accessible and laid out in the right order. First make sure that you have all the parts. Refer to any sketches made before the dismantling process was started. Make sure that you know where each piece fits.

Insert the back pivots into their holes, and slide the front plate gently into place, working the front pivots into position. Do not apply any pressure, or screw down the plate onto the pillars, until you are sure that all the arbors of the train are free to move.

Replace the screws or pins holding the plates to the pillars. If any pins are missing, broken or bent, they should be renewed. Taper pins can be bought from clock material suppliers, or they can be filed from steel rod. Tap the pins home with a punch and light hammer; hammering directly on the end of the pin may mark the surface of the plate.

Refit clicks, click springs and other small parts. In fusee movements, the chain or gut is wound on the spring barrel while the spring is let down, and the free end secured to the hole or holes at the end of the groove on the fusee; the hook at the barrel end of a fusee chain is formed with a tail or projection so that it lies flat on the barrel surface (the fusee hook is plain). The spring itself is set up with the ratchet on the arbor. If the amount of set-up was noted, it can now be wound to the same extent; if the

correct set-up is not known, one turn should be applied, which will normally be enough.

Oil all the pivot holes and moving surfaces, such as the ends of click springs, but not the wheel and pinion teeth. The oil must be the type specifically intended for clocks. Ordinary light machine oil must not be used, as it will age more quickly and tends to creep away from the pivots and leave them dry. Apply the oil with a piece of thin (about 20 G.) wire. One drop will be enough for most pivot holes. The oil sink around the hole should not be completely full. Oil the escape wheel teeth and pallets very sparingly, also lubricate the crutch at the point where it bears on the pendulum rod.

Replace the dial and hands, and fix the complete movement back in its case, then attach the pendulum and weights as appropriate. (*See* clocks for methods of setting up and regulating.)

Repair and restoration
Few clock repairs can be carried out by the amateur, as special skill and equipment are usually essential.

Broken and missing parts can be replaced by a repairer or restorer. The considerable cost of having a piece made should be measured against the great increase in the value of the clock.

The most common faults in clocks are caused by frictional wear on pivots, pinions and pallets. Worn pivots must be turned true on a lathe, and the holes drilled out to receive bushes of brass tube to form new bearing surfaces.

Replacement is the only cure for badly worn pinions, except where they are wide enough to allow the wheel to be moved along its arbor, bringing a new section of the pinion teeth into play. Lantern pinions can be fitted with new pins relatively easily. As a temporary measure the pins can be turned in the collars to present an unworn surface to the driving wheel.

Pallets can be resurfaced, but again the best course is to have them replaced. It is not enough simply to grind down and reface them, as the angles at which they meet the escape wheel teeth will be altered.

Fusee chains, which are often made in standard lengths, can be renewed, although they are now becoming difficult to obtain. The correct length of chain must be used, since too short a chain will not operate the stopwork, that is, the sprung finger which engages with a projection on the fusee to prevent the chain being stressed and possibly broken when the mainspring barrel has been wound to its maximum. Fusees made for use with a chain have a groove cut to a square section, while the groove on a gut fusee is rounded.

Movements sometimes show signs of past alterations. Early clocks with verge escapements were often converted to use with the anchor escapement after its introduction at the end of the 17th century. Similarly, small portable clocks such as carriage clocks may have had a lever substituted for a cylinder escapement.

It is now not uncommon for such movements to be converted back to their original forms, on the grounds that this will increase their value, although at the cost of performance.

Many clocks have also had their striking and repeating work removed. This will be obvious from the unused spaces between the plates and the empty pivot holes. (Note, however, that there will normally be a pair of holes in each plate which are not intended for pivots but were used by the maker to hold the plates together when drilling the pivot holes.) A skilled restorer can make a complete new striking or repeating train. This is an expensive undertaking, but again will be reflected in the clock's value.

immersed for a few seconds in a 5% solution of *nitric acid. After a brief immersion examine carefully to make sure that the acid is not etching into the metal. This can easily happen, particularly with copper coins. Be sure to rinse well afterwards in running water. If only part of the coin is tarnished or corroded coat the rest of it with *paraffin wax or grease. When all the acid has been rinsed off, rub in a little lanolin or *microcrystalline wax.

Heavily corroded silver coins often have very little silver left in them, so it is best to leave them alone.

Coins should be protected from the atmosphere and kept in special coin cabinets. These may be rather expensive, but a simple tray can be made from two identical pieces of hardboard. Cut circular holes a little larger than the coins in one, and glue the two pieces together. Cover the whole of the holed side with baize or velvet and cut circles slightly smaller than the holes above each hole. Glue the overlap down round the sides of each hole. Cut discs of the same material to fit the bottom of the holes and glue them in place. Then slip the coins into the holes.

You can also buy albums with transparent slides on each side of the coin recesses, so that both sides of the coin can be seen.

Coins, usually lead or tin ones, that are too fragile to be cleaned regularly should be embedded by an expert in a transparent thermoplastic or polyester resin block. They can be removed by soaking the block in chloroform, which will dissolve the resin.

COINS

In general, avoid cleaning collectors' specimens because it may detract from their value. Before you start, remember that the inscription may be more legible when corroded. If you must clean them, don't rub the surface with anything harder than cotton-wool or a soft silver brush.

Ancient coins can be cleaned in a nitric acid bath, but are best left to an expert.

Gold coins should be washed in soapy water, rinsed and dried with a soft cloth or leather. Silver coins can also be washed in soapy water or in a 10%*ammonia solution which must be rinsed off straightaway.

Bronze, copper and silver coins can be

CORAL

Coral is a hard substance composed mainly of calcium carbonate and found on the bottom of warm seas such as the Mediterranean. It is the skeletal remains of certain polyps, and varies in colour from deep red to pink.

Coral is used for ornaments and for jewellery.

It can be cleaned by sponging with a weak detergent solution. Stubborn dirt can be removed with a fine abrasive such as *whiting or *powdered pumice. Finish with a *microcrystalline wax polish.

Broken coral can be repaired with an *epoxy resin adhesive.

DOLLS

Many dolls with ceramic, composition or wooden heads and limbs have stuffed bodies. To replace a stuffed body, use a strong, closely-woven cotton that will last well, hold its shape and contain fine stuffing. A leather one can be made of a very soft kid.

The stuffing can be sawdust, rag, wood-wool, bran hair or a modern washable material such as kapok. Make sure that it is pushed firmly into place. Insert a piece of wood to prevent a long body from bending in the middle.

Never throw away the old clothes of a doll as they may be a valuable guide in dating it.

Remove stains and check that the dyes of coloured clothes are fast before washing them. If not, they will have to be dry-cleaned (*see* textiles).

When making new clothes try to use old materials. Check up in books, fashion plates and museums on the correct style of the period.

Ceramic dolls

Ceramic dolls are made of highly glazed white porcelain, or Parian ware, a very fine, high-fired, white clay that resembles marble, or, more usually, of bisque—unglazed porcelain. They are either made in one piece without movable joints and with solid or hollow limbs, or else they are joined with hollow limbs usually strung together with elastic. Ball and socket-jointed dolls usually have their bodies and limbs made of composition or wood, although their heads, and possibly hands and feet, are of a ceramic material.

Washing and mending. The ceramic limbs can be gently washed with warm, soapy water. For bisque dolls, add a little *ammonia to the water and brush gently with a soft toothbrush.

Breaks should be mended with adhesive, but it is better not to use an epoxy resin adhesive. This is because if you subsequently take the doll to an expert, he will be unable to work over the epoxy. A strong, colourless, easily soluble adhesive is suitable.

Noses and ears. Small missing parts like noses or ears can easily be replaced

A late 19th century china head doll. These dolls were made from c1750, and were particularly fashionable in the mid-19th century. Light-haired dolls like this became popular c1880.

with a stiff mixture of *filler, modelled either *in situ* or separately (*see* ceramic cabinet pieces). Dental plaster or a hard, white, modelling plaster is ideal. It is advisable to put a little blob of it onto the broken surface, so that the modelled missing part can adhere to it. The two pieces should merge perfectly and hold permanently if pressed firmly together. Smooth the join when it has hardened, with *glass-paper.

Head. If the head is much damaged, it is better to take it off the body. With a jointed doll, first remove the arms by un-hooking or cutting their elastic. Then you will usually be able to unhook the head with a button hook. If the body is made of cloth or kidskin, the head will simply be stitched on through holes in the ceramic shoulders.

Start working from the centre of the face and work outwards so that any irregularities are hidden by the hair. If the doll has to stand up to rough treatment, reinforce the head by lining it with a stout piece of Indian muslin.

The heads of jointed dolls often have a wooden dome at the bottom from which the stringing elastic goes through to the legs. It is difficult to replace this, if it is missing.

Improvise by using a button with a metal loop on the back. Line the hollow into which it will fit with kid or cardboard, and place it so that the side with the loop faces downwards. Then bend a piece of wire into an 'S' shape, and hook it, with the stringing elastic, onto the loop.

Bisque dolls generally have a large hole in the top of the head to facilitate inserting the eyes. It is covered with a dome of straw-board or cork. It can be replaced if missing by cutting out an angle from a circle of cardboard and forming the cardboard into a dome shape. You can make a more professional one out of papier mâché, shaped with the aid of a mould taken from the base of a cup or a bowl of the right size. Grease the inside of the mould before lining it with papier mâché about a quarter of an inch thick. Remove it when it has set, and then trim the lower edge of the dome, leaving it a little larger than necessary so that you can snip round it and turn it inwards to make a surface that glues smoothly onto the edges of the bisque hole.

Eyes. In order to repair damaged eyes and eye sockets, remove first the plaster behind that holds them in place. Remove the wig and soak the head in cold water to loosen the plaster. If one or both eyes are missing, you will have to enlist the help of a doll dealer. Old glass eyes are not easy to find, but he may have a supply. If only one eye is damaged, send its counterpart to the dealer as a pattern. If both are broken, need to be replaced, carefully measure the overall dimensions of the eye sockets before getting new eyes, as it is most important that the eyes fit perfectly. Otherwise the opening and closing mechanism will not work. Coat the outer edges of new eyeballs with a little melted wax to prevent them scraping against the sockets.

The eye units themselves are held in position by plaster at both ends of the horizontal eye-join wire, which is generally covered with putty and wax. If the plaster is broken or missing, the whole eye unit may be loose, so replace it, holding the eye unit in position with plasticine until the plaster has set, and first checking that the eyes are in the right position in their sockets. If the bridge behind the eyes has

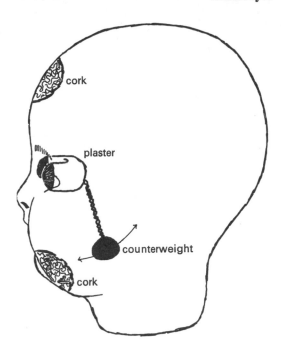

Common form of eye mechanism found in many ceramic dolls.

broken, it can be welded together with plaster. To repair the eye socket, first replace any missing pieces with filler. When dry, smooth it off with fine abrasive paper to prevent the edges scratching the eyes.

In most old dolls, the opening and closing mechanism is worked by a lump of lead or plaster fixed to the ends of the eye wires which are twisted together in the shape of a 'T'. A loose weight can simply be glued back onto the wires. Otherwise, make a new one of lead or with filler. It is very important to get the weight right, so that the eyes open and close properly.

Most dolls have pieces of cork inside them which the weight hits against when the doll opens and closes its eyes. These should be replaced if they have fallen out, as otherwise the eyes will move with a clacking sound, their balance will be disturbed, and eventually the eye wires will bend.

Eyelashes can be replaced with false eyelashes trimmed to a suitable length. Don't use the glue provided to stick them on, but colourless, easily soluble glue. Be careful not to apply too much. You will need a fine pair of tweezers and a magnifying glass for this fiddly job. Always replace the eyes if they have been removed, before gluing on the eyelashes. Otherwise the lashes will be caught when the eyes are eased into their sockets.

Painted eyes on porcelain dolls are much more easily restored. The delicate details can be painted in with a fine brush.

Hair. Porcelain dolls generally have painted hair, and bisque and composition dolls have wigs. If the hair is in a tangle, don't comb it as you would your own hair, as this will pull it out of its base. Instead, put a little cold cream or hair cream on your comb, separate a small lock of hair at the base, and gently tease the tangles out, working up through the wig.

Hair is normally washable, but always get the tangles out first. It is best to wash only wigs on canvas cap mounts, not those made of gauze. Lay the hair in the water to which you have added a little soft soap, washing-up liquid or a mild shampoo, and gently squeeze it. Never rub it. Hold it under the tap to rinse it. Never let the cap dry out fully whilst it is off the doll, as it will shrink. Make sure to put it back over the head whilst still damp, so that it retains its shape.

To make a new wig, make a skull cap out of tailor's canvas to fit the crown of the doll's head. Human hair is the best material for making wigs. You may be able to use an old wig of human hair. If so, unpick the strips of hair and oversew them around and round the cap. You might be able to benefit from friends who have suddenly decided to cut their hair. Or you can buy mohair from a doll or theatrical suppliers. This too should be oversewn onto the canvas cap. It is much softer than real hair and can be washed, but it will tangle easily, so always use a little cream rubbed into the palm of your hand when combing it out. Hair cream will give the hair a shine.

Limbs. Limbs are often broken at their ball and socket joints. The socket should be repaired with filler which can be shaped while still slightly soft by turning the ball in the socket. If a ball is missing, cast a new one from a mould taken from any round article of the right size, such as a plastic bead or a marble. Before reassembling the doll, lightly coat the socket with melted wax to make sure it moves easily.

Breaks in other places than the joints in solid limbs, can be repaired by dowelling (*see* ceramic dowelling), which will give the mend greater strength. A hollow limb in a doll is mended in the same way as porcelain statuettes with hollow limbs (*see* ceramic cabinet pieces). Provided the limb is not a part that is strung with elastic, it can be reinforced inside with a roll of tough paper or metal foil, firmly cemented in. The joint

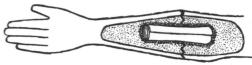

may have to be splinted to hold the two pieces together while the adhesive or filler is setting.

When replacing hands or feet, which are invariably solid, or even whole limbs when solid, it is much easier to find a model from which to take a mould. Use a flexible material such as rubber for the mould (*see* ceramic moulding). Include in the cast a wire loop or dowel for reinforcement (*see* ceramics: cabinet pieces). If only one hand is missing, you can use its counterpart, but be sure to remodel it while the filler is only partially set, so that you don't end up with two of the same hands. Alternatively, take a mould from a similar doll, and alter the size of the cast, if necessary, while the filler is still drying. If you can't find a model, you must build up the missing part free-hand, as for a porcelain statuette.

Retouching. In retouching porcelain dolls, follow the general instructions for *ceramic retouching. Water colours are best for bisque dolls. When dry, the texture of the bisque can be imitated by polishing with a very light wax polish.

Restringing. Always use special, round, thick elastic obtained from a doll's hospital to restring a doll. You can use underwear elastic, but it is not nearly so strong.

If the hooks for stringing are missing, make new ones by bending a piece of wire into a hook and anchoring it with filler or adhesive.

Measure from the hook on the lower leg joint (usually at the knee) to the neck of the doll and cut two pieces of elastic each twice this length. Then measure the length

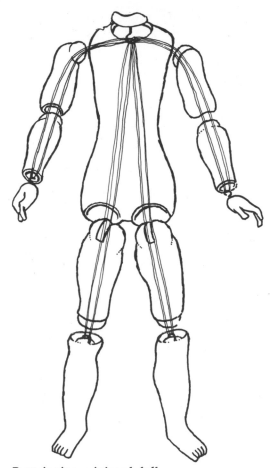

Restringing a jointed doll.

To clean composition dolls, wipe them gently with soapy water that has a few drops of ammonia added to it, or use a little grease solvent. Always try out such solvents first on a hidden part, such as the shoulders, in case the colouring comes away. If it does, it is probably better to rub the doll with breadcrumbs to clean it.

Cracks and breaks can be mended with a *cellulose filler or *plastic wood, of which there is a powdered form which is an excellent match for composition. It is often advisable to back the break with cardboard to reinforce the mend. Allow the filler to harden before sanding it flush with the surrounding surface.

To replace missing pieces, you can use papier mâché cast in a mould, if a duplicate is available. Be sure to coat the mould with a layer of Vaseline to prevent the papier mâché sticking. The cast piece can then be sanded smooth and painted to match the rest of the doll.

Tempera paints are best for retouching composition dolls, but be sure to match the original colouring even it it seems faded or dirty.

A German doll c1840 with a composition head and moulded hair. The body is made of kid with lower limbs of carved wood.

of both arms plus the width of the body and cut a piece twice this length. In both cases allow a little extra for the knot.

With a button hook or crochet hook start restringing by passing the elastic through the hook on one of the knee joints. Bring both ends through the hollow thighs and body and tie them to the neck hook. Both arms are attached to one piece of elastic that goes through the shoulders and chest. Don't let the elastic be too loose since then the limbs will be gangling, or too tight, which will prevent easy movement and may damage the limbs or body.

Composition Dolls

Since the early 19th century dolls have been made out of papier mâché and composition, which is a mixture of plaster of Paris, bran, sawdust and glue. Bodies and limbs of composition are often used with ceramic heads.

Wax Dolls

Wax has been used for making dolls since the latter half of the 16th century, and extensively in Germany, France and England in the 18th and 19th centuries. They may be solid wax. They are more likely to be hollow, made from a mould or made up of a wax covering on a composition base. Wax dolls may soften under exposure to excessive heat. Strong light will cause their colouring to fade. Ideally, they should be kept under glass domes.

Old and brittle dolls are so fragile and their restoration so tricky that it is best to take them to an expert, as you may easily ruin a doll unwittingly.

Washing. Superficial dirt can be removed by gently rubbing at the surface with a little cold cream. If the dirt has hardened and does not respond to this, try a little *turpentine on a cottonwool swab. Change the swab frequently if it gets very dirty. Use the turpentine sparingly, as it will soften the wax and may destroy the fine details of the modelling. It will anyway remove the colouring, which must then be reapplied. Turpentine in very small amounts will, however, keep the wax supple and prevent it becoming too brittle. When dry, polish very gently with a soft cloth.

Wax dolls' hair is generally rooted into the wax scalp. The hair can be washed with a little mild shampoo in cold water, but don't use warm or hot water which may loosen the hair from its roots. If the scalp is very black with dirt, gently clean it with a sparing amount of turpentine (see also dolls).

Mending. Cracks are most common faults with old wax dolls. Moisten a rag with warm turpentine and apply it to the crack. The wax will soften and the edges will merge together again. Another method which will have the same effect is to use a cottonwool swab moistened with hot water. If you add soap to the water, any dirt in the crack will also be removed.

Damaged faces should always be taken to an expert. You can mend the body yourself, because less irreparable damage can be done.

It is essential to become familiar with the

An English wax doll dressed as a bride. She has a calico body, glass eyes and mohair set into the wax.

use of molten wax if you are going to undertake repairs. Before starting, remove the doll's head, which is usually sewn on with linen thread.

If you need new wax, use *paraffin wax and *beeswax, melted together in equal parts. For a thin coat, melted candles can give a more translucent effect. Or mix candlewax and beeswax. The wax can be tinted with candle dyes, or old bits of candle or wax crayons, or else powdered pigments well mixed into the mixture. It is most important to achieve the right colour before commencing.

The new wax will not bond with the old unless the spot is well warmed first, but excess heat will melt it too much, dissolving the form altogether. So, first warm broken surfaces with a warmed tool, such as a knife. Hold them together, and lay a strip of fine gauze across them. Then apply the melted wax with a brush or heated tool over the gauze to the area of the break. Alternatively, dip the gauze into melted wax and place it over the pre-warmed surfaces, holding the pieces together until the wax hardens. Then brush on a little more melted wax to strengthen it. When the join is sufficiently strong, smooth the surface with a warmed spoon handle.

Missing parts can be built up by brushing on melted, tinted wax and shaping it with hot tools. If models are available, larger parts can be cast in rubber moulds and then stuck together. Alternatively, they can be modelled free-hand, using heated tools to carve the lump into the required shape.

When thoroughly hardened, the mended or replaced piece can be painted. Water-colours are generally the best type of paint. Any details should be painted in with a fine brush. To obtain the delicate shading of the flesh, it is better to rub the paint gently in with your finger, like with rouge, rather than using a brush.

Wooden dolls

Wooden dolls have been made since the earliest times. Most surviving examples date from the 19th century.

A set of seven 'Dutch Dolls'—this term was used to describe all wooden-jointed dolls, the word is a corruption of Deutsch (German).

To clean, wipe gently with a cloth moistened with warm water and mild soap. Experiment first on an inconspicuous area such as the shoulder. On very old dolls, it is often better to leave the faces alone, or you will disturb the patina of age. Occasionally you will find traces of woodworm (*see* Wood: furniture beetle). Each hole should be injected with an insecticide, and then filled with a *filler which can be painted over when dry.

Some wooden dolls have heads coated with gesso. If some of it has cracked and fallen away, replace with fresh gesso. Mix it to the consistency of cream before applying it with a soft brush in several thin coats. Allow each coat to harden before applying the next. Rub each coat smooth with fine *glass-paper.

Broken pieces can be repaired by building up in layers with *plastic wood (the powdered form is recommended). You can, of course, also glue on pieces of real wood, providing they match the original and are carved appropriately.

Joints usually consist of tongues that fit into slots. They are held in place and

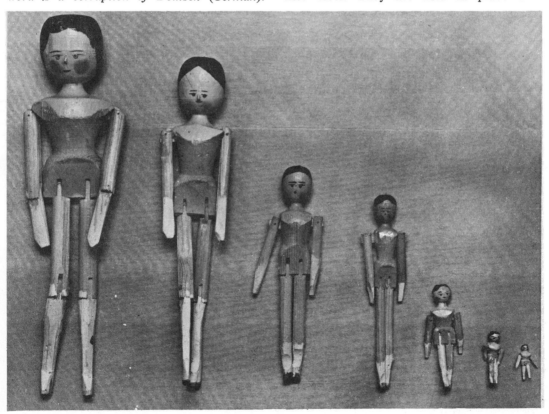

allowed to swivel by a wooden pin. Broken joint tongues should not just be glued in place. It is better to carve a new one. New hands and feet can be carved out of a piece of wood and then dowelled into the stumps.

For retouching, use watercolour or egg tempera paints. If a shiny effect is necessary, cover the paint with varnish. It is often possible to obtain the yellow colour of old varnish by first applying one or two coats of matt wood varnish, which is yellower than the usual varnish, and then a final coat of clear varnish.

EMBROIDERY

Fabrics were embroidered in the East at a very early date, and later by the Greeks, the Romans and Egyptians. There also exist early Christian embroideries dating from the 7th century. However samplers and canvas work (*petit-point, gros-point* and Berlin wool work) are among the most common embroidered objects found now.

These types of embroidery can be washed, provided that they are not in a delicate condition. The colours must be tested first. Do

this by damping a small section and pressing it between two sheets of clean white blotting paper. No hint of colour should come off the embroidery on to the blotting paper. Remember that one colour may be fast and another one may not, even on the same piece of work.

There are disadvantages to washing canvas work. The canvas itself has usually been stiffened with a water-soluble size, so that it will become limp with washing, and may even shrink.

Take particular care with upholstery, which is likely to change shape and so not fit when you want to replace it. Therefore avoid washing it unless absolutely necessary.

Special care must be taken with metallic thread, whether it is embroidered on or woven into the fabric. Test the effects of water before immersing it. It will sometimes wash clean. Silver thread is likely to darken again after washing almost immediately.

Tarnishing is often caused by acid on the

A typical example of Berlin woolwork, a form of embroidery on canvas popular from 1830.

hands. If you are handling material with metallic thread a lot, it is best to wear gloves.

Experts can sometimes clean metallic thread by avoiding the rest of the threads, but anything that cleans metal is almost bound to stain the rest of the material, and therefore should not be attempted.

For the general care and maintenance of embroidery *see* textiles.

ENAMEL

Enamel is melted glass with metallic oxides as colouring agents. It is powdered and fused by firing to a surface of metal. The process is most successful on copper or gold. The technique of enamelling was developed by the Greeks, Etruscans and Celts *c*600–300 BC.

There are various enamelling techniques. In *champlevé* the base metal is scooped out into compartments and filled with enamel, which is then polished level with the top of the metal field. It was popular in the 12th and 16th centuries, and revived as a technique in the 19th century. The most famous centre for this type of enamelling was Limoges in France. The effect of *champlevé* is very similar to *cloisonné,* in which thin strips of metal soldered on to the base metal in cells or enclosures are then filled with enamel to form the design. Then there is *guilloché,* where coloured, transparent enamel is laid over an engraved or engine-turned decoration on metal. It is commonly used on *watch cases. *Plique-à-jour* is a technique similar to *cloisonné,* but with the metal plate removed, leaving translucent metal windows. It is sometimes called 'stained glass' enamel.

Painted enamel, painting with enamel on metal, was perfected at Blois in France in the 17th and 18th centuries. The colouring is usually very vivid, and the work is covered with a glaze or flux which helps prevent deterioration.

Enamel used for decoration on glass and ceramics is applied as a paste after the production of the article to be decorated. This article is then re-fired to fuse the enamel with the surface. For general cleaning, treatment, etc., of such objects, *see* ceramics and glass.

In the ordinary way, enamel is one of

A late 18th century German carafe decorated with a gilt and enamel medallion bearing a coat of arms.

the most durable and permanent mediums used in the decorative arts. Most breakages, scratches and wear in modern times are incurred by general domestic maintenance. Decoration, especially gilding, on painted enamels can be worn away completely by excessive cleaning and polishing. Ideally, enamels should be kept under glass to alleviate the necessity for dusting and polishing. This is even more important with restored enamels.

Cleaning

Before attempting to clean any piece of enamelware, ascertain whether any previous restoration has been carried out. For the untrained eye the use of an ultra-violet lamp is recommended; the restored areas will show up as a light violet colour on a darker background which is the original one. Good restoration is expensive and is often worth preserving for its own sake, so don't use anything other than lukewarm water and soap for cleaning.

As a general rule warm water and soap is the best method of cleaning for pieces which are not too badly soiled. Biological powders are good, but don't use detergents. Ideally, painted miniatures should be removed from their frames, although this is sometimes difficult because they are often soldered in place with wire backings. Care should be taken when drying boxes with steel hinge-pins, as these tend to rust. Boxes with mirrored lids should *not* be soaked, as this encourages deterioration of the silvering. In such cases, *carbon tetrachloride or *acetone can be applied with a soft brush to the affected parts.

A *magnesium silicate pack can be used if the enamel is badly cracked and ingrained with dirt. Mix the magnesium silicate with distilled water and apply the resultant paste to the affected areas. When the pack has finished working, it will have a crazed surface. Now brush it off. This may have to be repeated two or three times.

*Hydrogen peroxide can be used for bleaching out stains in cracks. However, if the cracking is extensive and it seems likely that the white enamel may come away from the metal backing, it is advisable to have the cleaning done by an expert, for sometimes it is only the dirt and grime which holds the piece together.

Never use acid baths, they may burn away low-fired metal oxides.

Restoring

It is generally not known that enamels, especially opaque ones, lend themselves better to restoration than porcelain which is mostly translucent. This is because with opaque enamel there is very little evidence of cast shadow, and so the restored area has the same quality as the original.

Another advantage when restoring enamel is that no matter how extensive the damage, the metal base will most probably be intact, giving some evidence of the original finished shape of the piece.

All types of enamels *can* be restored. The

Mid-19th century Swiss watch with a painted enamel case.

most common processes are replacing flaked enamel; making good dented metal which has resulted in cracked and chipped surfaces; and retouching scratches. Firing cracks are not usually restored.

Refiring is impossible because the enamel has to be fired at a higher temperature than the oxides and doing this would destroy the original decoration. Re-shape metal parts, and repair damaged areas by using a *synthetic resin paste. Colour this with a low-firing enamel paint to match exactly the ground colour. Apply decoration on top of this, then glaze and treat to match the original piece.

Gilding is replaced by using a fine gold powder and burnishing it. Chips and missing areas in cloisonné work are made up in the same type of synthetic resin paste coloured to match the original enamel. This allows the restoration to be made without overpainting.

In general, transparent enamels on gold, silver and copper present more problems if an invisible restoration is required. There usually has to be some evidence of a join between the original and the new materials, as overpainting is not possible.

FLATWARE.

Knives

The most common fault with early knives is that the blade is often loose or falls out. This can easily be remedied by sticking the blade back with a cement made of 4 parts resin, 1 part *beeswax and 1 part *plaster of Paris. This cement will stick to the blade but at the same time fill the handle with the correct weight to supplement the lost pitch, so that an even balance is maintained.

Old iron blades are often rusted and pitted. The rust should be carefully removed by picking out the more severe areas with a pin. Then soak the blade in a penetrating oil mixed with paraffin. Then remove the rest of the rust with a mild abrasive.

Silver-plated steel knives which are 'peeling' should be replated. A copper surface must be 'flashed' onto the steel first (see Metalwork: electroplate), before the silver will adhere. This should be done by an expert.

Sharpening knives is a skilled job. It is normally done on a fine revolving grindstone with a mixture of tallow and emery. Domestic knife sharpeners should be used with caution, as the angle is often inaccurate and can damage the edge.

Forks

Uneven prongs can be altered to a uniform length. This should only be attempted by a skilled craftsman.

Spoons

Early silver spoons (17th and early 18th century) should not be touched by an amateur, as inexperienced tampering may destroy its value. If the bowl needs beating out, take it to a silversmith.

The *patina on early spoons is much cherished. Early spoons should be cleaned with warm, soapy water, rinsed well and dried with a soft cloth or chamois leather. Valuable spoons should be kept in a dry place. Chemical dips should *never* be used.

FOREL.

Forel is a vellum-like parchment with a visible grain. It is used principally for bookbinding, never for writing. For treatment, see parchment.

FRAMES

Clean varnished, polished and lacquered frames according to the finish. Don't clean plaster frames with water, which may disintegrate them. Instead, brush away loose dirt with a stiff brush and clean with a little *methylated spirit. Gilt frames can be wiped clean with a damp cloth; add a few drops of *ammonia to the water if the frame is exceptionally dirty. Polish with a soft cloth.

Broken and missing sections of moulding on wood or plaster frames can be restored. Use dental plaster to take an impression of a part of the moulding which matches the missing piece. Make a cast in this with gilders' composition or a *filler. Remove the cast from the mould when dry and clean it with a file and glass-paper until it matches the details of the original moulding. Cut to size. Fix the piece onto the frame with an *epoxy resin and then paint to match the colour or gild (see gilding).

You should always check that the framing of a picture is correct. Watercolours, prints, drawings, pastels, etc., should be glazed for protection against dust and dirt. The join between the frame and the back should be sealed with brown, gummed paper tape. Oil paintings do not need glass because they are normally varnished. Frames should not be backed with wood, which is susceptible to woodworm, but with hardboard.

It is best to use nylon cord when hanging pictures, as picture wire and chains are likely to corrode and break suddenly. Check these often, as falling can obviously badly damage a picture and ruin the frame.

Detail of a mid-Georgian gilt wood mirror frame.

FURNITURE

Minor blemishes and breakages can be made good in your own workshop. But it is not always easy for an amateur to decide what is serious and what is trivial, so examine the piece carefully first (*see* dismantling furniture). If in doubt, consult an expert *before* dismantling, as good repairs demand knowledge of period styles and methods of construction.

Generally speaking, a badly-done repair can do more damage than good to the value of a piece of furniture. So always give very careful thought to whether you have the capability to repair bruised corners on tables and chests, gaps in inlay, failure in drawer joints, small bubbles in veneer, worn chair and table stretchers, the replacement or splicing of unturned legs, and minor cracks and marks.

A plate from L'Encyclopédie *(1751–80) edited by Diderot and d'Alambert.*

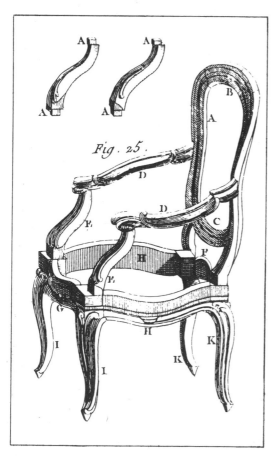

Structural damage, especially when it has been neglected, is serious. Chairs are particularly inclined to deteriorate badly, as one weak joint will quickly put increasing strain on the others. Perhaps the most difficult repair of all is a structural fault in the carcase of a veneered piece. For veneers may have to be removed first and then replaced after the fault has been rectified.

When tackling minor repairs at home, follow these rules.

First, repair as soon as possible. A fault will often throw a strain on other parts of the piece. Also, when the breakage is new, the edges of a break will be sharp and clean and therefore easy to join together. Time rounds corners and edges, calling for extra work in making the pieces fit together perfectly. If veneer or inlay becomes loose, repair straight away. If this is not possible, either remove the piece and put it safely away, or secure it temporarily in position with sticky tape. Better not to have to fit a new piece through the veneer being lost or becoming badly broken.

Second, when a missing piece has to be made, copy the original part as carefully as possible and always attempt to match the wood for colour and grain. If you don't know what the original part was like, sources of information include the furniture section of good libraries or museums, furniture departments of museums and National Trust houses. Study an actual piece of furniture if you can, as photographs don't give as good an idea. Matching grain is perhaps more important than colour, for if of a lighter colour, the wood can be stained to match.

It is better to make efforts to duplicate the original, than to make a repair which clashes with the character of the piece. It follows that it is a very good idea to save and collect pieces of old wood and veneers, from which you have a good chance of making a near match.

To repair blemishes on the surface of wood, *see* Wood: black spots, bruises, burn marks, cracks, heat marks, ink stains, scratches and spirit marks.

For details of the various processes used in dealing with wood, *see* Wood: bleaching, finishes, polishing, sanding, splicing, staining, stripping.

Dismantling furniture

When faced with the need to do repair work on substantial pieces, such as wardrobes, sideboards and chests-of-drawers, you will save yourself a lot of trouble by approaching the task methodically.

The general principle is: don't separate parts unnecessarily. Consider the neatest way of isolating the part, or parts, you want to work on. If you approach the job haphazardly, you will probably find yourself caught up in a chain reaction of quite unnecessary and possibly harmful work. For example, taking glued items apart always loosens the joints. And when you have needlessly isolated a member, you will also have to get rid of the old glue on it before replacing it.

When dismantling, make a point of marking every part so that it can be replaced in the right position and in the right order. Make sure that the member you wish to isolate is, or is not, screwed to any rails or brackets, before starting. Consider the order in which the members can most logically and effectively be taken apart. For sometimes you have to remove one part to get at another, and sometimes one part locks another in position.

When separating, never strike the wood directly with your hammer or mallet. If you do, you stand a good chance of bruising the surface, splitting the wood, and dislodging a joint. Always use a strong, flat piece of wood, holding it firmly against the part close up to the adjoining member before using the hammer. Thus the force of the blow will be spread, and the risk of splitting or breaking the wood removed. Alternatively, buy a rubber or nylon-headed hammer, or take an ordinary hammer and wrap some layers of thick cloth securely round the head (see woodwork tools). If you are tackling a chair or other lightly-made piece of furniture, rather than a heavier item like a wardrobe, the cloth-padded, or soft-headed hammer will prove far handier for knocking the joints apart than the flat piece of wood.

When the piece has been dismantled, always look to see what local repairs can be done in addition to the main job. And always try to do the minor jobs first. In any case, one cardinal principle is that you must get rid of all the old glue on all the joints. Use a cloth or small brush dampened with very hot water on the glue, and have a chisel or knife handy for scraping away any stubborn bits, taking care not to cut away any wood.

Make sure all joints are a snug fit before reassembling, for the glue must not be relied upon for filling gaps. Reassemble in reverse order, having applied fresh, hot *Scotch glue to the joints using cramps for a stronger fit (see woodwork tools: cramps). In cold conditions, see that the parts are warmed—stand them before a radiator or play a warm air fan on them—so that the glue does not chill too quickly. Finally, to test that everything is back squarely and properly, place the piece on a flat floor, then take a stick, ruler, or calibrated rod—the last for total precision—and fit it diagonally into each corner. This will show whether the piece has been put back properly.

If any glue has oozed out, wipe it off with a warm damp cloth. If it has set, remove it carefully with a chisel, taking care not to mark any polished surfaces.

Chair rails and slats

Loose chair rails and slats should be examined to see if there are any small gaps between the affected parts and the members to which they are joined.

If the gap is small, it can be filled satisfactorily with a thin slip of wood or a piece of veneer. Dip it into glue and work it carefully into the gap. Trim off and wipe away any surplus glue.

Another method is to glue and cramp the joint together firmly and then bore through the member and the rail end. Then drive in a screw so that the head is about a quarter of an inch below the level of the wood and fill the hole with a wooden plug or with *plastic wood stopping of the correct colour. Level off. Remember that plastic wood tends to sink as it hardens.

Both the vertical and horizontal slats in chair backs often work loose. If one of the mortice holes has become enlarged, use pieces of veneer glued into position to bring it back to its correct size.

If both holes are enlarged, and the slat is rather long and thin, glue one end of the slat firmly into its hole, but do not glue the other end, as a certain amount of freedom and flexing puts less strain on the glued end. The mortice holes should first be re-made to the correct size by gluing slips of wood or veneer as above.

A firmer repair would be to set a dowel about half an inch into the back surface of the supporting rail at one end, so that it passes through the slat. If the rail or slat has become loose because of a broken tenon, a complete new one may have to be made. Alternatively, the remains of the tenon can be sawn off, the mortice hole plugged, and a dowel joint made. Use the cut-off nail technique (*see* wood: dowelling) for positioning the dowels, and make sure that both the bored holes are in a straight line. Then proceed as described. If a curved chair rail has broken, you can strengthen the whole rail by gluing and screwing the break.

A loose rung or stretcher can often be sprung back into position by very carefully pulling the chairlegs apart. Gluing and wedging will hold the rungs firmly.

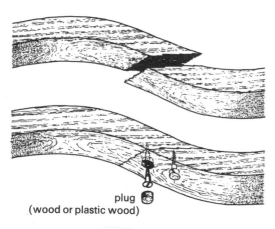

plug
(wood or plastic wood)

Repairing a curved rail.

Chair rungs

These are the turned rails set into the legs. They form the under-framing which strengthens them by keeping them the correct distance apart.

When the turned rail of a Windsor-type chair breaks, it may be possible to glue and cramp the two sections together, or bind them tightly together with cord. But if the chair is in constant use, it may be better to get a new rung turned by a skilled craftsman.

If the rung is of the same diameter along its whole length, buy a length of dowel of the same wood and diameter and cut it to size. You may find a suitable piece among your own stock, or shape it up yourself,

using the broken rung as a pattern.

First, saw roughly to size, then start shaping with a smoothing or surform plane and, perhaps, a spokeshave. Then use rough garnet paper, progressing to less rough paper, and ending with 1 or 0 grade glasspaper (*see* abrasives, woodwork tools). Next, glue the rung back into the sockets. This may require springing the legs apart (*see* diagram) to allow the rung to slip in. Do this with a gentle and even pressure, so as not to weaken the other joints on the chair.

To give extra strength, the ends of the rung can be cut and fine wedges inserted before gluing. The wedges are driven home as the rung is driven into the holes. Take care that the wedges are not too long or too thick, as it will be a difficult job to remove the rung again once the ends have been expanded by the wedges. Use a cramp or tourniquet to hold the joints firmly until the glue is set (*see* wood: cramping).

Chair and table legs

Chair legs usually break at the point where the rungs or under-framing go into them. They also split at the top where they are jointed to the seat rails.

If they are badly broken, or if a part is missing, a completely new leg may have to be made. This often requires considerable skill in getting a perfect match both in shape, colour and graining of the wood, and is best left to a skilled craftsman. Of course, if the leg belongs to an antique piece, a new one should only be fitted if absolutely necessary.

When repairing legs it is very important to have a level surface for the piece to stand on, to check that the legs are in the correct vertical position and of the correct length to prevent wobbling.

When doing the repair, make sure the legs are in the correct relationship with each other by testing the diagonal measurements. A thin, straight piece of wood marked exactly to the length of the diagonal or a calibrated ruler can be used. Check the measurement when cramping together, *before* the glue begins to set. Cramp the joints together firmly, using pieces of wood to distribute the pressure and avoiding bruising or marking the legs. Leave for 24 hours.

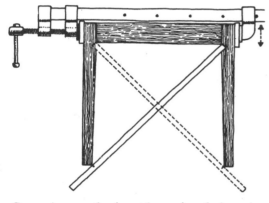

Cramping up the front legs of a chair, using diagonal pieces of equal length to check squareness. Adjustments can be made by moving the cramp until the diagonals are the same length.

Remember that chair legs are often made to slope outwards very slightly, and this fact must be taken into account when fitting a new leg.

Bear in mind that it is obviously better to make a new leg the correct length. Alternatively, start out by making it too long rather than too short. If it is too long you can saw off the excess from the foot. Take off slightly less than you need for the exact length. Test on a level surface, and mark

the amount required to be sawn off with a simple, improvised tool, such as a sharpened steel knitting needle, or a nail. Then smooth down.

If a leg is too short, cut a piece of wood to the correct size, shape and thickness, to fit the bottom of the leg. Then glue and nail with fine panel pins.

Turned legs and cabriole legs are best left to the expert for repair, especially on a valuable piece. The problem with breaks in turned legs lies in strengthening the repair by fitting a dowel in the right place to get the correct alignment. This calls for care before boring the holes in the two parts to take the dowel, and it is particularly difficult when the break is high up on the leg.

However, when the break occurs near the foot, the two parts can be glued together. After the glue has set hard, bore a hole from the end up to about $1\frac{1}{2}''$ past the break line, then drive in a glued dowel (see wood: dowelling).

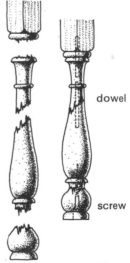

dowel

screw

Repairing breaks in a turned leg.

Cabriole legs generally have a lot of short grain in them, making them liable to fracture. As this will probably mean some rather complicated dowelling work, the splicing job needed is best left to an expert, unless it is simply part of the toe which has broken off.

If the toe or the foot of a leg has a broken piece which is missing, saw and plane the remainder back to give a flat surface. Then shape up a piece of wood to roughly the shape of the missing section and clamp it in place. You can then finish off the shaping with a rasp file, and finally glass-paper. If the chipped foot is elaborately carved, leave its replacement to an expert (*see* diagram).

the block is rubbed back and forth into position, squeezing out the surplus glue at the same time. You may have to round the corner between the two glued faces to get a true fit in the angle (*see* diagram).

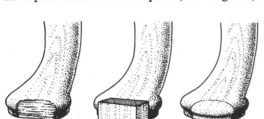

To replace a broken cabriole foot:
(a) plane the surface of the break smooth.
(b) using a cramp, glue on a block of wood, making sure to match the grain.
(c) carve and file the block to shape, finishing off with glass-paper.

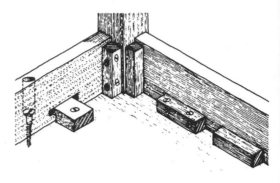

Table repairs. Table leg joints can be strengthened with wood blocks, either glued, or screwed and glued in place. Table tops can be fastened to framing rails with wood blocks or buttons secured in similar fashion.

If the foot, or any other piece, has broken off, look for evidence of *furniture beetle attack and treat accordingly before making a repair. This may mean cutting back to sound wood, or fitting a new leg, if it has been badly eaten away.

Table legs and framing rails are usually screwed directly to the underside of the table top or sometimes with wooden blocks called 'buttons'.

To correct any wobbliness, it may be enough just to tighten the screws.

If the screw holes are worn, put in a slightly thicker screw. Or glue in a wooden plug, and make a fresh screw hole. Be sure then to use a screw that is not too long or too thick, to avoid piercing or splitting the table top.

If the table frame has loose joints, remove any holding screws and lift off the top. Knock the joints apart with a *soft-headed hammer. Chip off the old glue, reglue, then clamp up, making sure the table is standing on a level surface. Check diagonals as with chairs. If the tenon itself is broken, a new one may have to be made.

A good way to strengthen the joints between legs and rails on tables is to glue small rectangular blocks of wood inside the frame at the corner where the legs and rails meet. Make sure surfaces are clean and dust-free, otherwise the adhesion will be poor. Two adjacent faces are glued, then

Do not move or jar the piece of furniture until the glue is completely set.

If the chair or table leg is suffering from a broken dowelled joint, you will have to saw off the broken dowels, bore them out, and fit new ones.

If the dowel has become loose in the hole enlarged by wear, take the dowel out, and glue in a plug. When the glue has thoroughly hardened, bore a hole for a slightly larger dowel. (*See* Wood: dowelling.)

Metal brackets are sometimes put onto chairs to hold the joints steady. If one becomes loose plug the screw holes and rescrew on the bracket. It is best to remove it and repair the joints as required. Re-glue according to the usual method.

A broken table or chair leg can often be repaired by splicing on a new piece. It is very important to make sure that the grain of the new piece matches and runs in the same direction as the grain of the old piece. Wood is inherently strong *with*, but weak *across*, the grain.

To make a spliced joint, cut a V with a fine tenon saw in the leg, then cut and shape the new joining piece to an exact fit with plane, file and glass-paper. If the leg is tapered, the joining piece must be carefully shaped so that the line follows through.

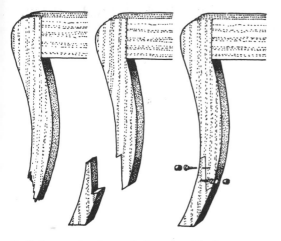

Splicing a broken chair or table leg.

Glue and cramp the new piece to the leg. When the glue has set, bore holes through from the back of the original part of the leg and into the new piece and drive in glued dowels. As an alternative screws may be used instead of dowels (*see* diagram).

Splicing on antique pieces should be done with care. It is particularly useful where it is not practical to take off the whole leg. You might be well advised to consult an expert, depending on the extent and shape of the fracture.

Desk and table tops

Many writing tables and desks have hide, skiver or morocco leather tops. These may become very worn, but can be replaced with a piece of new leather. This should not be done on an antique piece without consulting an expert first.

First, peel the old leather away, using a knife blade if necessary. Then clean the underlying surface until completely smooth, removing all old glue and stubborn patches of leather. Finally, rub down with a fine glass-paper wrapped round a cork block, taking care to work right up to the sides. Don't scratch the polished wood surround. Cut your new piece of leather slightly larger than the area it has to cover, because leather will shrink under the drying of the adhesive.

Next, spread the new adhesive onto both the desk top and the new piece of leather. The traditional adhesive to use is paper-hanger's paste, but *polyvinyl acetate emulsion is perfectly suitable. Do not apply too much adhesive, or it will come through and

stain the leather. Lay the leather slightly over the border, because of the shrinkage.

Smooth the leather down gently when it is in place to remove all air bubbles and wrinkles. When the surface is even, press the sides into the border recesses with your thumbnail. Trim off surplus leather with a sharp stencil knife and steel straight-edge so that the edges fit neatly against the sides of the recesses.

If you want to decorate the edges of the leather top, you will need a tooling wheel. This can either consist of a plain line or have a decorative pattern engraved on it. Heat the wheel and then wipe it with a piece of cloth moistened with a little *methylated spirit to prevent it from discolouring the leather. Try it out first on an odd piece of leather to find the correct temperature and the pressure required for a firm impression. It is a good idea to draw a guideline with a soft pencil and ruler, to make sure that the wheel runs straight. Then apply the wheel along the guideline. Alternatively, the wheel can be used against a straight-edge. This process is known as blind tooling.

Gold tooling is really beyond the scope of the amateur. The gold leaf is pressed onto the leather with the tooling wheel, using white of egg as adhesive.

Drawers

The earliest forms of drawers in furniture had fairly thick sides, very often with central grooves which engaged with runners fixed from the front to the back of the cabinet. The sides were either just nailed into a rebate or had crude dovetails to join them to the drawer front.

During the walnut period (1680-1740), neater forms of construction evolved. Dovetails became smaller and more numerous, though still rather crude, and the runners were on the bottom of the drawer. Drawer bottoms were mainly of oak, sometimes pine, with the grain running from front to back. The sides, too, were of oak, or of pine, which takes veneer better.

By the middle of the 18th century, drawer construction had become more or less uniform. The dovetails had become fine, although the best dovetail drawer joints are often found on 19th-century furniture.

The main troubles which afflict drawers

are broken or loose dovetail joints, worn sides, split and twisted drawer bottoms, and worn runners. After a couple of centuries or so, it would be highly unlikely that friction had not caused wear.

Sticking drawers. The cause of this is sometimes the warping or twisting of the sides of the drawers. First look for any physical obstructions, such as an obtruding nail or screw. Then look to see where the rub marks are on the drawer sides and take down any high spots with medium glass-paper.

A damp atmosphere can also often cause sticking. If the drawer still sticks after a period of dry weather, rub down the top and bottom edges with * glass-paper wrapped round a cork block.

The old trick of rubbing a candle along runners and sides can often work wonders for making a drawer run smoothly.

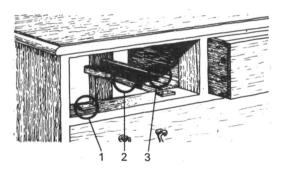

Common drawer faults:
(1) Drawer stops may be missing, causing the drawer to go in too far. (2) Drawer runners may be badly worn, so that the drawer does not run smoothly. (3) Drawer guides may be missing or worn, making the drawer work unevenly.

Loose drawers. Drawers which jog from side to side when being opened or closed usually have a badly worn or missing guide inside the chest. You can renew the guide by gluing in new strips of wood. Give the new guide a rub with a candle when in position.

Look at the runners the drawer slides on. If the constant to-and-fro movement has worn it unevenly, fill the identation with *plastic wood. If the wear has affected the whole of the drawer runner, try to raise the level of the track by gluing thin strips

of wood onto it, or renew completely.

If a drawer goes too far into the carcase, it means that the drawer stops have broken off. These stops are very simple to make. Cut small rectangles of wood and glue and nail them to the rail below the drawer, so that the back of the drawer front touches them when the drawer is in its correct closed position.

When the bottom edges of the drawer sides are badly worn, so that you have to lift the front of the drawer to get it all the way out, it is better to consult an expert. He will probably separate the parts, then plane the bottom edge to a line parallel with the grooves which hold the bottom. New pieces of wood can then be glued on, of a width equal to the combined thickness of the side and the drawer bottom slip, if there is one.

Loose drawer joints. These are best dealt with by dismantling the whole drawer and re-gluing. First, remove the drawer bottom by taking out the screws holding it in place, and slide it out of its grooves. Then tap the joints apart, and scrape off the old glue. Reglue and check for squareness. Cramping is not usually necessary if the dovetail joints are a good fit. If the joints are rather slack, drive in one or two fine panel pins after gluing and cramp up the drawer (*see* Wood: cramping).

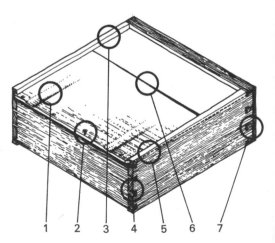

Check drawers for: (1) grooves worn by drawer stops; (2) projecting screws; (3) and (5) new strips of wood glued on to disguise worn bottom edges of drawer; (4) and (7) loose dovetail joints; (6) split bottom.

Drawer bottoms. Before plywood was invented, drawer bottoms were often made up of two or three thin boards glued together. The pieces may have become unglued, split, or twisted because of the weight of the drawer contents over the years. You can either replace the bottom completely with a piece of plywood. If the piece is antique, try to repair the existing bottom. Take the drawer bottom pieces out, and remove all the dust and dirt. If the split is very bad, break the bottom completely and glue together again. This is easier than trying to glue together the split. To reglue, warm the pieces and glue the edges, then lay them on a flat board with heavy weights on each end until the glue is set. Put a sheet of newspaper underneath to prevent the glued pieces from sticking to the flat board. Twisted wood can often be flattened by damping and putting it under heavy weights for a few days.

More elaborate repairs. Consult an expert about more elaborate types of drawer construction, involving lipped and shaped drawers decorated with fine veneering.

Lipped drawer fronts were introduced in the early 18th century. They made the drawers dustproof by overlapping the carcase and concealing the edges. Continued opening and closing over the years often results in the lipping being forced out or broken. This happens, for example, when the drawer stops are missing, because then the veneer gets damaged.

Cock beading round the fronts of drawers, which came into use slightly later than lipped edges, are less vulnerable. If they are loose it is a simple matter of gluing them back into position.

Handles and knobs
A loose wooden knob should first be carefully removed. Scrape off any old glue before re-fixing. To make a tighter fit in an existing old hole, wrap a strip of glue-saturated cloth round the dowel of the knob and push it all in so that it tightly fills the hole. If, however, the knob is tight but badly broken and a new knob is required, take care not to disturb or mark the adjoining surface of the drawer or door, especially if it is veneered. Cut away the shoulder of the knob where the glue grips the veneered

surface by gently tapping with a chisel. Since the grain of the knob is always front to back, the shoulder of the knob should chip away easily without the chisel touching the drawer front. Next, strike the dowel of the knob from inside the drawer to get it out. Get a new knob turned to match the others, stain if necessary and polish. To fix, or re-fix the knob, bore right through the wooden plug or make a dowel, then glue it in.

To fix brass handles to the drawers instead of knobs remove the old knobs as described above, then plug the old holes with a short piece of dowel stained to match the surrounding wood. If the front of the drawer has a decorative grain, you may have to recess the plug and glue in a carefully matched piece of veneer. Screw on the new handles, taking care not to burr either the screws or the handles.

Handles which faithfully reproduce old styles can be bought. But replacing old brass handles with plain wooden knobs has historical precedent. It was a common practice in Victorian times to 'modernise' pieces by removing the old brass handles and fixing wooden knobs.

Hinges
Troubles with hinges can develop in doors, fall-front desks and bureaux, and gate-leg tables. They are generally speaking easy enough to treat, with one exception. That is when hinges bind or pull because of shrinking, swelling or warping in the carcase of the piece. You can easily spot this, and the only treatment is to tackle the root cause. Correct the faults, and the hinging trouble will mend itself.

One of the commonest faults is binding, when the door either does not close, or springs open. This is often because replacement screws of too large a diameter have been put in not fitting flush into the countersunk hole, thus preventing the hinge from closing completely. Replace with screws of a smaller diameter, which will mean plugging the old hole with a piece of wood and then boring a smaller hole. Alternatively, deepen the countersinking so that the screw heads can go in flush.

Another cause of binding is the hinge recess being too deep for the hinge. This often happens when the original hinge has been replaced with one with thinner plates. It can usually be corrected by packing the recess with a piece or pieces of veneer, or with a slip or slips of card or paper. You can fit thicker hinges.

If the screw holes have been mangled over the years and no longer hold the screws in place, you will have to take the hinge off completely. Then make plugs to fill the screw holes. Fix the plugs firmly into place with *Scotch glue or an *epoxy resin adhesive. When the adhesive has set solid, bore holes of a suitable size and screw the hinge firmly back into position. You must always bore screw holes. Never simply make a hole with a bradawl or gimlet, because that way you risk splitting the wood.

If the wood around a hinge is split, broken or has a piece missing, you will have to make a really strong repair. Prise open the split, clean it, and then glue and cramp it together until the glue is set. Another method is to fit in another piece of wood, carefully matching grain and colour. The replacement piece is glued and cramped firmly into position. It may be necessary to cut a new rebate. Put the hinge back into place.

If a hinge has been screwed on slightly out of alignment, the door may not open, shut or even hang satisfactorily. Always check that the piece of furniture to which it belongs is not being twisted by standing on an uneven surface. If so, one corner may need a wedge or block under it.

If a hinge screw will not come out, this may be because it has rusted. First try gently tapping the screwdriver when it is in the slot of the screw. If this does not work, run a spot of oil round the screw, then hold a red-hot piece of metal—a large nail is ideal—in pliers against the head of the screw for a few moments. Take care not to scar the surrounding wood. This will usually loosen it.

If the screw head. is broken or badly burred, so that the screwdriver will not grip, the hinge may have to be cut or drilled away, so that the screw can be turned with a pair of pliers.

Mortice and tenon joints

Loose or broken mortice and tenon joints are often strengthened by metal plates and

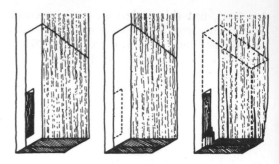

Repairing a broken mortice by splicing in a new piece of wood.

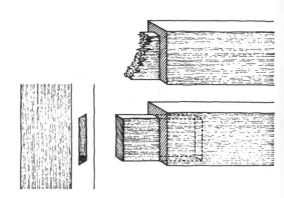

Making a new tenon.

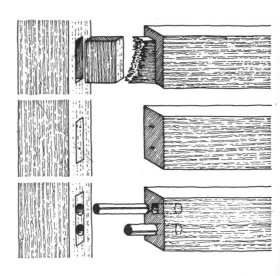

Replacing a broken tenon with a dowelling joint. Both parts of the joint should be planed flat. Nail ends, cut off with wire cutters, are used to mark the site of the dowel holes. It is important that the holes bored in.both halves of the joint should lie along the same axis.

brackets, but this makes an unsatisfactory and clumsy repair. If you are dealing with an antique piece, it will be truer to its character to repair the actual joint, provided that the member is sound. In the same way, it is best to use traditional *Scotch glue, which is more in accord with the nature of the piece, than modern adhesives.

First, remove the plate or brackets (if one has been fitted). Carefully remove the member with the broken tenon. Then clean out all the old glue and dirt from the mortice (the hole into which the tenon fits). If the mortice hole has broken away or is badly worn, carefully cut around it back to sound wood. Make a replacement piece or pieces to fit exactly in order to bring the mortice hole back to its original size and shape, (see diagram). Glue the replacement into position. Press a piece of wood the size of the tenon into the mortice hole and leave in until the glue is set; then remove. Saw off the broken tenon at the shoulder, so that none is left projecting from the end of the member. Make a new tenon twice the depth of the mortice hole which fits it tightly (see diagram). The reason for the extra length is that you next cut a mortice in the end of the member from which the broken tenon was sawn off. Put the joint together without glue to see that the loose tenon fits correctly. Then apply glue to both mortice holes and insert the tenon. Cramp together until set. Do not allow excess glue to set in the mortices, because this hinders the tenon from going completely home.

A tenon which is not broken, but slack in the mortice, can be thickened by gluing a piece of veneer to the face which needs building up. Allow the glue to set, then sand down the veneer until the tenon fits tightly into the mortice. Finally glue and cramp together. Take care to remove excess glue with a warm, damp cloth. It is easier to do this at this moment rather than when the glue is set and hard.

Upholstery

Upholstery became an integral part of chair design in the first half of the 17th century, when padded backs and seats were combined with the chair frame instead of loose cushions. Webbing or canvas was stretched and nailed to the frame, and the padding and covering taken right over the woodwork to form what became known later as a 'stuff-over' seat. The appearance of upholstered sofas and chairs altered greatly with the introduction of coil springs in the 1830s.

Valuable antique chairs and sofas should be re-upholstered by an expert using materials and techniques similar to those originally used. It is perhaps unnecessarily pedantic for a piece of less character and worth to replace old horsehair with new horsehair, or old flock with new flock, when latex foam and plastic foam are so readily available, and so much easier for the amateur to use than the traditional materials.

Latex foam comes in moulded cushion units, or in sheets sold by the square foot, with several forms of cellular structure for different degrees of comfort. Plastic foam also comes in a variety of thicknesses and densities, and is also sold by the square foot. Both sorts of cushioning should always be cut with a constantly wetted knife or breadsaw or a large pair of scissors, to give clean cuts without jaggedness.

There are two types of webbing: upholsterers' webbing, traditional in type and made of flax, cotton or jute, of which flax and cotton are the strongest; and rubber webbing which gives a more springy support.

To repair 'stuff-over' seats

First strip off the old upholstery until the seat frame is bare. Remove the tacks with an old screwdriver. Then fix the new webbing to the seat frame, interweaving it and spacing it as closely together as you feel will provide the best support for the new upholstery. Then stretch the webbing by 5-10%. You will find it easier to do this by tacking one end in position, then stretching the webbing by 10% and tacking down.

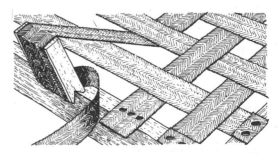

Fixing webbing, using a block of wood to strain the webbing tight.

If you are using rubber webbing, attach each piece to the frame with about four ⅝″ upholstery tacks, positioned at least a quarter of an inch from the end and sides of the webbing. Then cut off the extra. Do not tack hessian over rubber webbing because it restricts its stretching.

If you are using upholsterers' webbing, pull it very taut with a webbing strainer, or block of wood. Fold over the end and tack it to the frame with five tacks. Pull the webbing taut and use three tacks to fix to the frame. Then cut off the webbing, allowing an extra 1″–1½″. Fold this extra back over, and tack it down with two tacks. Tack a piece of hessian over the upholsterers' webbing.

Cut out a pattern of the seat in stiff paper, allowing an extra half an inch—or slightly more for a domed seat—all round. Lay this pattern on the smooth, top surface of the foam, which should be 1½″-2″ thick. Mark round the foam with a pen or piece of chalk. If the upholstery is going to be domed rather than flat, a piece of foam 2″-3″ smaller than the seat size will also be required, and of the same thickness as the other foam.

Cut out the latex or plastic foam, remembering to wet the knife or scissors. Then lay the foam on the chair seat, right side up, with half an inch overlap all round. Stick strips of calico 2″-3″ wide to the top edge, using a *contact adhesive. Put a thin coat of adhesive along half the width of the calico strips, and along a corresponding width around the top edges of the foam. The strips should overhang the edge by 1″-1½″. Allow to dry until tacky, then press the coated surfaces together. (If a domed seat is being made, lightly stick the small piece of foam to the underside of the larger piece.)

Pull down the foam and tack the strips to the seat rail to make the cushioned edges firm. Before finally driving the tacks right home, check to see that the foam is pulled down evenly all round the seat.

You are now ready to put on the covering material. Cut it at least 1½″ larger all round than the seat area, to allow enough for tacking to the underside of the seat rails.

The calico strips are of course tacked about half an inch up from the show-wood bottom edge of seat rails. The cover tacks must be close to the show-wood, as they are then covered with a braid or gimp, fixed either with gimp pins of matching colour, or with *natural latex-adhesive.

Lay the cover on the seat. Temporarily tack it to the centre of the underside of the front, and then the back rail, using one tack partly driven in. Then do the same for the underside of the side rails. The cover should now be correctly positioned, especially if striped or patterned, and under slight tension. Smooth the cover over towards each tack before driving each tack in, working from the centre outwards. Continue to smooth the material with your hand as you deal with each tack.

Trim off any spare material under the seat with a sharp knife or scissors. For the back legs, you will have to cut a V in the material to fit round the legs before tucking under and tacking.

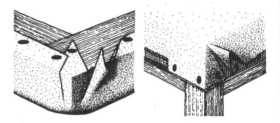

Double pleat corner for loose seat. Single pleat for square corner of stuff-over seat.

Repairing loose seats. Take off the old upholstery, then lay down the webbing (rubber or upholsterer's). If you are using rubber webbing, make sure that the sharp edges of the rails are rounded off with glass-paper, so as not to cut into the webs. If you are using upholsterers' webbing, don't forget to lay hessian over it (as described above). Then cut out the foam, which should be about 1″ thick, allowing an overlap of half an inch for doming, see above; use foam ½″-¾″ thick. Tape the edges of the foam with calico strips to attach the foam to the frame, as above. Then lay the foam on the seat, and, starting from the centre of each side, pull the calico strips down until you have a smooth line where the foam meets the wooden frame rails. Any lumps will show through. Put temporary tacks in first on all four sides, then put the other tacks in and drive them home.

Finally lay the covering material of your choice, allowing a 1½″ overlap for the underside of the frame for tacking. Holding cover and foam together, turn the seat upside down and put in three temporary tacks at the back and front to hold them in position. Now hold the seat on edge, and drive in three tacks along each side, smoothing with the palm of the hand from the centre of the seat towards each tack to strain the cover into slight tension. Then tack off at about 1″-1½″.

Do the corners last, and use a double pleat. The key thing to remember when upholstering loose seats is never to use covering material bulkier than that which you are replacing, otherwise the newly-covered seat may not drop into place.

Re-webbing. When only the webbing of a coil-sprung chair has broken, or is badly sagging, it can often be repaired from underneath, without having to strip away the seat covering. Remove the bottom hessian to expose all the old webbing.

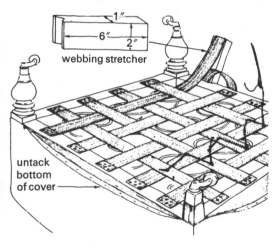

Rewebbing underside of chair.

Knock out the tacks with an old screwdriver. Then cut the twine holding the coil springs to the old webbing. (At this point make a note of the tying method.) Check that the tops of the springs have not penetrated through the hessian above the springs. If this has happened, it is best to call in an expert, because the whole chair will have to be stripped and re-upholstered.

If the springs are in good condition, and the top hessian is sound, re-web as described for 'stuff-over' seats. The webbing pattern should follow that of the old webs. Do not try to position the springs until the webbing has been completed.

Tie the springs to the webs with strong twine, using a half-circular needle. Look at the method used for tying while taking off the old webbing. Patience is required to ease all the springs into their correct positions on the new webbing. Each spring is tied to the webbing with four individual knots equally spaced round the circular base of the spring, so that they will not all come adrift if one knot breaks.

Loose arm and back joints; sagging. If an easy chair or sofa has loose arm or back joints, remove the outside cover to expose the wooden frame. Strengthen and make the loose joint firm by gluing and screwing a stout block of wood, which will not split, into the inside of the joint. Screws should go through the block into both frame members. Re-tack the outside cover in position after the glue has set.

Metal repair plates are not generally recommended for furniture, but an exception can be made for fully upholstered chairs and sofas where the frame needs strengthening and where the re-gluing of joints, or the fitting of wooden blocks, is not possible. There is a wide range of plate shapes and sizes at hardware shops. Always bore holes first into the wooden frame before screwing on the plate, to avoid splitting.

Another way to repair an easy chair or sofa which is sagging to the floor is to turn the piece upside down. Gravity will help to pull the bottom more or less level, though it may take some time. Afterwards, take a piece of thick paper, or cardboard, and make a pattern the same size at the bottom. Cut out a matching piece of plywood, $\frac{3}{16}$″ or ¼″ thick—*don't* use hardboard—and bore holes at about 4″-6″ intervals along the edges. Then bore slightly smaller holes into the bottom of the chair frame, and fix the plywood with screws long enough to give a good hold. This is an easier repair than tying springs to the webbing, though not one 'purists' would adopt. But it is often useful especially where the frame joints are rather weak and slack.

Warping

Warping can often be caused by damp being absorbed on one side, through not having been sealed or polished, and not on the other. It affects such things as solid table tops, desk lids, and door panels. The principle is to allow the convex side to dry out more than the concave, or hollow side. However old the piece, wood will flatten out as naturally as it will warp.

To prevent warping, make sure that the top and underside of a table or desk—and both sides of a vertical panel—have been well sealed with polish or wax (see Wood: finishing).

To repair warping, place the convex side facing a warm (not hot) radiator, and lay a slightly damp cloth on either side. Alternatively, make up a small platform to stand about 6″ above the radiator, and place the warped surface on that, hollow side down and wetted.

If that does not work, try placing the end of the panel on blocks and then place weights over the ends. If the panel is twisted as well as warped, distribute the weights judiciously. The important thing is to wet the concave side. Whatever method you adopt, make sure that both sides are equally sealed with polish or wax as soon as the panel is dry and flat, which may take a few days.

When faced with a warped door panel, detach it and apply the above method. An expert might well decide where the frame has also become twisted, to twist the panel into the opposite warp by wedging a block of wood between the bottom corner of the cupboard or wardrobe and the door, forcing the top back by carefully cramping into position for a few days, but this requires knowledge and skill.

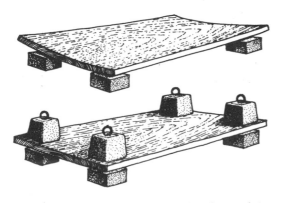

Correcting a warped and twisted panel by dampening, using corner weights.

GEMSTONES

There is a wide range of gemstones. If you are in any doubt about the identity of a stone ask the opinion of a jeweller or a gemmologist. Diamonds are very hard and one way of testing if they are real is to see if they will scratch glass. They should therefore always be prevented from coming into contact with other stones.

Most gem-set jewellery can be cleaned by soaking it for a few minutes in *methylated spirit or one of the special cleaning fluids now available. Brush gently with an old toothbrush to get any obstinate dirt out of crevices, then dry and polish with a soft cloth. You can also use warm soapy water, but make sure that it is only lukewarm. Stones such as aquamarines, emeralds, garnets and sapphires can be damaged by hot water.

Never immerse pieces in which the stones have a solid back setting. They are either held in place by a glue which could well be dissolved, or, as in the case of a lot of antique jewellery, the stones are backed with foil; water damages foil backings irreparably.

Stones which should never be washed or soaked in solution are opals and turquoises. Opals are very porous, and particularly sensitive to sudden changes of temperature, which may cause them to crack. The colour of turquoises is apt to be affected by washing. They should be dry-cleaned with a little *calcined magnesium.

Check jewellery regularly to make sure that no stones are loose. Opaque stones may be re-set with an *epoxy resin adhesive, but this is not advisable in the case of clear gemstones as it affects their appearance. Missing stones can sometimes be replaced, but it can be difficult and expensive to match them up.

Always make a point of removing gem-set rings before doing the washing up.

GILDING

This is a process for covering materials with an extremely thin film of gold.

There are basically four different methods of gilding: mercury gilding, electro-gilding, gold leaf gilding and the use of gilt waxes.

Mercury gilding was a very effective process. It was used from Roman times and involved forming an amalgam of mercury and gold which was applied with a brush. Subsequent heating drove the mercury off as a vapour, leaving the remaining metal evenly deposited. It survived until electro-gilding was introduced in 1840. It is now banned because of the terrible effects caused by mercury vapour. *Never attempt it.*

Electro-gilding was introduced by Elkington in 1836 and patented in 1836, 1838 and 1840. It is a process whereby a piece of gold is connected to the positive pole (anode) of a battery and the article to be plated is connected to the negative pole (cathode). They are both then immersed in a solution of double cyanide and the gold is deposited through the action of an electric current.

This should not be attempted by an amateur. The chemicals involved are extremely dangerous; also they are not easily available. Gold leaf gilding is the one type which can be undertaken at home. It requires a certain amount of practice to achieve a perfect result. Anything valuable should really be gilded by an expert.

The work must be done in warm, dry conditions and in as dust-free an atmosphere as possible.

First of all the article to be gilded must be absolutely clean. Wipe it over with a weak solution of *ammonia, and dry it. If you are gilding wood, it is essential that the surface is as dry as possible, because any moisture may cause slight swelling and folds in the leaf.

When the object is clean and dry, apply an even coat of *gold size. This is a special weak glue made from boiled linseed oil and ochre. It can be bought in two types: one dries in 2–4 hours, and the other in 8–12 hours. When the surface is slightly tacky, it is ready to receive the *gold leaf.

Position the leaves on the size, slightly overlapping and all pointing in the same direction. When the surface is completely covered, take a clean cotton cloth and rub gently over and with the overlaps until they have all blended together. New gilding can be toned down to match old gilding by rubbing it very gently with *flour paper or by experimenting with watercolour washes over the gold.

The leaf is now permanently in place and should now be burnished. It can be given added protection with a thin, clear coat of varnish.

Gilt waxes are very useful for touching up gilding and can be ued on wood, metal, plaster and plastic. They are available in a number of shades and are easy to use and harmless. They should be applied with a soft cloth on a clean, greaseless surface. They are quick-drying and can be buffed to a fine lustre. The wax should be sealed with an alcohol varnish before polishing. Never use a turpentine-based varnish, because it will lift the wax.

Never use gold paint to touch up old gilding because it won't match.

Don't regild pieces unless absolutely necessary, because the beautiful *patina of old gilding is one of its attractions and helps to distinguish an old piece from a reproduction.

Gilt objects should be cleaned periodically with soap and warm water applied with a sponge. Rinse afterwards, preferably with *distilled water, and dry with a soft cloth. Never use dips, brushes or abrasives.

Always store gilt objects in a dry place and avoid leaving metal objects such as pins in gilt boxes.

GLASS

Glass is not a true solid, but comes into the category of 'super-cooled' liquids. It is made from a fusion of silica, alkali and lime. When the mixture is melted in a crucible, it forms a syrupy liquid that hardens on cooling without crystallising. This is why it is transparent. The usual source of silica is sand, although crushed rock is sometimes used. The alkali in old glass used to be either from ash from burnt seaweed (soda glass), or from wood ash (potash glass). Lead as a flux was first introduced into ordinary glass by the English glassmaker, George Ravenscroft, in 1676. These three varieties have very different properties. Soda glass remains plastic for a long time while cooling, allowing the glass-maker to manipulate it into elaborate shapes. Potash glass changes from a liquid to a rigid state very quickly, allowing little time for manipulation so that it is usually decorated with carving, engraving or painting. Lead glass was originally intended as a substitute for rock crystal; its superior light-refracting qualities show up to the greatest advantage in cut glass.

Glass is easily discoloured by impurities contained in the raw materials. The Egyptians discovered that they could make colourless glass by adding a little manganese, but their secret was lost, and for a long period glass was coloured with metal oxides in imitation of precious stones. It was not until the Venetians rediscovered the technique in the 15th century that they were able to produce their clear, colourless 'crystallo', which was made in imitation of rock crystal.

Glass can be decorated with itself, as in mosaic, millefiore and the Venetian *latticinio* techniques. It may be embellished by enamel painting and gilding, and it may be cut and engraved.

The English had made window and simple utilitarian glass from Roman times until the reign of Elizabeth I, when Venetians came over and settled in London (late 16th century). The Venetian tradition continued until the late 17th century. Throughout the 18th century the shape and decoration of glass evolved continuously, particularly in the wine glass. Decoration on colourless glass consisted of wheel engraving or enamel painting; the stems were decorated with air or opaque twists. Opaque white and coloured translucent glass was also produced in the 18th century. Deep-cut designs of a geometric nature became the chief method of decoration between 1775 and 1880. Irish glass received fresh impetus about this time because of the arrival in Ireland of English glass-makers who had left England in order to escape the heavy excise duties. Thus Ireland became famous for its cut glass made in the English manner between 1780 and 1825.

The earliest American glass-house was set up in Jamestown at the beginning of the 17th century; window glass and crude utility ware was made. In the 18th century, glasshouses in New Jersey, Manheim, Pennsylvania, and New Bremen, Maryland, achieved distinction with the aid of imported European craftsmen. Some of the most imaginative glass produced in the 19th century was made at the Boston and Sandwich Glass Company, where new colours, models and patterns were created. In 1825,

the pressing machine was introduced into America, enabling a wide range of objects to be press-moulded with patterns deriving from the cut glass of England and Ireland.

Cleaning and general care

Glass not in use should be washed two or three times a year to keep it free of dust and grime which can cause deterioration. Wash each piece separately in warm water with a little fine soap or mild washing-up liquid. Plastic containers for this are preferable. Do not use very hot water and avoid powdered detergents. If the glass is very dirty, add a few drops of *ammonia to the water. Glass decorated with enamel, gilt, silver or platinum should be cleaned with cottonwool swabs dipped in the water, to which ammonia should not be added. Rinse with cold water. With frail pieces the change of temperature should be gradual. Dry with a soft linen or silk cloth, or an old chamois leather. Cotton cloths are not suitable, as they leave fluff.

Decanters or bottles should be filled with warm, soapy water and cleaned with a bottle brush or a long prod, such as a wooden stick wrapped in a cloth. If this does not clean them, fill them with water with half a cup of *vinegar added. Cover them and leave for about two days before rinsing. It is most important to dry out decanters. They should be left upside down overnight to drain. Then insert a drying cloth and rub it around. Make sure that the stopper is dry before you put it in, or it may get stuck.

For brightening dull glass, use a paste-type silver polish. You can make your own by adding *calcined magnesia to *benzene until a semi-liquid mixture is formed. Let it dry on the glass and then rub with a clean cloth to make it glow. Wash with warm, soapy water, rinse and dry.

Glass should be stored away from dampness, air-conditioning and heating vents, and protected from strong sunlight. Heat and damp can cause distastrous results. Do not store in tissue or other paper, both of which can harbour dampness. Keep all glass on shelves in well-ventilated storage cupboards.

Removing glass stoppers

Don't use force to try and remove the stopper of a decanter or glass bottle which is stuck. Instead, try soaking it in warm water. If this fails to loosen it, make up a mixture of 2 parts *alcohol, 1 part *glycerine and 1 part common salt. If these are not available, try cooking oil and *methylated spirit. Paint the mixture on the stopper, especially on the area where it enters the decanter or bottle. Leave it for a day. Then tap the stopper gently or wriggle it from side to side. It should then come away as usual.

Removing stains

Most stains can be removed by rubbing with *jeweller's rouge applied with a soft rag. Or else put some metal polish on the glass, allow it to dry, then rub it with a soft cloth.

Decanters and other containers for liquid are the most likely articles to become stained. They will show an opaque cloudiness on the inside if wine or water has been left in them too long, or if they have been repeatedly left damp. If the stains do not respond to a dilute solution of ammonia, try rubbing round the inside with a wooden stick wrapped in a cloth charged with a little fine *pumice powder. Use jeweller's rouge, which is a much finer abrasive, to finish it off. (Never use kitchen scouring powder, as this will scratch the glass.) Wine deposits can be cleaned with a mild acid solution of 5% *sulphuric or *nitric acid. After treatment, the decanter should be rinsed out at least a dozen times with clean water.

If all this fails, it is likely that the glass on the surface of the interior has literally broken down from being subjected to over-humidity. If this seems to have happened, take the glass to an expert who will remove the stained glass layer with hydrofluoric acid. This acid should never be used in the home, as both liquid and vapour can cause terrible burns.

It is not advisable to store liquids in antique glass containers, so do not allow wine to remain in decanters. If you do want to fill them for display purposes, use distilled rather than tap water.

Weeping glass

Humidity can seriously affect certain types of antique glass, especially if it is made of potash. It causes a loss of transparency and a cloudy or grizzled appearance. What happens is that when a layer of moisture forms on such a glass, the carbon dioxide in the moisture reacts with a substance in the glass to form sodium carbonate and calcium silicate. The resulting film will rapidly absorb more moisture from the air, producing droplets of liquid. Treatment for this is a matter for the expert, and the glass should be given to him as soon as possible. If it is left untreated, the process of disintegration will continue, until eventually tiny scales of glass begin to flake off.

Even contemporary glass can be affected if exposed for a long time to very damp conditions. To retard the disintegration, wash the glass thoroughly in running tap water, soak it for several hours in distilled water, and then dry it thoroughly as quickly as possible. Then give it a coating of *acetone or *celluloid varnish. It should be stored in a well-ventilated cupboard containing a stick of *silica gel or similar drying agent to prevent further damage.

Scratches

Scratches on glass can sometimes be removed by rubbing over them with a chamois leather impregnated with *jeweller's rouge. However this will take hours of labour. It may be better to take it to an expert, who will grind down the surface. A little *linseed oil rubbed into the scratches helps to make them less visible.

Grinding out chips and glass cutting

Chips in glass can be ground out by an expert, who will grind down the surface with a wheel and then repolish it.

Damaged cut glass can be disguised by expert re-cutting. The cutting is done by revolving wheels which grind away the surface, fashioning it in such a way as to leave prisms which refract light instead of allowing it to pass through the glass directly.

Repair

*Epoxy resin adhesives can be used to repair glass. *Polyvinyl acetate emulsion can also be used.

First make sure that the broken surfaces are clean and dust-free. Swab them with acetone if necessary to remove finger marks. Then apply a thin layer of adhesive to one surface only, as too much adhesive will only make the joint more visible, and stick the surfaces together. Use strips of self-adhesive tape, placed at right angles to the break, to maintain the correct position, but be careful that they do not exert undue pressure. Beware of unfired enamel or gilded decoration which could be pulled off accidentally when you remove the tape. When the adhesive has set and the tape is ready to be removed, you can prevent this happening by swabbing the tape with *white spirit which will dissolve the glue. The tape will then peel off easily without harming the decoration or the adhesive.

Remove excess adhesive before it hardens, with *acetone, or a split razor blade held at right angles to the glass to avoid scratching it. Glass-paper or steel wool will scratch the glass.

Do not heat glass, to hasten the setting of adhesive, but leave it to cure naturally.

Missing pieces should really be replaced by an expert, but this is expensive, and if you want to do your own, use a transparent polymethacrylate resin. This is a powdered resin which when mixed with a liquid sets to a hard, almost clear, transparent compound. However it does have a slight amber tint. Coloured acrylics are also available. When mixing, take care to avoid stirring air in with the mixture or the result will not be clear. As the resin has no great

adhesive quality, a little adhesive should be applied to the broken edge beforehand. The glass should be warmed very slightly before applying the acrylic, as heat is generated in the curing which might cause cold glass to crack.

Although liquid acrylic readily assumes shape of a mould, it also absorbs colour, so always use a colourless mould. Moulds of white modelling clay or plaster of Paris are best. The mould must be coated with silicone grease or the acrylic will stick to it. Pour the mixture into the mould, taking care that there are no air bubbles present. To prevent air being trapped in the acrylic, it is better to build up the required thickness in a series of layers, allowing each to harden before applying the next.

Surplus acrylic should be cleaned off immediately while still liquid. If you wait until it is hard, rubbing with abrasives will dull the surface and you may scratch the glass.

Because acrylic lacks adhesion, and also has a tendency to discolour, you might prefer to build up the missing pieces with colourless epoxy resin.

If the enamelled decoration has been damaged, you can repaint it with either acrylic paints or dry powder pigments mixed with polyurethane. A protective coating of a glazing material such as polyurethane is generally necessary with the former.

Before and after. Even with the resources of a museum, damaged glass cannot always be completely restored.

For restoring gilded decoration, use either gold leaf or gold paint, with a protective coating on top (see ceramics: retouching).

HANDLES AND KNOBS see Furniture

HINGES see Furniture

HORN
The outer sheath of horn is made of keratin. This becomes pliant when subjected to heat and moisture and so it can be moulded or flattened. Horn was valued for its translucency and used for lanterns and horn books (where a sheet of horn protected the paper or parchment). It was also used, among other things, for inlay, drinking vessels and boxes. Objects were often mounted in silver or decorated with etching into which colour was rubbed. Horn is frail and porous and so should not be exposed to extreme changes of temperature, dryness or damp.

Wash it in warm soapy water, but do not soak. Dry it quickly.

Horn is usually thin and hollow with a tendency to flake. The surface can be strengthened by impregnating it with *polyvinyl acetate. If it will not show, the inside surface can be reinforced with a plastic tape. For repairs, use *cellulose adhesive.

INK DRAWING AND MANUSCRIPTS
The oldest writing ink is carbon ink, which was first used by the ancient Egyptians. It is made of soot with a binding of oil, gum or glue size. Chinese and Indian inks are also of this type.

The other kind of ink is iron ink, which was first used c. 200 BC.

As a general rule, a carbon ink will be blacker and permanent. It is usually used in drawings. Iron ink tends to turn yellowish or brown, is impermanent, and is more often used for signatures and manuscripts. Coloured inks, especially old ones, are usually impermanent.

When cleaning ink drawings or written manuscripts remember that there is no easy way of discovering which kind of ink has been used, so don't embark on any washing or bleaching process without doing a small test section. If this is impossible, assume the ink is fugitive and seal it with a thin wash of an *acrylic resin solution such as 5% *polymethyl methacrylate in *acetone. This can easily be removed afterwards with a little acetone when the drawing or manuscript is dry. Test a sample first to see that this solution does not cause the ink to run. When this has been done, clean and restore as for *paper.

IVORY
Ivory is composed of a hard tissue called dentine. There are various types, but they all share the same characteristics and are virtually indistinguishable when worked. The types are elephant tusk, walrus tusk (particularly used in the 11th and 12th centuries), mammoth tusk (excavated in Siberia in the 19th century), and teeth from sperm whales and hippopotami which have an enamel coating that must be removed before working.

Plastic, celluloid and plaster of Paris can all be treated to look like ivory but do not have the 'grain' which is visible in true ivory. The striations radiate from the centre of a tusk in the same formation as a tree-trunk.

Prehistoric carvings in tusk have been found. Ivory has also been used by the Assyrians, Egyptians, Greeks and Romans, in Oriental art and in Europe from early Christian times to the present day. Its texture is suitable for the finest carving, and it can be etched, stained, painted, gilded and inlaid with metals and stones. It can be used as an inlay itself and as a veneer.

Ivory should be kept in reasonably humid conditions, and away from excessive heat, cold or damp.

Before cleaning ivory it is important to remember that it yellows naturally with age. Also look out for traces of original colouring, which should not be cleaned off. Netsukes (carved Japanese ornaments), for example, are often shaded with grey or brown to highlight the carving.

A brush is probably the quickest way to remove dirt. Surface dirt can also be removed with soap and water, provided that the objects are in good condition. Make sure that the ivory is left wet for the shortest possible time because of warping and cracking. If the ivory is cracked, it should be dry-cleaned with a solution of *spirit soap in *white spirit or *trichloroethane. This

An 18th century Japanese ivory netsuke, an ornament used as a 'toggle' on a belt or sash.

can be brushed onto the ivory and the dirt removed. The object should be finally wiped with the solvent to ensure no soap remains. A little *microcrystalline wax can be applied after cleaning to restore the shine and to protect the surface.

Warping and cracking is caused by excessive cold, heat or damp. Don't attempt to fill cracks, because under different conditions the gap may close. If, however, a small piece is missing or chipped off, the space can be filled with a mixture of *beeswax and *carnauba wax tinted with oil-paint to match the ivory.

Ivory knife handles often fall off. This is caused by washing up with hot water and detergent which loosens the old animal-based glue. To mend, first clean off all the old glue from the spike of the knife and from the inside of the handle. Glue the two together again with a synthetic rubber adhesive.

Breaks in ivory can be repaired with a nitro *cellulose adhesive. This can be easily removed with a solvent, and so adjustments can be made to a delicate repair. Before mending keep all fragments for a period of time at the same humidity, or the pieces may shrink different amounts.

If an ivory piece is in a weak state and becoming powdery, an expert can consolidate it by impregnating it with a 5% solution of transparent *synthetic resin.

Similarly, soft and wet ivory can be strengthened with a *polyvinyl acetate emulsion, though this condition is only likely to occur with archaelogical pieces.

JADE

Jade is a hardstone. It was extensively used by the Chinese for small carvings. There are two kinds of stone generally recognised as jade: nephrite and jadeite.

Nephrite, a silicate of calcium and magnesium with a granular structure, has been known since earliest times. In its pure form it is white, but owing to the presence of chemical impurities it takes on a characteristic range of colours, ranging from whitish grey to a dark green, with many intermediate shades of blue, yellow and green. When polished, it has a rather oily lustre, unlike the vitreous appearance of most jadeites. Its main sourse was Khotan or Chinese Turkestan in Central Asia.

Jadeite, a sodium aluminium silicate, has a fine fibrous structure. It is often the finer in quality, being harder and more vitreous in appearance than nephrite, and a translucent deep emerald green in colour. There is no evidence that it was used in China before the 18th century, when it was introduced from Burma, but since then it has surpassed nephrite in popularity.

A third variety, a chloromelanite of alumina and soda, usually called 'Siberian jade', has a blackish-green colour unlike nephrite or jadeite. It was not often carved by the Chinese, but the Russian court jeweller, Fabergé, used it occasionally.

Jade is an extremely hard material. It has to be cut by abrasives such as quartz sand, powdered garnets or corundum. Jade is hard enough to scratch glass, which is a useful test of the nature of the stone. The resonant character of jade, and the fact that it will not warm in the hand, when combined with its proper translucency and colour, are also sign of genuineness.

Jade carving was probably introduced into China in the late Neolithic period, when ritual objects and small pieces of jewellery were made. Later, carving became more intricate, and workmanship reached a high level of refinement in the figures of animals and monsters, vases and cups, and vessels in imitation of bronze forms. During the Ming dynasty (1368-1644), irregular lumps of jade were carved to represent mountains with such details as pine trees, pagodas or human figures, and there was also much imitation of earlier styles. Under the Ch'ing dynasty (1644-1912), a new style arose in which virtuoso craftsmen produced intricate carving.

Jade has also been worked extensively in India, where jadeite was the most popular material. The most common articles were bowls with very thin, translucent walls, often mounted with rubies and other precious stones.

In New Zealand, greenstone, a type of nephrite, has been used in primitive Maori art, principally for making axe heads and flat pendants, carved into distorted human forms, called *tikkis*.

Most surviving specimens of Mexican jade show considerable skill in carving, and included small pieces of jewellery and, occasionally, masks.

Imported jade has also been worked in different parts of Europe, including Switzerland, France, Belgium and Italy.

Cleaning

Jade should be washed with warm, soapy water, thoroughly rinsed and dried carefully with a soft cloth.

Mending

Broken pieces of jade should be mended with a strong adhesive such as an *epoxy resin or a *polyvinyl acetate emulsion. The broken surfaces must be scrupulously clean and dry before the adhesive is applied. Cover the surface with the least possible amount of adhesive. Firmly press together the two parts in the correct position. Remove any excess adhesive with *acetone on a cottonwool swab. The mend must be very tightly clamped with strips of self-adhesive tape or heavy weights during the setting period. Dowelling can be used if there is much strain on a break, but it is best avoided, especially in the more translucent parts.

If there are any pieces missing, make a filler out of *synthetic resin mixed with *French chalk and the appropriate powdered pigments to obtain the required colour. Either model the filler into the necessary shape, or, if a duplicate is available, take a mould. Glue the cast piece into position.

Alternatively, sealing wax of the required colour can simulate the surface of polished jade closely. Melt the wax into the site. Smoothing it out with a flat tool heated above the melting point of the wax. When the filler has set, polish the surface with a mild chrome polish.

JAPANNING see Lacquer.

JET

Jet is a form of fossilised wood found in bituminous shale. It used to be plentiful in Saxony and England, particularly in the Whitby area of Yorkshire, where there were many workshops turning out jewellery and small objects such as egg cups, paper-knives, thimble cases, etc. It was very popular in the mid-19th century for mourning jewellery, and also in the 1880s when coloured stones were out of fashion.

There is a cheap substitute known as French jet, which is really black glass. It was used particularly for objects with sharp-edged decoration.

Jet was carved, faceted and engraved.

It can be cleaned by rubbing with fresh breadcrumbs, or with soap and warm water taking care not to immerse the piece in water.

Any broken pieces can be repaired with an *epoxy resin adhesive coloured black.

JEWELLERY

Jewellery should be kept clean and inspected regularly to see if any repairs are necessary. Check that beads are still firmly threaded and that no stones have become loose in their settings. Clasps and pins should also be examined to make sure that they have not weakened.

Some types of loose stones can be re-fixed with an *epoxy resin adhesive (see gemstones) but most repairs will need to be done by a jeweller.

Soldering broken pins, earring wires, etc., is a very tricky job, because stones have to be removed first. Unless you are very experienced in soldering, it is easy to damage the piece or produce an unsightly repair (see Metalwork: soldering).

Jewellery should be stored with care, and the pieces kept either in their separate cases or in a proper jewel case. Make sure that they do not come into contact with each other, as diamonds will easily scratch other tones. Pearls in particular are easily damaged.

*Pearls and beads are generally threaded with a knot between each bead, so that if the thread breaks, the knots hold the beads and prevent them from falling off. When re-threading use a strong thread such as silk or Terylene. Select a thickness according to the size of the hole drilled through the bead. Use a blunt needle to draw the thread through the holes. To make the necessary knot, tie a loop round a pin, and with the pin guide the knot until it is tight against the bead; repeat for each bead.

Advice on cleaning and restoration will be found in the following entries: amber, cameos, coral, enamel, gemstones, gold (*see* metalwork), ivory, jade, jet, marcasite, niello, palladium (*see* metalwork), pearls, pinchbeck (*see* metalwork), platinum, (*see* metalwork), silver (*see* metalwork), tortoise-shell, watches.

JOINTS *See* **Furniture** (mortice and tenon joints).

LACE

There are three techniques of lace-making. It may be made on a pillow using bobbins to hold each thread (e.g. pillow lace, bobbin lace). It is also done with a needle and varied by cutting and drawing out threads and the use of embroidery (needlepoint lace, *point de venise, reticello, guipure,* darned net and cutwork). Finally, it may be crochetted or knitted, which involves a continuous thread that can be completely unravelled. Lace was developed around the 16th century, and is usually worked in cotton or linen thread. It is obviously very delicate and must always be treated with great care.

To clean it, first soak the lace in several baths of *distilled water, which will loosen the dirt. It can then be washed in warm water with a few drops of *Lissapol N and then carefully rinsed in warm water. If it is particularly delicate, it should be supported by stitching it (with large stitches) to a piece of fine lawn or muslin. If the piece is

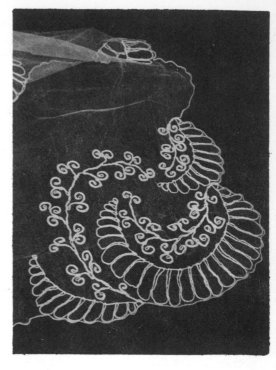

Lace wedding veil, of silk darned through net, c1875. Treasured family lace like this is best kept wrapped in acid-free tissue paper, and stored in a box.

very large, it is easier to fold it into a manageable size and lightly stitch it together. This will stop the weight of the water damaging the lace.

Lay the lace to dry on clean white blotting paper and pin it down into shape. Make sure that the pins are stainless steel, or they will leave rust marks.

If the lace is lying on a pillow, or for some other reason cannot be immersed in water, it can be dry-cleaned by sprinkling powdered *French chalk over it. Brush it off with a camel-hair paint-brush.

See textiles.

LACQUER

Lacquer was introduced to Europe between 1650 and 1700 from the Orient. Shades of black, red, green, yellow and white lacquer were most common. It is highly decorated, often with gold either in relief or incised, and frequently inlaid with *mother-of-pearl.

At the end of the 17th century and beginning of the 18th century, imitation lacquer work, known as japan was produced

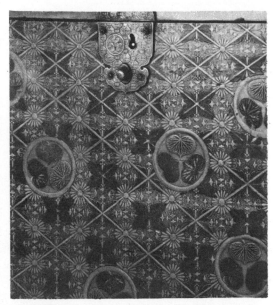

A detail of a Japanese lacquer cabinet with a pattern of formalised chrysanthemums and leaves.

in Europe. In France, because this imitation lacquer was developed by the Martin brothers, it was called *vernis martin.* Lacquered objects include screens, tables, chairs, cabinets, boxes and trays.

When cleaning lacquer, *never* use a damp cloth, because moisture can cause the lacquer to peel. For a light cleaning for smudges and fingermarks, use a little household spot remover on a soft, clean cloth. Wipe it on and remove it instantly.

Scratches or chips can be touched in with black shellac polish, or white polish to which powder colour has been added (*see* French polish).

LEATHER
Leather can be tanned in three ways. The oldest method, a mineral process, involves steeping the skin in a solution of salt and alum. In another process, called chamoising, the leather is treated with oils and fats; brains were often used. The most common method is a vegetable process which uses tannin, a substance naturally present in bark, wood and leaves.

After tanning, leather can be treated in a variety of ways: dyeing, staining, embossing the surface, plating (producing a very shiny surface), 'boarding' to bring up the natural grain patterns, enamelling to produce patent leather, and finally, scraping to give a suede finish.

Washing and cleaning
The vegetable-tanned leathers, such as heavy hide leather as used on harness, trunks and boots, are cleaned with *spirit soap as a 2% solution in *white spirit. Rinse with white spirit alone. When dry, it should be protected and polished with a *microcrystalline wax. Give very brittle leather an application of *British Museum Leather Dressing.

Leather of this type is particularly susceptible to red rot. In the early stages this can be recognised as a pinkish tinge, particularly on the flesh side of the leather and on cut edges. If you see this, immediately treat the leather with a *potassium lactate solution. In the advanced stages of red rot the colour darkens to a deep red, by which time the leather is disintegrating. All you can do to stop further disintegration is to impregnate the leather with an *acrylic resin solution. Dilute the resin by adding to 1 part resin 2-3 parts *trichloroethane. Brush the solution onto the leather. It will quickly be absorbed and set within a few minutes. If the surface is left unnaturally shiny, rub it with a little trichloroethane.

Cuir boulli, or objects of moulded leather, such as buckets, tankards and jugs, were made by steeping the leather in cold water, moulding it into shape and sewing it together while still damp. Produced since medieval times, objects are likely to be brittle. The only suitable treatment is a light application of British Museum Leather Dressing. When dry, apply microcrystalline wax, which will clean and help to preserve the leather.

Light leathers such as morocco, made from skins (goat, sheep, calf and pig), can be cleaned with British Museum Leather Dressing and microcrystalline wax. Light-coloured leather should be tested before treating with the dressing, as it can darken the colour.

Velvet or suede finishes should be cleaned with a *granular cleaner, which will remove dirt without affecting the surface. If any stains remain, trichloroethane can be tried. Do not use British Museum Leather Dressing or microcrystalline wax.

Decorated leather, sometimes known as 'Spanish' or 'Cordoban', which has been gilded, painted and embossed with heated metal plates, was used for screens, hangings and upholstery. It was produced from the 15th to the 20th centuries. The leather is likely to have become very brittle and possibly split.

The first step is to expose, if possible, the 'wrong' side of the leather, which is the side that you treat. Be very careful to support the leather if you are removing it from a frame, and assume that it will be in a fragile state. Try to keep any original nails or studs; new ones will not look as good. If the leather is backed with canvas or wood, it is best to seek expert advice as separating it can be a very difficult job; doing it wrong will split or damage the leather.

Check for signs of red rot, and if present treat accordingly.

Remove all surface dirt from both sides with spirit soap, and when quite dry treat the undecorated side with British Museum Leather Dressing. Beeswax can be omitted from the recipe, as a polish is not necessary. The dressing will not penetrate the painted and metallic surface.

The gilding on this type of leather is usually produced by coloured glazes over burnished tin or silver. If this has deteriorated, it is possible to retouch with a clear varnish (a synthetic resin type soluble in white spirit) tinted to match the original with a spirit-based aniline dye.

Finish with microcrystalline wax. Fragile leather can be backed with canvas if its condition is very bad. Stick it down with a *polyvinyl acetate adhesive.

Holes and tears can be patched from behind with thin leather placed grain side downwards.

Reptile leather (crocodile, watersnake, python and lizard), shagreen (ray fish skin dyed green) and fish skin are hard and tough, and only need cleaning and polishing with microcrystalline wax.

The very thin leather known as skiver, which is made from the surface layers of sheep or goat skins, has often been protected with a 'leather varnish'. This is *shellac dissolved in *methylated spirit. If the surface is very scratched and waxing has no effect, remove the old varnish with methylated spirit. Either revarnish the surface with shellac and methylated spirit or rub it with microcrystalline wax.

Mineral-tanned leather in an undressed state is most likely to be found in archaelogical specimens and made up into purses, pouches and gloves. When dressed to give greater suppleness, it was commonly used for womens' shoes and gloves, though not often after the 18th century. It is important not to use water on it, as it can revert to an untreated state. It has often become very stiff, but can be softened by gently kneading the leather. Clean with trichloroethane or spirit soap and white spirit, making sure to rinse soap traces away with white spirit. Test the effect of these two methods on the colour of the object before using them.

Oil-tanned leather is made from cattle, horse and deer hides. It is sometimes called doeskin. One type, 'buff' leather, is pale yellow with a suede finish, and is used for military uniforms, boots, gloves, saddle seats, etc. Try cleaning it with a granular cleaner. If this is not successful wash with soap and water or with spirit soap in white spirit or water.

Chamois leather or wash leather tends to become stiff with age. It can be softened with a 10% solution of purified neat's foot oil in trichloroethane. If the object is not too fragile, it can be kneaded afterwards. Clean with spirit soap in white spirit.

Rawhide is untanned cattle hide which has only been de-haired and de-fleshed. Being light and tough, it is often used for luggage, cases and other containers, where it is usually stretched over a wooden frame. The following dressing will keep it in good condition. Dissolve 3 of *gelatine and 15 of *polythene glycol wax in 250 ml of distilled water; add 5 ml of *glycerine to the solution.

Repair

The following repair operations are common to all types of leather.

Stitching can be resewn if the leather is in good condition. Match the thread as far as possible and wax it before using it.

Leather should be glued with a *polyvinyl acetate adhesive. If the object is of moulded leather (cuir boulli) it may be very brittle and you may use an *epoxy resin. Don't use adhesive tape, which will damage the surface of the leather.

Fungus tends to attack vegetable-tanned leathers. This can be prevented by brushing the surface with a 10% solution of *ortho-phenylphenol in methylated spirit. Don't use any other type of fungicide without checking that it doesn't leave a stain.

Insect attack (woodworm, book-lice and silver-fish) can be prevented with *paradichlorbenzene.

Iron stains can be lessened and sometimes removed with a 25% solution of *oxalic acid in water (although normally the metal should be lacquered to prevent contact with the leather). Damp the area with water and then apply the oxalic acid solution. As the leather dries the stain should fade. Try it a second time if there has been no improvement. When the leather is dry, rinse it by wiping a damp cloth over it. When the leather has dried again, rub it over with a mircocrystalline wax.

LEATHER TOPS See **Furniture** (desk and table tops).

LOCKS

The history of locks dates back to Roman times. In the 14th and 15th centuries locksmiths began to make locks with elaborate, chiselled ornaments. French locks with the face divided into compartments by buttresses surmounted by pinnacles were characteristic of this period. They were usually rectangular. German and Spanish locks splayed outwards.

European locksmiths were very conservative, and it was not until the late 16th century that Gothic styles replaced the Renaissance styles. In the 16th century, a new sort of lock was invented with an inside mechanism. This became more elaborate and functional but less ornamental during the century.

Up to this time locks had been mostly of iron. By the late 17th century the fashion had changed and locks in enclosed brass cases as we still have today.

Until the 19th century the lock was still very much part of the decoration on furniture and doors. Firms like Bickfords of London and John Wilkes of Birmingham produced locks with fine brass tracery in conjunction with blued steel.

When restoring locks, remove them from their surround and strip them down com-pletely. It is advisable to make a drawing of where the pieces go as you do it. Clean the pieces according to the metal. Take care not to damage intricately detailed working with too harsh an abrasive.

Rust on ferrous metals can be removed with a rust-removing oil or a proprietary solvent.

Simple locks can be oiled with natural sperm oil. More intricate mechanisms should be oiled with *graphite, which doesn't attract dust.

Bent pieces on iron locks should be annealed before restoring (see metalwork: annealing). Do this while the piece is still attached to the lock if the mechanism is simple, although additional cleaning will then be necessary.

If you have lost the key or it is missing, you can try other keys, but be very careful not to force the mechanism. You can buy new keys from most locksmiths, but you will need to remove the lock and take it along to them.

MARQUETRY see **Wood**

MARBLE

Marble is a metamorphic rock formed by the action of heat or pressure, or both, on limestone. By this action the limestone loses its original nature, and it becomes an aggregate of calcite crystals which, in its pure state, is white, but may be coloured, veined or black when impurities are present.

Marble was used by the sculptors of ancient Greece and Rome. The Greeks generally employed white marble, although they often applied colour to it. The most famous of the white Greek marbles was the close-grained pentelic, quarried at Mount Pentelic in Attica. The coarser-grained, translucent, white marbles from the Aegean islands of Paros and Naxos were also popular. The Romans worked with coloured and patterned marbles. They used the pure white Carrara marble from Tuscany, as did the Renaissance and Neo-Classical sculptors.

Nowadays, the most popular coloured marbles are Apollino, a white and green banded marble, Rosso Antico, varying in shade from pale to purplish red, liver and blood red, Verde Antico, a green mottled serpentine marble, and Belgian Black, a compact, fine black marble, previously

A mid-19th century lifesize marble figure of the goddess Diana.

known as Tournai marble. The last is much used by modern sculptors.

Marble is comparatively easy to carve and capable of taking a high polish, but it is porous and therefore easily stained by damp, rust, or by contamination from smoke, dirt or dust in the atmosphere.

Weathering causes the surface of marble to change, becoming warmer in tone and more translucent with the years. This patina is an essential feature of old marble, and should be kept. It will survive the general cleaning described below, but would be destroyed by the use of abrasives or acids.

Cleaning

Marble needs to be dusted regularly as the accumulation of soot and iron particles in the fine details of the modelling of white marble sculpture will cause staining. Use a feather duster or a soft-bristled brush rather than a cloth, which will tend to grind the dust into the stone.

Washing may be necessary occasionally, but be careful with white or light coloured marbles. Test a small, inconspicuous area before you start. It is important to use warm water that is free from iron and preferably distilled. Do not use soap, or cleaning powders or pastes, as they can easily damage the patina. As pale marbles are very easily discoloured, avoid using coloured cloths and rusty buckets.

After thorough dusting, begin washing from the bottom, doing small areas at a time and preventing the dirty water from lying in hollows or running down in rivulets over the marble. Dry each area thoroughly with a clean, white cotton rag or ample supplies of cottonwool as you go.

If greasy dirt has accumulated over many years and become ingrained in the surface of the marble, washing will not remove it. Apply a methelene chloride paint stripper with a soft brush, using a stippling action so as to work the solvent into the crevices of the marble. This will remove most of the dirt.

Some dirt may remain in the pores, which can be removed by a mud-pack.

The mud-pack is made of a *magnesium silicate powder mixed to a paste with distilled water, and applied to the surface by hand to form a layer about 15 mm thick. It has no chemical effect on the marble, but acts as a poultice to keep the surface wet without saturating the body of the stone. Leave in position for about 24 hours, by which time it will have partially dried. When the surface begins to craze, it is ready to be removed. Do not leave it too long, or it will fall off the surface, but do not take it off too soon or it will not come away cleanly. Remove a little at a time and immediately wash the newly exposed moist surface with distilled water, using nylon brushes and wiping with a sponge. Do not remove too much at once, or part of the surface will dry out before it can be washed, and the ingrained dirt will harden again on the surface and prove difficult to remove. This is why the pack should not be left until it falls off the marble. Make sure that no traces of the pack remain on the marble.

This method is so succesful that the cleaned surface is likely to look rougher than it did beforehand because of the removal of dirt which had been filling the minute pits in the surface caused by natural weathering. The appearance of the cleaned marble can, if necessary, be improved by brushing on a layer of *microcrystalline wax dissolved in a 10% solution of *white spirit. This coating gives some protection against dirt. It is soluble in white spirit, so that it can easily be removed during any future cleaning.

Painted marble is best cleaned with saliva applied with a cottonwool swab. Rub the areas quite vigorously, unless it is flaking. For retouching, use tempera paints. When dry, apply a layer of picture varnish to restore the gloss. When this has hardened, after 24 hours, apply a layer of micro-crystalline wax. This will reduce the gloss of the varnish, matching the surface sheen more closely with that of the marble.

Removal of stains

White or light-coloured marble can very easily become stained. The most common stains are due to dust, which leaves traces of soot and iron. Anything damp that is coloured will transmit a stain to the marble, so beware of packing materials, straw, newspaper, corrugated paper. Even clean, white cloth, if damp, encourages fungoid growth which will stain. (If you plan to store a white marble object for any length of time, it is best to pack it in a wooden box constructed with brass screws, and to use wooden bars, padded with white cottonwool covered with polythene, to hold the article in place.)

In general don't use abrasives such as emery or sandpaper on marble, as they will damage the patina. Also, don't use acidic solvents, as all acids disintegrate marble. If slightly alkaline solvents are used, they should not be left on the marble for too long and they should be washed off very thoroughly, as they can cause yellow stains. Neutral organic solvents are safe.

Staining is often difficult and sometimes impossible to remove. Most stains should respond to a 2% solution of *Chloramine T in water, which should be rinsed off thoroughly after use. Exposure to air and sunlight may also help to bleach the stain away.

If Chloramine T is unsuccessful, apply a weak solution of *hydrogen peroxide (100 vols peroxide diluted to approximately 1 part peroxide to 3 parts water) containing a drop or two of *ammonia. Make sure you wash it off well afterwards.

Organic deposits caused by lichens and algae may be softened and removed with a weak solution of ammonia. If they cover a large area, spray with *formalin first. Then wash stained areas with a 5% solution of a *fungicide, which also helps to protect against mildew or other fungus.

If the stain remains, try the paper-pulp method. First, boil some good-quality blotting paper in distilled water. Then beat it thoroughly in a bowl until it is reduced to pulp. When the pulp has cooled, put a layer of it, $\frac{1}{2}"-\frac{3}{4}"$ thick, over the blemish or stain and leave it until it is completely dry. The moisture from the pulp sinks into the stone, loosening the stain, and then as evaporation takes place, the moisture with the impurities is drawn out of the stone into the paper pulp. If necessary, apply more pulp.

You can also use this method for oil or wax stains. A blob of oil-paint should be softened with paint stripper. Chip away any surface lumps or wax. Dry the pulp out completely, then soak it in a mild solvent such as white spirit and place it over the stain. The mud-pack method, using white spirit rather than water, can also be used to remove oil and wax stains.

Note that it is virtually impossible to eradicate the oily ingredients which have been absorbed into the pores of the marble, leaving a grey or brownish residue.

Certain dark areas of stains will remain. Carrara marble is particularly difficult, as the stains penetrate deep into the pores where they cannot be reached by solvents or bleaching agents. Hide any stains that cannot be removed by rubbing a little coloured chalk over them.

Repair

If marble is subjected to undue heat, the crystals that make it up may expand at different rates in different directions and lose their power of cohesion. This causes the surfaces to have a granular appearance. The affected parts show up as a staring white, as they reflect more light than the surrounding stone. In extreme cases the statuary may be worn down to a shapeless mass of loosely adherent crystals looking like granulated sugar.

Marble in such a condition should be treated by an expert, who will consolidate the surface by impregnating it with wax or lime.

Undue heat will also cause marble to warp, for which there is no treatment, so marble is not really suitable for fireplaces, despite tradition.

Small broken pieces, chips, cracks and holes can be repaired with a *polyvinyl acetate emulsion. For larger breaks, an *acrylic resin is advisable.

Thoroughly clean and dry the broken surfaces. Then apply the adhesive. The two pieces should be securely tied or clamped together during the setting period. A filler can be made a trough along the break line by mixing polyvinyl acetate emulsion with marble grains. Veining can be painted in with acrylic colours after the filler has set to stimulate the natural veining.

Marbles of all kinds can be seriously damaged by acids in the atmosphere. Marble objects kept indoors can be coated with a layer of *microcrystalline wax dissolved in a 100% solution of white spirit to provide protection against dirt. No satisfactory protective coating has yet been discovered for marble statuary kept outside, so it is always better to keep it inside, away from the damaging effects of the weather.

MARCASITE

Marcasite is made up of small crystals of iron pyrites. It is cut like gemstones and usually set in silver. It was widely used from the 18th century onwards for jewellery, buckles and buttons, and was sometimes set on an enamel background in imitation of diamonds.

Marcasite can be cleaned by rubbing with an impregnated silver cloth. If it is very dirty, it should be brushed gently with a paste made of *French chalk, *methylated spirit and a few drops of *ammonia. A tooth-brush is an invaluable aid for this.

Marcasite should be kept away from heat, which can damage its sparkle

MEDALS

The value of medals depends on their condition, so handle them as little as possible. Don't polish them unless you have no intention of re-selling them. Before handling them, always make sure your hands are very clean and hold them by the edges.

Silver medals should be washed periodically in soap and warm water and dried with a soft cloth or tissue. Wipe them very gently with cottonwool moistened with *petrol, to protect against dampness, before you put them away. Silver medals develop a bluish bloom or *patina in time. It should not be removed, because it does not diminish their value, and may even increase it.

Copper and bronze medals should only be treated with an occasional gentle brushing with a soft bristle (not nylon) brush to remove dust.

Medals are best protected from the atmosphere by keeping them in their original cases or in suitably-sized boxes or drawers, laid between two wads of cottonwool. Coin cabinets with shallow drawers with baize or velvet-lined wells are ideal, but expensive.

For details of how to make a simple tray for holding medals, *see* coins.

METALWORK:

BELL METAL
An alloy of copper containing 20%–25% tin. A little zinc was sometimes added to give superior casting properties.

Bell metal was originally used for bells, but the tone of a bell is actually influenced more by the soundness of the casting than by the composition of the alloy. It is now mainly used as a beating bronze.

There are two schools of thought about how to look after bells made from bell metal. Some collectors prefer to keep them in the condition in which they are found. Others like to restore the original clean, glowing appearance.

If you decide on cleaning, treat as for *copper. In no circumstances buff the bell, as this could remove any of the original markings cleaning often reveals.

It is also important that the *patina of early oriental bells should never be removed. Wash these in soapy water to remove superficial dirt.

BENARES WARE
This is a form of brassware made in India and stamped or hammered to give a dappled appearance. Typical objects are trays, vases, bowls, mugs, cups and doorstops.

Clean as for *brass: brush an ammonia solution into the chased and embossed areas with a toothbrush. Then wash in a detergent solution and rinse thoroughly in clean warm water.

Benares ware can be kept clean with an ordinary proprietary metal polish and regular polishing with a soft cloth, or it can be lacquered to save work.

Benares ware is difficult to mend because it tends to be brittle.

BRASS
Brass is an alloy of copper and zinc, with 65% copper and 35% zinc. It is probably the most widely known decorative alloy, and has been used since Roman times. Typical brass objects are fire-irons, fire-dogs, fenders, candlesticks, horse brasses, warming pans, trays, furniture handles, etc.

When cleaning furniture fittings, it is best to remove them first if possible, as the chemicals may damage the wood.

To clean brass, first wash it with an ammonia solution to remove all grease and dirt. Thoroughly rinse afterwards. Next prepare a solution of *oxalic acid and salt. As oxalic acid is poisonous, it is safer to use *vinegar, which makes a good substitute. Use one heaped tablespoon of salt and two tablespoons of vinegar to every pint of water. Clean the brass in this solution, and rinse it thoroughly in distilled water. Then polish with a little oil or a proprietary metal polish.

Badly corroded brass can be cleaned in a fairly strong, warm solution of washing soda. Brush or wipe it away afterwards and the corrosion should come away. Stubborn spots can be removed by rubbing with *emery powder on a cloth or fine steel wool. Always work in one direction only. Scratches can be polished out with *jeweller's rouge afterwards.

Brass can be hard-soldered with spelter or soft-soldered with silver solder (see soldering). The silver solder can be coloured with one of the metallic coloured waxes used for regilding so that it matches the brass. Hard-soldering should be left to an expert, because the melting points of spelter and brass are fairly close, so that there is a danger of destroying the object. Holes and cracks can be patched with a *synthetic resin mixed with fine brass filings.

Brass can be lacquered to avoid the need for frequent cleaning.

BRITANNIA METAL
This is an alloy of tin containing small amounts of antimony and copper. It often looks like *pewter, but it is a harder, stronger, more resilient metal. It was made in sheets, and could be shaped by die-stamping or lathe-turning. It was introduced c.1770, and used for cutlery, coffee-pots, teapots, candlesticks, dishes, cake baskets, etc.

With the introduction of *electroplate, Britannia metal objects were often silver-plated, and may be marked E.P.B.M. The plating tends to wear off, but it is very difficult to have pieces replated.

For cleaning and repairing see pewter or electroplate, depending on whether the piece is plated or not.

BRONZE
Bronze is an alloy of copper and tin. The proportions vary considerably according to requirements of use and colour. Modern statuary bronze contains 75% copper, 20% zinc, 3% tin and 2% lead, whereas ancient bronze often contained up to 15% tin. The colour of new bronze varies from light gold to dark brown.

Bronze is ideal for making castings, so it was often used in the past for the manufacture of tools and weapons with work-hardened edges.

Bronze is very susceptible to corrosion. It turns green or blue when exposed to the air, but this patina is often thought of as one of its great attractions. You should usually be careful not to remove it.

However if you do you want to remove the patina, flake or scrape it off with a brass wire brush. A 10% solution of *acetic acid in water will remove any obstinate pieces. It will leave a red discolouration which can easily be rubbed off. Wash off the solution thoroughly, using *distilled water for the final rinse. If you are considering removing the patina of an old piece, it is best to ask the advice of a museum expert first.

You can produce a green-coloured patina by applying a weak solution of common salt and copper nitrate followed by immersion in a bath of 100 parts weak vinegar, 5 parts *ammonium chloride and 1 part *oxalic acid. The process takes several days to complete.

A brown patina can be produced by heating the object gently and brushing it with *graphite. Or you can boil it in a solution of 30 parts copper acetate and 30 parts ammonium chloride in 10 parts of water until you get the colour you want. These processes, however, require a certain skill and experience and are best not attempted at home.

For ordinary cleaning, wash bronze pieces in distilled water; dry, and then polish with a *microcrystalline wax. Or you can degrease and lacquer them.

Bronze can be soldered in the same way as *brass.

Bronze disease

Bronze disease takes the form of light green spots on the surface. The spots are caused by the action of salts which attack the metal. The disease is only found in ancient bronzes that have been buried for a considerable length of time.

If you have an ancient bronze with bronze disease, it is best to ask the advice of museum experts who will be able to suggest the best way of preserving it, taking into account the state of the patina, encrustations and the actual degree of decay. In the meantime, however, wash the piece in *distilled water and keep it dry with *silica gel crystals.

Some bronzes which have been buried for thousands of years may have only a limited degree of decay. This is because an equilibrium has been established between the corroded bronze and the earth. This may be disturbed by excavation, so that corrosion sets in again. In such cases it is imperative to get expert advice as soon as possible.

CAST IRON

Cast iron is a mixture of iron and small amounts of carbon, silicon, sulphur, manganese and phosphorus. As its name implies, it is poured into a mould. It may be distinguished from *wrought iron by its duller grey finish and more porous appearance. It is also less smooth than wrought iron.

Cast iron has been used for garden furniture, railings, fire-backs, mileage posts, gates and gateposts, domestic ware, kitchen ranges, lamps and lamp posts and fire-dogs. It is particularly plentiful in Regency towns such as Brighton.

The two problems you are most likely to come across when restoring cast iron are rust and over-painting. (For how to remove rust *see* iron and steel.) Over-painting can be removed with paint stripper or burnt off with a blow-torch. Don't get the metal too hot. When the paint is liquescent brush it off with a steel brush. The object can then be either burnished or repainted. If it is likely to remain outside at all, use a lead-based paint to prevent rust. Be careful when applying it not to lose the detail of the casting.

Well-worn fire-dogs and fire-backs may be brittle, so you must avoid cracking them during the treatment.

Older, more utilitarian pieces can be heated just sufficiently to open the pores. The rust will rise to the surface, which can then be brushed off with a wire brush. While the object is still warm, oil it with a mixture of 4 parts *turpentine to 1 part *linseed oil, plus a teaspoon of paint drier. Alternatively, seal it with a *microcrystalline wax or a lacquer. This will help preservation.

COPPER

Copper is a lustrous, reddish-brown metal. It is one of the most useful non-ferrous metallic elements. It has been widely used since it was first discovered about 8,000 BC.

In its pure form copper is malleable and ductile. It can be hammered and worked without fracture, although pounding leads to work-hardening. *Annealing will restore its malleability. Copper is an excellent conductor of electricity and resists the action of the atmosphere and sea water pretty well, although if it is exposed to the atmosphere for long periods a patina of green copper carbonate forms.

Copper is widely used in domestic hollow-ware. It is also the basis of many alloys, including brass and bronze. It is a common foundation metal for silver substitutes such as Sheffield plate .

Copper should be kept in a dry atmosphere, because damp and oxygen form a film of tarnish. Although this is unsightly, it will not actually damage the piece.

Don't cook anything containing vinegar in a copper pan, as the acid will react with the metal.

In order to remove the bluish-green tarnish, make a paste of *methylated spirit and *French chalk, and rub it on with a soft cloth. Finish by polishing the copper with *crocus powder or fine *whiting and a proprietary metal polish.

Remove small spots of corrosion with a 5% solution of *oxalic acid. As this is poisonous, you may prefer to use a 5% solution of *citric acid. Don't use harsh abrasives, as copper is easily scratched.

Water spots can be removed with a paste made of whiting and *turpentine. You can try the traditional method of rubbing with a piece of lemon dipped in salt.

Copper can be lacquered to prevent tarnish. Old lacquer or varnish should be removed with a 5% solution of *caustic soda in warm water, taking care to protect your hands with rubber gloves.

Copper can be brazed and welded, but it should be left to an experienced craftsman because it is easy to overheat an article and melt it.

Copper can also be soft-soldered. First clean the joints thoroughly of all grease; turpentine is good for this. Copper can be repaired with *epoxy resin adhesive, which will avoid harming the patina.

Loose handles on copper pots, warming pans etc. can be refitted by riveting. This is best left to an expert, particularly if the pan has to be waterproof.

Before trying to knock out any dents or bends, the piece must be annealed by heating to red heat and quenching (see annealing). This will make the copper supple again. Use a wooden mallet on a wooden base, and always radiate out from the main body of the piece.

ELECTROPLATE

A general description of base metal objects, usually of *brass, *bronze, or German silver, on which has been electrolytically deposited a thin layer of a more valuable metal, e.g. *gold, *silver, *rhodium, *copper or nickel (see metalwork processes: electroplating). The most common electroplated articles are silver-plated domestic ware—coffeepots, teapots, flatware, etc.—manufactured widely in England and the U.S.A. from c1860. In English examples a set of stamped initials frequently appears on the underside of an object, indicating its composition, e.g. E.P.N.S. (electroplated nickel silver), or E.P.B.M. (electroplated Britannia metal).

Electroplate should never be cleaned with abrasives or chemicals, for these will remove the metal coating; instead it is best to rub it with a little *French chalk, moistened with *methylated spirit and a few drops of *ammonia, using a soft cloth. Silver-plated ware tarnishes more easily than sterling silver and should be protected, when not in use, by wrapping in tissue paper, or a proprietary anti-tarnish paper. Any dents, scratches or repairs likely to require the replating of an article should be left to an expert. It should be remembered that in the U.S.A., electroplated silver is often referred to as silver plate, a term which in England is technically applied only to sterling silver. For a test to distinguish electro-plate from sterling silver see Silver.

GOLD

Gold is the most precious of all metals. Its colour cannot be imitated by any other metal. It is untarnishable and remains bright and free from surface films of oxide at all temperatures. It is also one of the best conductors of electricity.

Gold will dissolve in a mixture of nitric and hydrochloride acid, but in no common mineral acid. Pure gold is very soft and malleable and is seldom used in its pure form. It is usually alloyed with copper and silver for greater hardness and strength.

The strength of gold in an alloy is expressed in carats, that is, the number of parts that are pure gold. Thus, 22-carat gold is an alloy of 91·7% gold, and 4·2% silver and 4·1% copper; 18-carat gold has 75% gold, 12·5% silver and 12·5% copper; and 9-carat gold has 37·5% gold, 31·25% silver and 31·25% copper.

You can test the carat strength of gold by putting a drop of *nitric acid on the surface. Golds of less than 9 carats will turn green. Golds of up to 18 carats should be tested with *aqua regia, which will turn the gold pale. To distinguish between white gold and stainless steel, let a drop of aqua regia eat into the surface a fraction and then absorb it with blotting paper. The stain on both metals will be similar, but if you add a drop of stannous chloride to the white gold it will turn black, whereas stainless steel will not.

Gold is used for the manufacture of

jewellery, ornaments, coinage, wire and gold lace, thread for cloth, gilding and decoration inlaid into other metals, and numerous *objets d'art*.

There are also coloured golds. White gold is an alloy used for jewellery, in which the gold is combined with silver, copper and zinc, or by adding palladium. Red gold is combined with copper and produced in both 9-carat and 18-carat standards. Green gold, which is really a pale yellow, is a mixture of silver and was much used in the Art Nouveau period for jewellery. Blue gold contains iron as an alloying metal. Purple gold is alloyed with aluminium and is very hard.

Gold can usually be cleaned with water and mild soap or a pure detergent. If it has a stubborn tarnish that will not come off, it means that it is not pure gold; a solution of *ammonia will probably clean it. Failing that, use a 2% *sulphuric acid solution. After cleaning, polish with a soft cloth or chamois leather to bring out the shine.

Any scratches should be removed with *jeweller's rouge and fine grains of *crocus powder followed by *swansdown cloth.

Repairs to gold should be carried out by an expert.

GUNMETAL

Gunmetal is an alloy of copper and tin in the ratio 16 : 2. Its use as an alloy for guns became obsolete almost a hundred years ago with the manufacture of steel ordnance.

The term gunmetal is now applied to a family of copper-based alloys containing between 2-11% tin and 1-10% zinc. Leaded gunmetal contains up to 7% lead, and nickel gunmetal up to 6% nickel.

Gunmetal was employed for castings, for example, the doors of Hildesheim Cathedral, cast in AD 1015, as well as the founding of memorials and statues such as the Grosser Kurfurst statue in Berlin. Its most important uses today are for valves and pumps, fire-fighting equipment, horse couplings and marine equipment.

Gunmetal alloys have good casting and founding characteristics. They are highly resistant to corrosion under most atmospheric conditions and in sea and fresh water; they are easily machined; and they are not affected by sub-zero temperatures. Gunmetal also produces pressure-tight cast-

ings with an accurate detailed finish capable of a high polish.

All gunmetal alloys can be soft-*soldered. However, brazing or silver-soldering should be carried out by an experienced craftsman.

Gunmetal undergoes superficial tarnishing with the formation of brown, black or green patinas which protect the metal from further corrosion. The *patina takes a long time to form; it is often artificially produced on statues.

For cleaning gunmetal, *see* copper.

IRON AND STEEL

Iron is an element and is never found in a pure form. Pure iron is relatively soft and ductile, and can be cold-worked and forged. The two main types of antiques are made from *cast iron and *wrought iron, which cannot be hardened by heat treatment.

From 1856, when the Bessemer furnace was invented, steel largely superseded wrought iron. Basically, steel contains more carbon than wrought iron and less than cast iron. The impurities of pig iron are initially removed. Steel is alloyed to other elements to produce a wide range of metals with various degrees of strength, hardness, malleability, ductility and heat-resisting qualities.

All iron and steel is attacked by rust when in contact with air and water. This can be prevented. First thoroughly wash and dry the article. Then apply lacquer, oil, *microcrystalline wax or Vaseline, any of which establish a thin protective film.

Surface rust can be removed with a fine *emery cloth. Rub in one direction only. Any stubborn areas can be picked at with a small chisel or penknife. A 9% solution of *oxalic acid or a commercial *rust remover can be used to release the rust. Wash it off afterwards, and dry.

Holes caused by rust can be filled with fine filings mixed with an *acrylic resin, which can be filed down when set.

More serious rust can be divided into two sorts. In the first, complete oxidisation has taken place and there is no free metal remaining. Here no chemical tratment is necessary because a stability has already been achieved. However, the piece can be preserved from further corrosion by being impregnated with lacquer.

In the second, the rust is so bad that its

removal might cause the article to collapse. It should be left to an expert.

Scratches can be removed by *burnishing, or filing and rubbing with an emery cloth. Hold the file across the work with the emery cloth attached to it so that a flat surface is always maintained.

Both iron and steel can be soft-soldered (*see* soldering). Remember that any heat will alter the hardness of carbon steel, which will have to be heat-treated to the correct stress.

JAPANNED TIN WARE *See* Tin

A thin coating of clear wax will protect fine examples of japanned tinware such as these.

LEAD

The most common lead objects are garden ornaments such as statues or urns.

Objects which have become encrusted with a layer of whitish powder (carbonate of lead) should be boiled in water which should be changed several times. Then immerse in a 10% solution of *acetic acid in water. Then soak it in a weak solution of *sodium hydroxide and rinse in *distilled water.

The dull grey appearance of lead indicates a thin film of oxide which forms a protective *patina. If this patina is blistered or not apparent, it means that the lead has been attacked by organic acids or paint fumes, and active corrosion will follow. The piece should be treated with electrolytic reduction. It can be soaked in a 10% solution of *hydrochloric acid followed by a 10% solution of *ammonium acetate. Thoroughly rinse and dry and apply a protective coating of a *microcrystalline wax.

Lead should not be stored in wooden cupboards unless the timber has been well seasoned or lacquered, because wood tends to give off acidic organic vapours. The best method of storing small objects, e.g. toy soldiers, is to keep them in polythene bags.

NIELLO

Niello is a compound of lead and silver. It usually contains copper and sulphur. It has been used to ornament silver with a black inlay in engraved designs since as early as 1500 BC.

It is sometimes difficult to recognise niello on heavily tarnished objects. So if you think it is present, proceed carefully. Don't use electrochemical methods or a dip, which could eat it away.

Clean with a gentle metal polish, or with a paste made of *French chalk, *methylated spirit and a few drops of *ammonia. Apply with cottonwool, twisted on a matchstick so as to get at intricate parts. Any remaining tarnish or corrosion should be picked off with a needle.

For protecting from further tarnish, *see* silver.

ORMOLU

The word ormolu comes from the French *or moulu*, ground gold, and is used to describe any highly finished gilt bronze or brass casting, as well as the gold leaf, and various toning lacquers applied to it. It was used as a decoration from the 18th-century on French furniture and furniture in the French style, clock cases etc.

Always remove the ormolu from the furniture before cleaning. Take care not to lose any of the original screws, pins or fixing devices. Clean it with a weak solution of *ammonia applied lightly with a brush.

Old lacquer can be removed with *acetone.

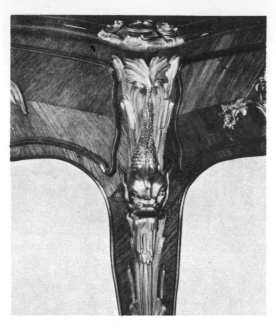

A beautiful example of ormolu: this dolphin mount comes from a French 18th century king wood bureau plat.

After washing, rinse in *distilled water, dry thoroughly and then either burnish very lightly (*see* burnishing) or degrease with acetone and apply a *cellulose lacquer.

The mounts are usually gilded. If no gilding is detectable, it might mean that they have been badly cleaned at some stage. They can be regilded (*see* gilding).

PALLADIUM

This is an important metal in the *platinum group. It closely resembles platinum in all its properties and colour, although it is substantially lighter.

Palladium jewellery became popular when platinum became scarce in the Second World War. It is now often used instead of white gold in the multi-coloured effects of the low-carat, coloured golds.

For cleaning, *see* platinum.

PATINA

The patination on metalwork is a product of corrosion on copper or copper-rich alloys which have been exposed to the moist air or have been buried in the soil. It is normally dark green in colour, and it is formed by the oxidation of copper sulphate and the action of sulphuric acid in the air. The deposit

accumulates slowly and normally offers a good protective resistance to further corrosion. It may have aesthetic qualities which are impossible to imitate.

Taking away dirt and tarnish should not remove the patina, if you use the correct polishes and abrasives. If you have an old piece replated, remember that the old, mellow shade of the patina will be replaced by the harsh, bright colour of a modern piece.

PEWTER

Pewter is an alloy of tin and various amounts of lead, antimony, copper and bismuth. In the finest pewter the lead content is virtually nil.

There are pieces of Roman pewter in many museums, but the vogue for pewter was at its height in the 17th century, and thereafter declined. Most pewter ware consists of domestic or church plate.

Opinions differ about how much pewter should be cleaned. Some collectors like to see it bright and gleaming like silver, whereas others prefer a dark grey *patina. Pewter should be dusted regularly. Minor stains can be removed with a mild abrasive such as *jeweller's rouge or *rottenstone applied with an oily rag.

It should be washed every few months in hot soapy water, rinsed in *distilled water and dried with a soft cloth. After washing, give it a thin coat of Vaseline to protect it. Or degrease it with *acetone or *methylated spirit, warm it gently with a hairdryer, and give a small protective coating of *microcrystalline wax.

Old pewter often has small spots, or warts, on the surface. They should be left alone unless they are actively corroding the pewter, because when you try to remove them you will expose a fresh surface to oxidation and corrosion. If they are active, however, they should be removed by an expert who will use *electrostripping.

You can restore a piece which has been left for a long time and is badly corroded by applying a dilute solution of *hydrochloric acid, working it in with the split end of a piece of bamboo. Take great care when applying the acid, and in particular protect your eyes and hands from splashes.

Corrosion can also be removed by prolonged soaking in *paraffin. Don't rub the surface afterwards with any but the mildest abrasives, because it can very easily be damaged.

Re-shaping or hammering out dents should not be attempted unless you have had some experience in metalwork. It is unwise to tackle any pieces on which the marks of the original hammering can still be seen, as these should be preserved. The dents should be placed over suitably shaped pieces of wood or a sand-filled canvas bag, and hammered with a plastic-covered or leather-topped hammer.

If the piece is really valuable or you are at all doubtful about how to approach it, leave the job to an expert.

Broken parts can sometimes be repaired with an *epoxy resin adhesive. Pewter can also be soft-soldered, but don't attempt it if you have no experience of soldering, because it has a low melting point (see soldering).

Pewter is very susceptible to acid action, so don't keep it in oak drawers or cupboards. If possible, keep it in a closed case. At the very least keep it behind glass where it will tarnish less.

PINCHBECK

Pinchbeck is a brass alloy which consists of 83% copper and 17% zinc. It was invented by Christopher Pinchbeck in the 18th century. It was used on small boxes and for Georgian and early Victorian jewellery, and watch cases.

Pinchbeck was known as 'poor man's gold' because of its colour. If in any doubt about its genuineness, test as for *gold.

Pinchbeck articles should be cleaned, etc., as for *brass.

PLATINUM

Platinum is a precious metal. It is slightly greyer and less lustrous than silver. Its great advantage is that although it is slightly affected by sulphuric acid at high temperatures and by combinations of hydrochloric acid, including *aqua regia (see gold), it is resistant to all alkalis, salts and oxides and so is untarnishable. It has a high melting point and has the ability to retain its colour at high temperatures.

Platinum is sometimes confused with stainless steel. It can be identified by dropping a little aqua regia on the surface and absorbing it with blotting paper. If there is no stain to be seen, the metal is undoubtedly platinum.

Platinum was not generally available until discovered in large quantities in the Ural Mountains in 1819. The use of platinum for jewellery rapidly increased at the turn of the century, when its colour and strength made it a popular setting for diamonds.

Platinum for jewellery is usually alloyed with 3% copper to improve its working and wearing properties.

To clean platinum, wash it in warm, soapy water.

Scratches can be removed by polishing with *jeweller's rouge. Any other repairs should be left to a jeweller. Platinum requires too high a temperature for soldering by an amateur.

RHODIUM

Rhodium has been known since 1803. It is very much harder and resistant to wear than platinum, especially when electro-deposited.

It is mainly used to electroplate silver, white gold and other metals. When resistance to corrosion and abrasion is important.

Rhodium is resistant to every known acid including aqua regia. It can only be corroded by fuming sulphuric acid concentrated at 300°C (572°F).

SHEFFIELD PLATE

Sheffield plate was made for approximately a hundred years from the 1740s to the 1840s, when it was superseded by *electroplating.

It is made by fusing a fairly thin sheet of sterling silver onto a copper ingot which is then rolled out into sheet form. It differs from all other types of plating in that it is the only one where the silver is fused to the copper before the object is formed. Towards 1850, some Sheffield plate was made of a base metal called German silver instead of copper.

Up to 1763 the under and inner surfaces of some Sheffield plate objects were left as copper. Occasionally, however, the surfaces were coated with tin, for instance those of teapots, coffee-pots and jugs. Plating on both sides began about 1800.

Constant polishing and rubbing often wears down the silver surface, exposing the copper. If the copper gets badly worn and makes the article unusable, it is worth having it electroplated. However the attractive mellow appearance of the old plate will then disappear which will slightly detract from its value. Of course if it had been in a really bad condition, the value may be increased. Replating Sheffield is in fact very much a matter of individual taste.

To clean Sheffield plate, start by giving it a good wash in hot, soapy water. This should remove most of the surface grease and dirt. Next attack any black parts with a paste of *ammonia and *whiting. This should be applied with a good bristle brush. Don't use an old toothbrush, which may scrape the surface.

Remaining stubborn areas can be tackled with a silver dip applied with a brush. Never immerse the object in a dip. Always wash the dip off with running water. Don't leave it on too long, because it will begin to etch the surface, and after a number of washes the copper will be exposed.

Dry thoroughly and apply a long-term non-abrasive silver polish with cottonwool swabs. Dusters are not suitable because they are apt to pick up particles of dust which are then rubbed in and wear the surface. A dry chamois leather is good for polishing.

Sheffield plate should be kept as clean as possible, because each polishing removes a minute portion of silver. Pieces therefore are best kept behind glass, where they will tarnish more slowly. Also try to avoid keeping them in rooms with coal or gas fires. Pieces not on display should be wrapped in polythene bags after being cleaned.

Leaks in teapots and jugs can be stopped with resin or soft-soldered. This is best left to an expert as it is often a tricky business.

SILVER

Silver is the finest and most malleable metal after gold. Fine silver is extremely ductile, and can be hardened by cold working such as rolling and drawing. Once it is hard, it can be returned to its natural state by *annealing.

All British silver has to be hallmarked. The hallmarks on a silver article tell you when and where the piece was assayed and how much pure silver it contains. Standard sterling silver contains 925 parts of pure silver out of 1,000. The Britannia standard contains 958·4 parts.

The lion passant has been the standard mark on English silver since 1545. In 1697 the lion's head erased and a full-length figure of Britannia were adopted. They replaced the crowned leopard's head and the lion passant until 1719, and were also used to indicate the higher standard of silver. In 1719, the old standard of sterling was restored, becoming operative in 1720.

There may be no evidence of a hallmark. In the USA, for instance, they are voluntary and silver does not bear date letters. The hallmark may also be indistinguishable. In either case you can establish whether an article is silver by applying an acid test. First clean a small, inconspicuous area and make a scratch of sufficient depth to expose any base metal. Put on a spot of *nitric acid. Sterling silver will produce a light, creamy-grey deposit; sub-sterling silver will have a dark grey deposit; and a base metal will cause a greenish effervescence. Wash the article thoroughly in running water as soon as the test has been completed.

Silver resists the attack of a wide range of alkalis and acids, which is one of the reasons why it is used for culinary and domestic purposes. It is attacked by most sulphur compounds and becomes covered with a yellow-brown or black sulphide film of tarnish.

Occasionally the formation of this chloride may reach the point of corrosion. If the corrosion is severe, the metal needs to be treated with sodium hydroxide and zinc, but this is a job for an expert. Small amounts of corrosion can be removed by soaking the piece in a solution of ammonia for a day or two.

Small areas of tarnish can be removed by applying a paste made of *French chalk, *methylated spirit and a few drops of *ammonia. Rub on with a soft cloth.

A dip is particularly useful for neglected tarnish and cleaning up ornate decoration. You can buy a proprietary brand, or make up your own by placing the silver in contact with a piece of aluminium foil and covering it with a 5% solution of *caustic soda (washing soda is a good substitute). There will be an electrochemical reaction with some fuming and effervescing. Remove the piece when the tarnish has cleared, wash it under warm running water, and thoroughly dry.

Long-term brands of silver polish are generally excellent. If you really want to prevent tarnish you will need to store articles very carefully (see Sheffield plate).

The restoration of damaged silver takes years of training and experience.

Scratches can be removed and the article brightened by *burnishing. The burnisher should always be highly polished. The work should be lubricated with soft soap and water or saliva. Hold with the burnisher blade towards you. Turn the work constantly, stroking in different directions until the surface is quite smooth.

Silver inlay

This is usually found in wood or lacquer.

Don't clean the silver by methods which may harm either the surrounding material or the silver. The safest is to pick or chip the tarnish, corrosion or dirt cautiously off the silver. Use an ordinary needle or an etcher's drypoint needle for picking. For chipping, make a range of chisels and scrapers from pieces of silver-steel rod of round, square and rectangular cross-sections. Harden them by heating ¾″ at the sharp end to red heat and quenching immediately in water. Don't overheat. Polish the points on *emery paper. Alternatively, use engravers' chisels, which should be used with a small jeweller's hammer.

If the inlay can only be cleaned by chemicals, isolate it from the surrounding material by a wall of clay or modelling clay and apply the silver cleaner locally with swabs of cottonwool.

Don't use this method if it is impossible to rinse the chemicals off afterwards without the fear of damaging the surround, for example, when silver is set in lacquer. Try an abrasive cloth, e.g. *swansdown cloth very carefully, but remember it could damage the surface of the silver as well as removing tarnish or corrosion.

SILVER GILT

This consists of a very fine coating of gold on silver objects. It ranges in colour from pale lemon to deep reddish gold. It is found mostly on wine labels, spoons, jewellery mounts, the insides of bowls, salt cellars and tumblers. It was originally made by coating the silver with a paste of gold and mercury, and heating to drive off the mercury. Nowadays it is done by *electroplating.

Silver gilt should be cleaned periodically with warm water, soap and a sponge. Rinse,

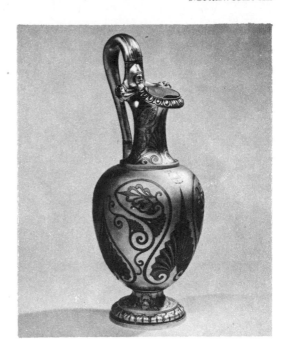

A parcel gilt Victorian silver wine jug, 1856.

preferably in *distilled water, and dry with a soft cloth. *Never* use dips, brushes or abrasives.

Usually it is sufficient to polish silver gilt with a soft cloth only. If necessary, use a soft polish which won't wear away the gold.

Regilding should be done by a silver or goldsmith. Make sure the original shade is matched; regilding tends to be done in a darker shade unless you insist on pale. Don't have spoons regilded; it will depreciate their value. Many collectors find worn gilding more attractive (*see* gilding and silver).

Store silver-gilt objects in a dry place.

TIN

Tin was first used as early as 3500–3200 BC. The Romans used tinned copper vessels. Tinned iron vessels did not appear until the 14th century AD.

Tin is non-toxic, soft and pliable, and is easily adapted to cold-working by rolling, extrusion and spinning. It is a silvery-white colour. It tends to have a yellowish tinge when cast, which is caused by a thin film of protective oxide. When polished, tin has a high reflectivity and retains its brightness well. It has a comparatively low melting point in comparison with other metals.

Tin imparts hardness and strength to alloys. Thus, one of the most important uses of tin is as an alloy with other metals.

The second major use of tin is for canning, which is outside the scope of this book. However, its beginning can be seen in the coating of tin which tea caddies, coffee-pots, boxes and saucepans had in the 18th and 19th centuries.

*Sheffield plate was often silvered only on the outside and tinned on the reverse to prevent tarnish and corrosion.

Under normal atmospheric conditions tin does not corrode, but if it is exposed to oxygen and moisture for a long period it is subjected to oxidation and becomes grey and granular in appearance. This is particularly so when it has been buried.

Solid tin objects are fairly rare. A wash in soap and water may be enough to clean them. Rust or incrustations can be removed with a very fine emery cloth. A coat of *microcrystalline wax will, in time, create a new patination which will protect the metal and lengthen its life.

These objects should really be cleaned electrochemically (see electro-cleaning) with caustic soda as an electrolyte. If they are very badly corroded, electrolytic reduction will be necessary. Both these processes are jobs for an expert.

Most antique objects of tinware date from c1820 and include candle boxes, coffee-pots, jelly moulds, umbrella stands, letter racks, plate warmers, etc. These are mostly copper or iron-based, with a thin coating of tin for protection. The rust, which is from the iron, should be carefully picked off with a needle. Then wash the piece in soap and water. Polish with wax. Do not use chemicals as these may remove the thin film of tin.

Japanned ware including Pontypool and Usk ware consists of a lacquer which is applied to a tinned surface of either copper or iron. Try not to remove any of this coloured lacquer when cleaning.

If the object is crazed, pitted or chipped, scrape off the paint or lacquer over the patches until you reach the base metal. Then rub it with extra fine steel wool dipped in *paraffin to remove rust. Probe any small holes with paraffin-impregnated steel wool on an orange-stick. Then wash with soap and water, rinse and dry.

The lacquer or paint can be touched up with artists' antique oils, available in specially weathered hues. Leave for 2-3 weeks to allow to dry and harden. Then protect the surface with a coat of lacquer or a *microcrystalline wax polish.

Soldering tin is a tricky operation because the melting point of the solder is only just below that of tin. So be sure to buy a low-temperature tin-lead solder containing 63% tin. See soft soldering.

If you want to solder cooking vessels coated with tin, clean them first in a 15% *nitric acid solution for 2–5 minutes. Wash off the acid thoroughly. Sprinkle hot *flux such as ammonium chloride on the surface and rub with a piece of pure tin which will distribute itself over the surface. If it doesn't, wipe it on with a pad. Alternatively, the article can be dipped in a reservoir of tin-lead solder. If the tin is likely to come into direct contact with food, use a high-tin-ratio solder (95% tin, 5% antimony).

WROUGHT IRON

Wrought iron is produced in a puddling furnace by mixing the iron with slag. It is almost pure iron with a small amount of carbon. It has superior welding qualities.

It is highly resistant to shock and corrosion. For this reason it is the most popular metal for gates; it was also once used for railings. Door furniture, knockers, hinges, signs horse-shoes and farm implements are all made in wrought iron.

Over-painting and rust can be removed with a paint stripper. Alternatively, use a blow-torch. Heat the metal just sufficiently to melt the paint and then brush it off with a stiff wire brush. The heat will also open the pores and any rust will erupt to the surface.

If you want to bend wrought iron, heat the piece to red heat first and then bend it while it is hot, otherwise a fracture may result.

To retain the natural colour (a dark brownish-black to carbon black), protect the cleaned surface with an oil mixture, a *microcrystalline wax polish or lacquer (see cast iron).

Wrought iron kept out of doors should be painted with a lead-based primer and top coat. Ensure a good coverage but do not over-paint, because the hammer marks of the original smith are much sought after as a finish and should be visible.

A fine pair of 19th century wrought iron entrance gates.

METALWORK PROCESSES:

ANNEALING

When working non-ferrous metals, it may be necessary to anneal, i.e. soften, the work at intervals to avoid fractures due to work-hardening, a brittle condition arising from compression of the metal's molecular structure. To anneal metal, heat it uniformly to red heat, using a gas torch, and then quench (immerse) it in cold water.

Keep the work between fireproof bricks, in a well ventilated room, away from any strong source of natural light—a darkened room will enable you to see at once when the metal turns a dull cherry red, indicating that the correct temperature has been reached. In a professional workshop, a pickle bath may be used instead of cold water: it is made up of a dilute solution of *sulphuric acid in the proportions of 1 part acid to 6 parts water. Its advantage is that it cleans off the scale created by the heating process. However, even diluted, sulphuric acid is terribly corrosive: however stringent the precautions, this method

105

should not be considered by the amateur.

Hardened steel can be annealed by bringing it to red heat, and allowing it to cool as slowly as possible, preferably by placing it in a bed of warm ashes. The metal can then be worked with a file. Steel tools with chipped or broken blades are best refaced on a grindstone or *oilstone; it is inadvisable to try to anneal and reharden them. Most ironmongers will sharpen and grind tools at a very low cost.

*Brass should be left to cool slowly in the air after annealing.

Aluminium does not glow red; when annealing it you should hold a matchstick against the metal. When the matchstick begins to char annealing point has been reached.

Zinc and *lead may be annealed by placing them in boiling water for a few minutes.

BLUEING
This is the production of a film of hard oxide on the surface of steel to prevent the formation of rust. Blued steel is widely used in clocks and watches and in metalwork generally.

The piece is polished, either with the traditional 'red-stuff' or, following modern practice, a corundum or aluminium oxide compound (see abrasives). Then it is washed thoroughly in *benzine, heated in an oven to a temperature between 540°F (purple) and 640°F (blackish-blue) and allowed to cool gradually.

Although the process is straightforward, considerable skill is needed, as uneven heating, or the presence of dirt and moisture, will spoil the result.

In the past clock-makers used a blueing pan shaped like a frying pan, which often contained a layer of brass filings for better heat distribution. The pan was held over a flame.

BURNISHING
Burnishing is a polishing process used on gold, silver, copper and its alloys, and steel. There is no record of when it was first used, but there is evidence that it has been used since earliest times.

Burnishing is carried out with two tools: first, a polished, hardened steel tool with tapered, straight or rounded curved blades.

Then, a highly polished curved or rounded agate or bloodstone burnisher.

The entire surface of the metal is worked over, holding the blade towards one and altering the direction of the strokes until a completely smooth surface has been produced.

The tool should be repeatedly moistened with soapy water to prevent the metal 'picking up'. The burnisher should be constantly rubbed with *putty powder and *jeweller's rouge to make sure that it continues to bite. Chain burnishers are very seldom used nowadays, and only for coarse work.

Small scratches and rust spots can be removed by burnishing, and *gold leaf should be burnished to bring up its full lustre.

ELECTRO-CLEANING
This is a technique used by museums and laboratories, and it is outside the scope of the amateur. It is used to remove dirt, grease, and oxides from metals.

An alkaline solution is prepared by mixing 1 oz oakite with 1 quart water. The object is suspended in this solution by a 20 G. copper wire attached to the cathode bar (see electroplating).

The solution is heated to 82°C (180°F) and a 6-volt current is passed into the object and the solution. Occasionally the anode and the cathode are reversed.

The hydrogen and the oxygen in the solution are violently agitated, dislodging any dirt, while the alkaline emulsifies any grease.

The object is immersed for about 25 seconds, and then rinsed in cold water and dipped into a pickle bath of sulphuric acid and water (see annealing).

The object is then removed and thoroughly rinsed in cold water. The surface of the metal must not be touched, as this would defeat the whole purpose of the process. The object is now ready for electroplating.

ELECTROPLATING
Electroplating is the technique of covering one metal with a thin layer of another by electrical deposition. It was first used commercially by Elkington, c.1860, although it had been patented in 1836. The advantage was then that objects could be plated after

manufacture instead of before, as in *Sheffield plate. It was also responsible for the decline of the Sheffield plate industry, although at the same time it facilitated mass-production.

The plating metals normally used are gold, silver, copper, nickel and rhodium, while the base metals are usually copper alloys, brass, bronze or German silver.

Electroplating allows a current of electricity from a dry cell, a battery, or a DC generator or rectifier to flow through a cyanide solution between two metal units placed in the solution at the positive and negative terminals of a direct current circuit. The current flow releases metal particles or ions from the positive pole (called the anode) into the solution and deposits them on the negative pole (called the cathode).

A gold, silver or copper plate or rod of the desired plating material is suspended as the anode, while the cathode is the object to be plated. Soluble anode plates in gold, silver or pure copper and nickel can be bought.

The electric current must be between $\frac{1}{2}$ and 12 volts DC; different currents are used for different effects.

The plating solution varies according to the material being plated.

The temperature is not critical, but varies according to the solution used.

The most important factor is the condition of the surface before plating. It must be absolutely clean and free from grease and oxides. This is best done by *electro-cleaning.

Once the deposition has taken place, the object has to be thoroughly washed in running water, dried and polished.

Electroplating cannot be undertaken at home. All cyanide-containing solutions are highly poisonous and should only be handled in a laboratory or well-equipped workshop by an expert.

For cleaning electroplated objects *see* electroplate and gilding.

ELECTROSTRIPPING OR ELECTROLYTIC REDUCTION

This is a process used by museum experts to remove old plate and surfaces on articles before replating.

In effect, it is the opposite to *electro-plating. The article becomes the anode, while the cathode used to collect the particles is usually a piece of brass. The metal deposited on the brass can subsequently be reclaimed. The solution is usually made of cyanide, but varies with the type of metal. After electrostripping, the article has to be very thoroughly rinsed in water.

ELECTROTYPING

Electrotyping is an application of *electroplating. It is used mainly to make accurate facsimiles. By distorting the current, temperature and agitation, it can also be used to produce special effects of size and texture. Thus extended immersions often make an object grow in size as new metal is deposited.

Electrotyping is a dangerous process and should only be attempted in a well-equipped workshop with fume extractors.

It involves attaching a mould of the object to be copied to the cathode and the plating material to the anode and suspending them in the appropriate plating solution. An electric current of between $\frac{1}{2}$ and 12 volts DC is then attached to the poles and the deposition begins. Normally the article is left in for about 4 hours, but this depends on the deposition required.

PLANISHING

The hammering of metal objects, usually copper or silver bowls in the final stage of their manufacture. The aim is to remove unwanted marks and replace them with a regular series of neat hammer marks over the whole surface.

It is done with a planishing hammer, a special, highly polished, expensive, hardened-steel hammer with two flat faces, one circular and the other square.

The object is held up against an anvil and the hammer brought down on it in a true line. A curved object has to be placed on a curved surface. Special shapes are available for differently shaped objects.

Planishing is a skilled job which should be left to a craftsman. In addition, the expense of the tools required would not be justified for the odd job.

SOLDERING

Soldering is one of the most versatile and easy methods of joining two metals. It falls into two categories, hard and soft.

Soft or 'common' solder is basically an alloy of lead and tin. It has a melting point below that of the original components depending of course on the proportions.

Hard-solder with an alloy containing more than 50% silver has a melting point of about 1,750°F. Those solders containing less than 50% silver have a melting point of about 1,300°F. Hard-soldering on precious metals should be left to an expert, as the critical temperatures are too close.

Soft-solder should never be used in conjunction with precious metals. This is because its base nature lessens the value of the article, and because the chemical interaction between tin and lead has a deleterious effect on silver and gold and their alloys. If these are overheated, the resultant damage can only be repaired by cutting or scraping the affected areas or replacing them with new metal. Soft-soldering, although not as strong as hard soldering, can be carried out by a careful amateur.

For successful soft-soldering, the surfaces to be joined must be cleaned thoroughly. Abrade them with a scraper, file or emery cloth, so that you can see the bright metal and be sure that the joint is clean. The surfaces should then immediately be covered in flux and soldered as soon as possible.

*Flux is a chemical agent that prevents an oxide film from forming on the metal surface when heating. There are two types for soft-soldering: zinc chloride and ammoniac (ammonium chloride), sometimes called killed spirits, and rosin, a non-corrosive flux suitable for electrical work. Both are commercially prepared and can be bought as a greasy paste, a liquid or a powder.

Secure the joint with soft iron wire and heat both pieces to a temperature equal to the melting point of the solder. Use either a torch or a soldering iron (see metalwork tools).

When using a soldering iron, make sure that it is clean. If it is new or has a residue of previous use, file it down to the bright metal and then dip it in flux. Then heat it either electrically or with a blow-torch, until it reaches the melting point of the solder. 'Tin' the iron by dipping and rotating it in the solder.

The parts to be joined should be suitably fluxed first. Place the point of the iron at one end of the joint and hold for approximately five seconds. Don't overheat, as pits may form in the join by the solder burning out or combining with the flux. Be sure to distribute the heat evenly. This allows the heat from the iron to spread through the joint and permits the solder to flow. Remember that the solder will always flow to the hottest part. When it starts, gradually draw the iron along the joint. If you need more solder, introduce a thin rod of solder on the top surface of the iron as you draw it along. On long joins it may be necessary to reheat the iron, but it is better if you can complete the operation in one draw.

When you have finished soldering, allow the seam time to cool. Then, remove the flux with hot running water. It is essential to do this, as all flux is chemically active and can damage the metal.

If you are using a blow-torch, cut and flux small pieces of solder (pallions) about the size of a grain of rice and place them evenly along the join, which must also be fluxed. With a soft flame and a fanning motion, heat the metal to the flow point of the solder and when the pallions curl up and shoot through the seam, work down the joint to assure uniformity.

Solder paints—soft-solder combined with flux—come in a variety of sizes and are ideal for the amateur. You only need to clean the joint, paint on the substance, hold together and heat to form a perfect joint.

Hard soldering needs a more powerful torch, fire-bricks to reflect the heat, and more precision. The silver-based alloys form a highly mobile film which is difficult to control in comparison to the sluggish mass of soft soldering, which can be drawn or pushed into place. Unless you have had experience, do not attempt to hard-solder anything valuable.

Gold and silver objects should always be left to an expert, but iron and steel can be joined comparatively safely. The strength of the joint will depend on how well the thin film of solder fits, so don't attempt to solder ill-fitting joints.

The most commonly used hard-soldering technique is called the feed-in or stick-feed method. It is used for soldering bases onto bowls and for relatively large soldering operations.

First assemble the two pieces, holding

them securely, for instance between asbestos blocks. Clean the surfaces thoroughly and flux them with *borax, which changes from a whitish powder to a slightly brownish, glass-like material at 1,400°F, and so is an excellent temperature indicator.

Begin heating slowly with a soft flame to dry off any moisture in the flux. Increase the flame, making sure that both elements to be joined reach the flow temperature at the same time. Continue until the flux melts and the metal is hot enough to receive the solder. This is normally when it is a dull, glowing red.

Next introduce the solder, which comes in stick or wire form and must be dipped in flux. The solder will run through the joint immediately, and you will recognise a bright thin line. Just touch the joint in one or two places, since the solder runs on its own.

Allow the piece to cool slowly. Quench in a pickle bath (*see* annealing) to remove any excess flux. (The presence of iron and copper salts in the bath will deposit a thin film of copper on silver, so be sure to use a fresh bath when quenching silver.)

MINIATURES
Miniature portraits first appeared in the 16th century, when they were often worn as jewellery. They continued to be popular until the beginning of the 19th century. They are painted in watercolour or gouache on card, ivory or vellum.

Continental miniatures are sometimes painted in oil-paint on a copper base (*see* oil paintings). There are also miniatures in *enamel.

They should be protected, like all watercolours from strong light. They should frequently be inspected for any signs of mildew or other fungus.

They need expert restoration, because of their extreme delicacy. Missing or rubbed sections can be effectively retouched by a specialist.

Care should be taken to prevent miniatures on *ivory, which is very fragile, from warping. This can be achieved, hopefully, by avoiding extremes of temperature and humidity.

Indian and Persian miniature paintings
The first Indian and Persian miniature paintings were done on palm-leaves in the

Lady Isabella Durrell by John Smart, 1785. This oval miniature is framed with a border of brilliants.

11th century, but on paper after its introduction in the 14th century. The medium was watercolour and gouache, but white and red lead pigments were often used which tend to blacken in the atmosphere of towns.

This can be treated with ethereal hydrogen peroxide. Shake equal quantities of *hydrogen peroxide and *ether together in a bottle. The layer of ether will rise to the top, but will contain enough peroxide to remove the blackening. Dip a brush into the top layer of the mixture only and stipple this onto the affected area.

Alternatively, a piece of *plaster of Paris can be impregnated with hydrogen peroxide and suspended over the painting. Don't apply it directly. because it will corrode the painting.

If the blackening does not disappear under this treatment it may be that the original colour was silver, which was often used in Persian painting to represent water. There is no way of treating this.

Flaking paint can be stuck on with an adhesive of *soluble nylon and *methylated spirit.

See frames, mounts.

MIRRORS

The earliest type of mirror, which was used from Greek, Roman and Etruscan times up to the Middle Ages, was a thin metal disc, usually of bronze, polished on one side and decorated on the other.

The method of backing glass with thin sheets of metal was known in the 14th century, but the Venetians finally developed it in the 16th century, producing glass with bevelled edges and silvered with an amalgam of tin and mercury.

The discovery of plate glass in 1691 improved the quality of mirrors, but the method of mixing them remained unaltered until 1835, when it was discovered that a thin film of real silver could be laid on the glass.

To identify how a mirror was made, look at the back: The mercury and tin method gives a grainy, metallic appearance. The silver method is finished with a protective coating of red lead or chocolate brown paint. An early mirror tends to go grey if exposed to damp, and circular patches appear where the metal has isolated itself and formed tiny granules. The silver film of the later type will flake off in patches and tarnish.

If a piece of furniture or a frame contains a piece of old tin and mercury glass, it should on no account be replaced with modern glass. The piece will be more valuable if it contains a mirror that, even if it is not contemporary, is of the right type. If you cannot see the back to check it, the softly bevelled edges, the thinness of the glass itself and its imperfect reflection should help you to identify it.

Mirrors of the modern type can be resilvered, but has to be done at a glass-works.

The glass can be cleaned with a proprietary window cleaner or with a mixture of equal parts of water, *methylated spirit and *paraffin. Take care not to get any moisture inside the frame, as it will cause unattractive spots.

Japanned, needlework, straw marquetry, tortoise-shell, verre eglomise, papier mâché, giltwood and silver mirror frames have all been fashionable, and they should be given the care and treatment suitable.

MOTHER-OF-PEARL

Mother-of-pearl comes from the linings of the shells of fresh and salt-water molluscs such as the oyster and the nautilus. It is composed mainly of calcium carbonate, and can be carved, incised or etched.

Mother-of-pearl was used as an inlay and for small, decorative objects such as card cases, trinket boxes, paper-knives, knife handles, fan-sticks, etc.

Mother-of-pearl should be protected from any kinds of acid, which will cause it to decompose.

It can be cleaned with a paste made of water and precipitated *whiting. Rub this on, let it dry, and then polish off with a soft cloth. Wash in warm, soapy water, rinse and dry.

Small chips can be filed smooth with a fine file and then polished with *jeweller's rouge. Missing portions of inlay can be replaced by cutting out new pieces with a fine saw. This is a tricky job and needs a lot of patience.

An unusual butterfly brooch c1860. The mother-of-pearl wings and body are set with rubies and green garnets in gold.

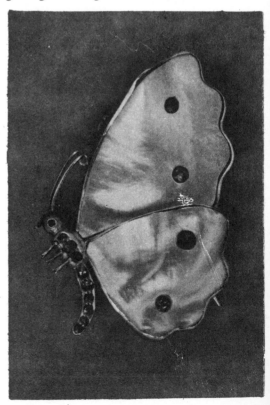

MOUNTS

*Prints, *watercolours and *drawings should always be correctly mounted, as this will help to preserve them in a good state.

A correct picture mount consists of the following. First, the background is stuck to the picture with a paper hinge (see diagram); this is done along the top edge of the picture. The mount should then be cut to size and attached to the top of the backboard, again using a paper (or linen) hinge. This method ensures that the mount can be lifted up to inspect both the front and the back of the picture. The mount can be cut either to reveal all four edges of the picture, or if there are larger margins, to cover the edges. Mounts should have bevelled edges and the bottom should be at least half an inch wider than the other three sides. This is tradition rather than necessity, but is based on what shows the picture off to best advantage.

Mounts and backboards should be of the highest quality, preferably ragboard. Only soluble paste should be used. The mounts can be treated with*thymol to avoid mould growth and foxing (*see* paper).

A properly mounted print will always reveal the plate marks. These are the impressed lines caused by the edge of the copper plate during printing. Nothing should be so closely mounted as not to show the edge of the picture.

Pastels, chalk and charcoal drawings should have thick mounts to ensure that they do not touch the glass.

If you have a watercolour or painting with something else on the reverse, or with an interesting inscription or watermark that you would like shown, it is possible to have it double glazed, i.e., with glass on either side.

Self-adhesive tape must never be used in mounting because it causes irreparable stains and damage.

Mounts should never be glued onto a cardboard or paper backing, because the adhesive and the backing, which may be of inferior paper or cardboard, can stain and cause the picture to deteriorate. It will also immediately reduce its value.

Cardboard can be removed as follows, if water is not harmful to the medium. Remembering that cardboard must be taken off the paper and not vice versa. With a

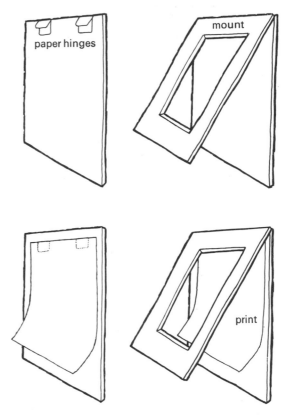

Mounting a picture:
(1) Fix paper hinges to background. (2) Stick picture to hinges (never to background). (3) Cut mount to size, and attach to backboard with paper or linen hinges.

long knife, split off the first layers of cardboard, leaving two or three behind. Hold these in the steam of a kettle until they are soft, and then lay the paper down on blotting paper and ease off the remainder of the cardboard. Make sure that the paper is sponged clean of all adhesive. Dry between sheets of a clean white blotting paper under glass. If the backing is not laminated cardboard but strawboard, it will have to be removed by wetting and then gently rubbing it off. A paper backing cannot usually be moved by steaming, but needs soaking in a bath of warm water. A few drops of detergent might help.

MUSICAL BOXES

Musical boxes were developed from musical movements set in clocks and watches in the mid-18th century. By 1825, the Swiss invention of a brass revolving cylinder with pro-

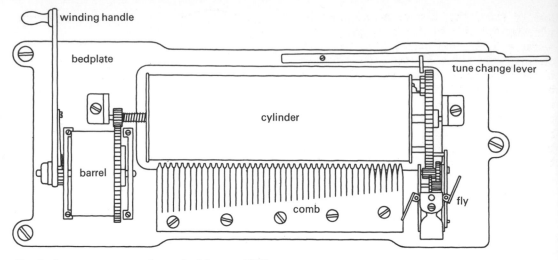

Typical arrangement of musical box, c1870.

jecting pins acting upon a tuned metal comb had been developed and the musical box industry was well established.

Musical snuff boxes

These were particularly popular *c*.1780–1850. Early examples were made of *silver or *silver-gilt, either left plain and polished, or elaborately chased, engine-turned or enamelled. These snuff boxes were specially made to contain small musical movements, but were also used to hold snuff.

Gold boxes were also popular, with enamel lids or with precious and semi-precious stones set in the lids.

Later snuff boxes were made of a black bone composition or *tortoiseshell with a picture or medallion embossed on the top. Although these boxes had space for snuff, after 1830 it is doubtful whether they were still used for this purpose. Cheaper versions were made of *papier mâché and tin with pictures stamped on the lids.

These musical snuff boxes should be treated according to the material of which they are made.

Large musical box cases

Large musical movements were originally put into plain wooden cases most commonly made of elm, cherry and rosewood. After 1830, these cases became more elaborate, with inlaid lids and veneered finishes. The best-quality cases were made of rosewood or walnut. Many were veneered on to cheaper woods.

For cleaning, care and restoration, treat according to the type of wood of which the case is made.

General care

A musical box is susceptible to damp and heat. It should ideally be kept in a warm, dry room well away from any direct heat such as radiators, open fires and heaters, and out of direct sunlight.

Heat will damage a musical box in the following ways. Direct heat makes the wooden case crack and warp and can destroy inlay on a box by causing pieces of the inlay to pop out. If this should happen, treat as for *marquetry. Too much heat will melt the waxen cement inside the cylinder that keeps the pins rigid. If this happens, the box will make hollow sounds while being played. The cylinder will stick on its spindle and not revolve easily. Re-cementing a cylinder, which is done by gently melting all the cement and rotating the cylinder until the inside is re-coated, is a process which can only be done by an expert restorer.

If a box has been left in cold conditions, it should on no account be wound and played until it has been allowed to warm up slowly for several hours in a warm room. Sudden changes in temperature can cause the teeth of the comb to break off or even snap the spring.

A musical box should be serviced by a watch-maker from time to time. A box needs servicing when it shows a permanent loss of speed that cannot be adjusted by winding. This may be due to clogging of the works with dirt and dust. In this case only cleaning and oiling is necessary. However it can mean that the spring is tearing or breaking. The box should be checked immediately, because if the spring snaps, the mechanism will 'run', whirling round rapidly out of control. This ruins the box by breaking the teeth of the comb and bending the cylinder pins. If this happens, only expert repairs will put it in running order again.

Never leave a musical box stopped half-way through a tune. When you have finished with the box, wind it just enough to end the tune so that no pins are contact with the comb. Then stop the box. If a box *is* left halfway through a tune and is then picked up and tilted, the cylinder will slide on its spindle, damaging the small dampers under the points of the comb. The points themselves and the cylinder pins can also be damaged under these circumstances.

It is essential to keep a musical box oiled, but not over-oiled. If it is not in constant use, it will only require oiling once a year or every eighteen months. Only the best clock oil should be used, and great care should be taken in applying it. The best method is to flatten the end of a small length by hammering or filing. Apply the oil with this flattened end. If this is not possible, use a toothpick instead. Dip the wire into the oil and shake free the drop on the end so that only the bare minimum of oil is applied. Too much oil attracts dirt and dust. All the bearings, pinions, cogs and the endless screw should be oiled (see diagram), as well as both pivots of the endless screw. When doing this, *do not remove the garnet endstone* to oil the top pivot. This can make the bottom pivot come out, releasing the spring and causing a 'run'.

The comb

If the mechanism of a musical box has 'run', the steel comb will be damaged and some or many of its teeth broken. If only two or three teeth are missing, a restorer can cut new teeth into the existing comb. However, it is very difficult to tune new teeth without having the original scale to which the comb was tuned.

A comb should be checked regularly for

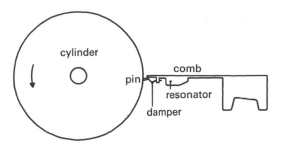

Section showing comb and cylinder.

damaged points on the teeth of the comb. These can be replaced, but if too many are broken, the problem again arises of tuning the comb after repair.

It is important to bear in mind that rust can be removed from a comb, but *combs should never be filed or drastically abraded,* because in this way part of the metal will be removed, throwing the comb permanently out of tune. The only treatment that can be applied to a musical box comb to remove rust is as follows.

Remove the comb from the box. Note that most early musical boxes have hand-chased screw threads so that each screw is intended for one hole only. To avoid confusing screws, it is helpful to punch the lid of a cardboard box with holes corresponding to the position of the screws that are being removed. The screws can then be dropped into their appropriate positions on the lid as they are removed. When replacing the screws it will then be easy to put them into their original positions. Loosen the rust by soaking overnight in thin oil.

Scrub the comb with a fine wire brush such as a suede brush. *Always work with the direction of the teeth, never across them.*

If there are any very stubborn patches of rust, a *mild* abrasive may be cautiously applied.

Never be tempted to use *acetic acid on a comb as this will eat into the steel.

When the comb is clean, rub the upper surface with a little oil and replace. Carefully check that the cylinder has come to rest at the 'end of tune' position, otherwise the comb tooth points may be damaged as the comb is fitted. Make sure that no dirt is trapped between the comb plinth and the baseplate, otherwise the comb setting will be altered.

When first re-fitting the comb, it is a good idea to only fit in three or four of the screws, so that it is easy to adjust the comb if necessary.

The cylinder

This is made of brass and set with steel pins which act upon the steel comb of the musical box to create the music. It is essential to check the state of the pins on the cylinder. If they are damaged, the box will be useless as a musical box until they are repaired. Cylinder pins should stand out proud from the cylinder, though in some cases they are raked slightly forward. If the box has 'run', the pins will be bent over or flattened. In early makes, cylinder pins are hard and brittle and impossible to straighten out. In some of the later makes, if the pins are bent out of action, they can be carefully straightened out as they are made of a somewhat softer wire. However in the majority of cases this is not possible.

The only repair is to have the cylinder re-pinned, an expert and expensive process. The cement is removed from the inside and the spindle is taken out of the brass cylinder, which is soaked in sulphuric acid for approximately six weeks, during which time the pins are eaten away. It is then rinsed in clear water and immersed in a lime bath to neutralise the remaining acid. The cylinder is then ready for punching with new pins.

Cylinders can become dirty, stained and tarnished. The best way to clean a cylinder is to do so with it in place in the box. Don't remove it unless absolutely necessary.

Remove the comb. Take off the motor and gear train so that the cylinder spins freely.

Wash off the old oil with *benzene or *surgical spirit applied with a clean nail-brush or small scrubbing brush. *Never* use a cloth, as this will only shred on the pins.

If verdigris is present on the cylinder, brush the affected area with a fine wire brush such as a suede brush, using a circular motion. *Don't* scrub too hard or the pins will be damaged.

Dab on a liquid metal polish with your fingertips. This should be put on sparingly, taking great care not to let any run onto the spindle.

Leave the polish to soak for a minute, then start to brush off with a clean bristle

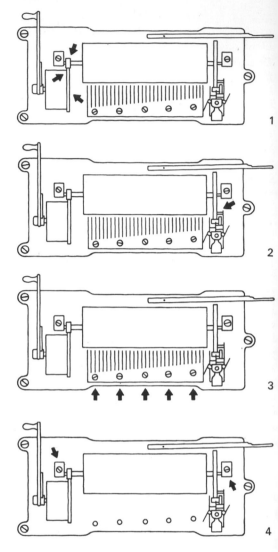

Dismantling musical box:
(1) Make sure that spring is completely run down. (2) Make sure that tune is completed by running it through by hand. (3) Remove comb carefully, and keep it in a safe place. (4) Remove end bearings and lift out cylinder – store it carefully.

nail-brush. The cylinder should be brushed lengthways, then across, and finally diagonally in both directions. The cylinder should be rotated while brushing.

If necessary, apply more polish and repeat the process.

Burnish the brass with a stiff bristle scrubber. A new short-bristle shoe-cleaning brush is best. This often takes a little time. No more polish should be applied.

Alternatively dust the cylinder with a little talcum powder, which acts as a fine abrasive, and brush until the brass is gleaming.

Oil the pins. Only a thin film of oil is necessary. *Apply oil sparingly,* as when oiling all parts of a musical box. Bend some thin card, e.g. a postcard, in a bow shape and spread some thin clock oil over the convex side of the card. Then pass the oiled card over the pins while rotating the cylinder. Do not get oil onto the cylinder itself, as this will only attract dust.

Avoid touching the cylinder with your hands once cleaned and oiled.

If the cylinder will not revolve, *don't force it.* The spring is almost certain to be fully wound and any sudden jolt could trigger off a 'run'. A common cause for the jamming of a cylinder is that the garnet endstone or jewel is missing from the endless screw. If this is the case, no amount of pressure will move the cylinder. It is a simple job get a watch-maker to fit a new stone. Excessive wear in the bearings and cylinder pinions can also prevent a cylinder from revolving. In these circumstances some repairs can be carried out by a watch-maker.

On all occasions when a cylinder will not revolve and the spring is fully wound, always remove the comb until the box is repaired. In this way, if a 'run' occurs, the comb and cylinder may avoid being damaged.

Dampers

These are fitted underneath the bass points of the comb to prevent vibration and ensure a 'clean' sound to each note. In musical snuff boxes they are made out of feather quills fixed with shellac under the comb. Larger movements have steel dampers. If any are missing or are not working properly, this will become apparent when the box is being played as the box will squeak, buzz and click.

Dampers can be fairly easily replaced by a watch-maker.

Resonators

These are small lead weights fixed on the underside of the bass notes of a comb to improve the volume of the sound. A dull bass note indicates that the resonators have corroded together.

The leads can become powdery, losing some of their weight and thereby impairing the tone of the box. This powdery corrosion can be cleared by passing a piece of *wet-and-dry paper between the leads.

An application of very thin oil will prevent this type of corrosion re-forming. Great care must be taken that the oil does not unite the resonators, as this will dull the tone.

Any dirt lodged between the resonators can be removed by passing a small piece of card between them.

If the leads have gone beyond treatment, it is very difficult to replace them.

OIL PAINTINGS

Oil-paint came into general use in the early 15th century. It is made by mixing pigment with oil, usually linseed, and then diluting it with essence of turpentine (or spirits of turpentine). Varnish is also added as a medium.

Oil-paints were developed and perfected by Flemish artists, although the Chinese probably used the technique much earlier. It quickly became the most popular medium of painting due to its flexibility and durability.

The bases were usually canvas and wood, although ivory, slate, copper and zinc were also used. They were first covered with the ground or priming, which makes a suitable surface for the paint. On completion, the painting was varnished.

The restoration of paintings is really a job for an expert, because of the immense variety of materials used in grounds and the differing constituents of the paint. Also, the damage that can be done by the wrong treatment of a painting is always irreversible. An expert will be aware of the problems involved and knows what pitfalls there are in any particular period or artist's work. Cracking or *craquelure* on a painting may be caused by any of the following: paint drying at different rates, i.e., a top coat put onto a wet undercoat; inadequately mixed paint; butumen; the ground cracking (this happens particularly with gesso); the varnish cracking; the picture having been varnished before it was dry; the ground either too absorbent or not absorbent enough; incorrect framing; or a thin layer of paint over a thicker one.

If the painting is on canvas, first place it on a flat surface. Put something underneath the canvas to prevent any strain being placed on it.

Surface dirt can be cleaned in two ways. If the painting is more than fifty years old and the surface therefore totally hardened, apply *white spirit or *turpentine substitute gently with cottonwool. Another method is to clean with *microcrystalline wax in very small amounts on swabs of cottonwool or a piece of silk. Polish it off after an hour, with clean cottonwool. Constantly check that no colour is coming off and that there are no loose and flaking areas of paint.

Any dirt or discolouration that remains after this treatment is within the varnish layer or the paint layer. Before synthetic varnishes were invented, the basis of varnish was either copal, dammar, copaiba or mastic resins. These cause the varnish to darken with age, crack and 'bloom', and also absorb dirt from the atmosphere. An expert restorer can remove this old varnish layer and revarnish the painting, but it is difficult because the solvent for varnish is usually the same as for paint.

Paint layers may darken because the oil itself darkens. If a painting has been kept in the dark, it may be particularly bad. The colour can be restored to some extent by exposing the picture to sunlight, which bleaches the discoloured ingredients in the oil.

If the painting is on metal, slate or ivory, it may be prone to mildew. Put in a dry atmosphere and dust the mildew off. You can protect a painting against fungus and mildew by putting a sheet of thick paper impregnated with a fungicide behind the frame. The glass can also be sterilised by a rub over with *formalin.

If the painting is on a panel which has been attacked by woodworm, the best treatment is fumigation, which should be done by an expert.

An expert restorer will also be able to stick back flaking and bubbling paint. It is done with a gelatine, beeswax and resin adhesive and a heated tool. In extreme cases, the painting can be transferred to another support.

A canvas can be strengthened with extra canvas in strips around the edges. A painting can also be entirely relined, which means backing it with a new canvas. Holes and tears can also be mended and the painting retouched.

Never hang paintings unprotected with glass over a source of heat, because of the rising dust and fumes. A painting should not be hung in direct sunlight either, as this can affect the varnish. The ideal conditions are a relative humidity of between 45% and 60% and no extreme changes in temperature.

PAPER

Paper was first made in China in the Second Century A.D. from silk or vegetable matter. Paper made from mulberry fibre was widely used. In general, paper made in the East was soft and absorbent, as it was used for brush-painting, writing and woodcuts. Paper came into use in the West in the 13th century, and was harder because it had to take quills and engravings.

Best-quality paper was, and still is, made of cotton and linen rags sized with gelatine. A lower-quality paper was developed using straw fibres, c1800 and wood pulp, c1840, and sized with rosin and alum.

Ideally paper should be kept at a constant relative humidity of around 16°C (60°F). If you are doubtful about the dryness of conditions, protect the paper against fungus and mould by interleaving with impregnated paper to sterilise it. Make impregnated paper by immersing white blotting paper in a 10% solution of *thymol in *alcohol. Replace it every six months, as its effectiveness wears off. In the cast of a print, the back can be painted with the thymol solution for protection.

To clean paper try dry methods first. Remove dirt with a gentle rubbing with a soft gum rubber (not an india rubber, which removes the surface of the paper). Try also a proprietary powder, which picks up the dirt without disturbing the paper's surface. You can also rub lumps of the doughy centre part of a white loaf along the surface of the paper. Discard the pieces as they become dirty, or the dirt will be rubbed in.

You can also wash the paper by immersing it in water. Lay it on a support of glass or polythene and soak it in a bath of cold, distilled water for an hour or so. Follow with a bath of hot water. Photographic trays are ideal for this job. If the dirt doesn't move, try soap. Lather it on with a soft paint-brush. Rinse carefully because the paper will yellow if the soap is left in. Alternatively, soak the paper in a non-ionic wetting-agent, such as *Lissapol N, for approximately half an hour and then rinse it. Don't lift paper by the corners when it is wet, as it tears very easily. Dry it between two sheets of clean white blotting paper and under glass to keep it flat.

Individual stains can be dealt with as follows. Oil, fat and tar stains can be moved with *benzene, dabbed on with cottonwool, or *pyridine. Another method is to place several thicknesses of blotting paper on either side of the paper and then put a hot iron on top to draw the stain off. This method can be used for wax, which is susceptible to *carbon tetrachloride and benzene as well. Dab on and then blot carefully. Remove coffee and tea stains with a 2% solution of *potassium perborate. First dampen the area with cold water and then dab the solution on the stain. If you leave the paper in the sun to dry, the stain should have almost gone within two hours. Rinse and dry. Any slight stain left can be bleached out with a *Chloromine T solution.

Fly stains may be removed with *hydrogen peroxide. Make a solution of equal parts of alcohol and hydrogen peroxide (20 vols) and dab onto the marks with a fine camel-hair brush. The method for removing ink stains will depend on the type of ink used (see ink drawings and manuscripts). Try brushing with a 2% solution of Chloromine T to bleach it out. Alternatively, a 5% solution of *oxalic acid or a 10% solution of *citric acid, might be successful. Wash the paper thoroughly afterwards.

Fungus and mould marks are often found on paper, because it absorbs moisture from the atmosphere and because size and bookbinders' paste are good food for fungus. Very bad fungus spots may be blackish in colour. The most common is 'foxing', which is orange-brown. Infected paper should be treated immediately, as fungus spreads. Some fungus marks and mould spores can be removed by brushing. Then leave the paper out in an airy sunny room to prevent any further growth. Washing will remove some stains.

Foxing. A plate from The New Newgate Calendar, *Vol. IV, by Andrew Knapp and William Baldwin, published c1810.*

Any subsequent remaining stains will have to be bleached out. The safest and mildest bleach to use is Chloromine T, because it leaves nothing corrosive in the paper. Mix the powder with *distilled water to 2–3%. Submerge the paper in cold water and then tranfer it into a bath of Chloromine T for a few minutes. Lift the paper out and dry between sheets of white blotting paper under glass. Alternatively, individual stains can be bleached by brushing the solution onto the patch with a soft paintbrush. An expert may use stronger bleaches. However, great care should be taken not to over-bleach paper and prints to an unnatural whiteness.

Creases can be removed by immersing the paper in water and then laying it on piece of clean glass. Remove all the excess water with blotting paper, and then leave it to dry.

It is also possible to iron paper with a hot iron. Place another sheet of paper on top of the creased paper before you start, so that there is no danger of singeing it.

Tears in paper should be mended with a *flour paste. Apply it to the paper thinly and evenly, not in dabs. Dry the join under a sheet of glass or in a press. An easier alternative is to use a ready-made paperhanging paste. Small holes in paper can be filled with a cellulose powder mixture. Back the hole with mulberry paper or acid-free tissue paper, then make up the filler with a *cellulose adhesive and *distilled water. Match it to the paper colour with tea or watercolour. Never use self-adhesive tape, because it discolours badly, for which no remedy has been discovered. It also tends to crack after three months.

Matching paper on a larger scale is an expert job needing experienced knowledge of the many types of paper in existence.

PAPERWEIGHTS
These are usually of glass, and may be washed in warm, soapy water. Examples with glued-on bases should be wiped, rather than immersed. Rinse and dry thoroughly.

Use silver polish occasionally on dulling paperweights. Rub it on and let it dry to a fine white powder, then buff it up with an old chamois leather or soft linen cloth. If you wipe the polish off well, there is no need to wash it afterwards.

Broken glass paperweights are best taken to an expert.

PAPIER MACHE
The basis of papier mâché is 'mashed' paper, which is mixed with glue, chalk and fine sand, moulded, baked, and then lacquered. It was originally used in the 18th century for ornament and architectural moulding. An improved technique was evolved in the 1770s which made it harder and more resistant. Its popularity grew during the 19th century, and methods for covering wood and metal with papier mâché were invented. By the end of the 1870s it was out of fashion and no longer manufactured.

The finish is recognisable by its smooth lacquer decorated with oil painting (usually of flowers), gilding and, after c.1825, inlay with mother-of-pearl. It is nearly always black, but other colours and 'marbled' finishing exist.

Characteristic objects are desk sets, boxes of all types, fire-screens, trays, candlesticks, canterburys, chairs, small tables—and occasionally more ambitious furniture.

Papier mâché is best cleaned with a liquid furniture polish and a soft cloth. Take care not to rub the decoration too hard, as the painting and inlay are liable to flake off.

Breaks can be mended with an *epoxy

English glass paperweight, c1880.

A detail from a papier mâché tray in superb condition.

resin. Chips on chair-backs or corners of trays can be filled with *plastic wood and retouched with oil paint. It is important to match the black carefully. You may need to add tones of brown, indigo, blue or green.

Do not attempt to replace any parts of a small article, as the finish cannot be reproduced and restoration will immediately be apparent. Do not try to replace pearl inlay or to regild.

For woodworm, the safest method is *fumigation. It is important to remember that if the lacquer surface is cracked or bits are missing, the article will be subject to the same attacks as *paper.

Structural faults, in furniture, should be treated as in ordinary furniture. You will see that the papier mâché has been placed on a wooden base.

Take care never to put anything hot on the surface, as heat damages the lacquer. *Mother-of-pearl inlays are particularly vulnerable to heat, and even mildly corrosive substances.

PARCHMENT

Parchment originated in Asia Minor *c*.150 BC. It was prepared from animal skin, usually sheep, by a process which consisted of treating the surface with lime, removing hair and flesh, splitting the skin, stretching and scraping it, and finally rubbing both sides with pumice. Parchment used to be used for deeds, documents and books, but its use declined after paper was introduced.

Parchment must not be exposed to extreme conditions, and should be kept as dry as possible. Metal safes and deed boxes tend to be damp; if the parchment is kept there, it should be well wrapped in cotton-wool or fabric.

Don't attempt to spot with water, as wetting parts of the parchment will cause cockling.

Don't try to bleach stains out. Parchment naturally yellows with age and the bleached sections will not match.

Grease and wax marks can be removed with *benzene. First very gently scrape off any excess wax with a sharp knife.

Warping and wrinkling as a result of damp are the most likely problems. These and creasing can be removed, provided there is no gilding or colour present (in which case it is a job for an expert). First,

fix ink onto the parchment with a thin wash of *acrylic resin solution (*see* ink drawings and manuscripts). Test that the ink shows no sign of running by slightly wetting a small sample. If it does, abandon the project. If not, sandwich it between two sheets of damp blotting paper and press lightly. When the parchment is limp, but not too wet, place it on a sheet of glass which has been previously polished with *French chalk to remove any traces of grease. Then cover the parchment with a sheet of dry blotting paper, and press it against the glass by placing weights on top of the blotting paper. Ideally, the weights should be in strips, and they should not be too heavy to prevent the parchment from moving slightly and flattening. This is a very delicate process, and it should not be tried on anything valuable without practice first. And remember that parchment is hardly ever completely flat, as it is usually not evenly thick, so only attempt to flatten extremely warped pieces.

Tears can be mended provided that the edges are chamfered. Paint the edges with a minute quantity of dilute *acetic acid (10% solution) which will gelatinise the fibres. Then press the torn edges together between two sheets of blotting paper. Cuts and missing corners should be patched by an expert.

Fungus must be dealt with by expert fumigation. However, mould spores can be softly brushed off at home.

PASTELS

Pastel is pigment bound with chalk and gum tragacanth. It is very fragile, and the gum in its composition makes it very prone to mould growth. It became popular in the 18th century and was much used in France.

Pastels should be kept in a dry place and mounted so that there is no chance of the pastel touching the glass. Fixative solutions can be sprayed on, but although they do prevent the pastel powdering off the paper, they can reduce the brightness and blow away some of the detail and highlights. The spraying is best done by someone with experience.

In an old pastel it is possible that the colour may have become fixed into the paper. It can be cleaned by washing. This is, however a decision for an expert

Mould growth can be picked off very

carefully with a fine camel-hair brush dipped in alcohol.

See frames and mounts.

PEARLS

Pearls can be real, cultured or imitation. They have been popular for jewellery and adornment since early times. Real and cultured pearls are produced by oysters, the latter from artificially planted 'seeds'. This process was perfected by the Japanese at the end of the 19th century. Real or cultured pearls can be recognised because they feel gritty to the teeth. Imitation or artificial pearls have been made by a variety of methods by the French, Germans, Italians and Chinese. In the 19th century, blister and baroque pearls, of strange, uneven shapes, were much used in Arts and Crafts jewellery. Fresh-water pearls, produced by pearl-bearing mussels, were popular in mid-19th-century Celtic jewellery.

Real or cultured pearls can be cleaned with warm, soapy water. It is better, however, to dry-clean them. Place them in a tin, cover them with *calcined magnesia, and shake them gently. Wipe the powder off with a soft cloth. Real or cultured pearls should be worn as often as possible, as they gain lustre and colour from being in contact with the skin. Wipe them gently after wearing with a piece of chamois leather.

Artificial pearls are apt to be fragile. Their coating sometimes peels off. They should be cleaned by wiping gently with chamois leather.

Pearl necklaces should be restrung regularly. Pearls should be kept away from other jewellery as they get scratched easily.

Really valuable pearls should be cleaned by an expert. If badly discoloured, they can be peeled, but this, too, obviously demands the skills of a professional.

PENCIL DRAWINGS

Pencils are made of black lead or graphite, and have existed in their present form since the 17th century.

It is feasible to immerse a pencil drawing in water for cleaning. Don't attempt any dry-cleaning methods, because pencil is easily rubbed out or smudged.

For cleaning and restoration, *see* paper.

See frames and mounts.

'*Life at the seaside, Ramsgate*', *a Victorian engraving by C. W. Sharpe.*

PRINTS

There are three sorts of prints that may be termed 'antique'. The first, relief, is an impression from a carved wood block where the uncut parts print black. The second, intaglio, is achieved by printing on paper from inked metal plates; the cut or etched sections print black. The third, surface or planographic printing, depends on the natural antipathy of grease to water. Before you begin to do anything to a print, make sure that you know exactly what it is. If in doubt, get an expert opinion from a museum or dealer. Start on something of little value, as any mistakes will be irreversible.

No print should ever be trimmed down around the edge, as this will reduce its value.

When cleaning prints, take care not to overbleach them, as the paper becomes chalky white and much of the richness of the black is lost.

Woodcuts are the oldest form of prints and have been used since the late 14th century when paper became generally available, although textiles were printed with woodblocks as early as the 12th century. The blocks are cut on plank wood (usually fruitwood). If the engraving is to be coloured, as in the case of Japanese prints, there may be as many as twenty blocks cut, each for a different colour. The term wood-engraving usually refers to the process developed by Thomas Bewick in the 18th century. The cutting is done on the end-grain, usually on boxwood which is particularly hard. This allows the engraver to achieve finer lines and more precise detail. Like intaglio prints, woodcuts and wood-engravings are usually printed with oil-based inks. They may therefore be cleaned and restored like *paper.

Intaglio printing covers aquatints, engravings, etchings and mezzotints. The methods of preparing a metal plate vary, but the general idea comes from silversmithing. Engraving evolved in the middle of the 15th century. The earliest etchings date from the beginning of the 16th century. The design of an engraving is drawn directly on the metal plate with a hard-cdgcd tool. For an etching, the plate must first be covered with a wax ground. The design is then drawn onto this and the plate plunged into an acid bath; the acid eats away the metal along the lines of the drawings. The ground is then removed. The lines in an etching have a softer and more irregular quality than the hard lines of an engraving.

In the 18th century mezzotints and aquatints were developed. The plate is prepared for a mezzotint by covering it with minute indentations which will print a dark ground; the light of the picture is the result of the smoothing and scraping of this surface. An aquatint has a grainy effect caused by sprinkling resin, sugar, salt or powdered asphaltum onto the ground, and fixing it to the plate by heating it and then dipping it into acid. All intaglio prints are printed with an oil-based ink.

Intaglio prints can be cleaned and restored like *paper. There is probably no danger from immersing them in fluid. Check the following exceptions first. Check that there is no ink signature. This is likely to run when wet and should first be fixed onto the papeer (see ink drawings and manuscripts). Check for the existence of watercolour, since many 18th and 19th-century prints have been hand-coloured with watercolour, particularly sporting prints and fashion plates. These can be gently cleaned with *Chloromine T and cold water, but they may fade slightly. If the colouring is crude, this will not be detrimental; if it is good, treat the print as for *watercolours.

Prints of this period were often varnished. It may or may not be possible to restore the print to normal. It will depend on the type used. Oil varnish becomes insoluble with age, but spirit varnish can be removed.

The surface should first be rubbed over with damp cottonwool. Then test a small section with *methylated spirit to see if it has any effect on the varnish. Failing this, try a section with an *ammonia solution (1 part liquid ammonia to 50 parts water).

Having decided on the solvent, lay the print, face up, on a sheet of glass and flood it with the methylated spirit or ammonia solution. Brushing should help to agitate the varnish off.

When the varnish has been removed, the print will probably be stained. If so, rinse it in water and bleach it slightly by placing it in a bath of 1 part *acetic acid to 10 parts water. Dip in and out quickly. Don't leave it to soak. Rinse in distilled water.

If the print has been coloured and varnished, the colour will probably be damaged by the varnish removal process and would be weakened by subsequent bleaching. It is worth thinking whether you would prefer to have faded colour and no varnish.

The exceptions are chiaroscuro and Japanese prints. Chiaroscuro prints were popular in the 17th century and were printed entirely in tones of black, grey and brown, in imitation of grisaille painting. They are printed partially with water-based inks which are not necessarily permanent. They should be cleaned like *watercolours.

Japanese prints were first printed in black as book illustrations. The complicated colour prints first appeared in the 18th century and throughout the 19th century. The early prints were printed with vegetable dyes which are impermanent. The later cruder colours were produced with aniline dyes. They were printed on mulberry paper, which is very thin and soft.

The surface should not be rubbed, even with the softest eraser. Washing is also, obviously, out of the question. Luckily this type of paper is not prone to foxing or mildew.

Surface dirt can be cleaned off by laying the prints face down on a sheet of glass.

Cover it completely with a sheet of tissue paper, and then sponge the tissue with plain water. The moisture will soak through the tissue, and the dust on the print will adhere to it. The front of the print can also be cleaned in the same way. However, certain colours such as mauve and heliotrope, are easily damaged and should never be dampened.

Torn prints and very fragile ones can be pasted down with *flour paste onto another sheet of paper. This should also be mulberry paper and as close to the original in quality and weight as possible. Japanese prints, particularly the early ones, should never be hung in strong light, as some colours will disappear altogether within a matter of months.

Lithography was invented by Aloys Senefelder at the end of the 18th century as a purely black and white printing process. In 1826 he invented colour lithography. The drawing is done in reverse on a lithographic stone with a greasy crayon. The stone, which is porous, is wetted and then inked. The oil-ink remains only along the greasy areas of the drawing, which is then printed. For a colour lithograph several different stones are used. For cleaning and restoring a lithograph, see paper.

RUSHWORK

Rushwork has been used for seating from earliest times. Stools with rush seats were found in the tombs of the Egyptian Pharaohs. It was popular in England from the Middle Ages, but particularly in the 17th century. Since then the shapes of chair frames have changed but little, and the technique of rushing a chair remains unaltered.

Rush seats have a tendency to sag. The rushes begin to break down after 20 or 30 years in dry conditions. If this is what is wrong with your chair, nothing short of re-rushing will restore it. You can, however, improve matters if the rushes are not badly broken by taking the chair outside, spraying the rushes with water, and leaving it to dry in the open air. This has the effect of tightening the rushes and reducing the sagging look.

It is perfectly possible to re-rush a chair yourself. Practice makes perfect; the third chair you do will be a great improvement on your first. Rushes are available from various craft centres in England. You require $1\frac{3}{4}$ lb for an average chair. Soak the rushes in cold water for 10 minutes. Remove them, place them under a cloth and leave for 24 hours. The cloth prevents the rushes from drying out. During this time they become 'mellow', that is, pliable and ready to use. Make quite sure that the rushes are not too dry, because if they are they will crack once you start work.

Cut away the old rushwork from the frame. If when you have done this, you see that the whole chair frame needs cleaning and treatment of its own, e.g. for woodworm, scratches, etc., do it first (see Wood).

Before you start work, decide what thickness of strand you require. One strand of rush can be used, but two twisted together is better. Lay the rush (one or two strands) over the left-hand side of the front bar of the chair frame, hold it firmly against the inside of the front bar with your finger. Then tightly twist the rush. Twist rushes away from you, rather than towards you. Always keep the rushes tightly twisted as you work, particularly those strands on the top of the seat where they are seen. Twisting is not necessary for the strands when they pass under the frame. Pass the long end of the rush under the frame, up and round the left-hand bar, thus securing the short end of the rush. Then take the strand across the frame to B, passing it round the right-hand bar, making sure that you bring it up behind the strand you have just brought across. Pass the strand down over the front bar close to B, taking it under and across the open frame to C. Take the strand over the back bar, then up and over the right-hand bar close to C, under the right-hand bar and finally across to point D. Pass the strand over the left-hand bar, up and over the back bar, and pass it under and back to your starting point, completing one round. This process is repeated until the frame is filled. Tie fresh strands of rush, as you need them, on to the strand you are already using. Make a reef knot (see diagram) to attach on the underside of the frame.

As you work round the frame, a space or 'pocket' forms between the top and bottom layers of rushes on each of the four sides. You should pack these 'pockets' very tightly with all the short or broken rushes you have to hand. A tapered piece of wood will be found useful for ramming home the packing. This packing keeps the rows in position and

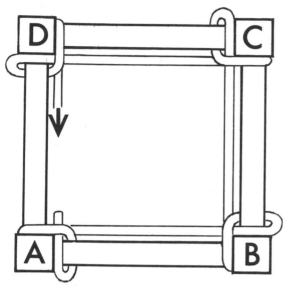

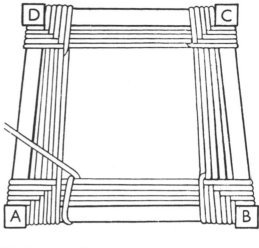

Re-rushing chair seat, step 1.

Variant seat shapes.

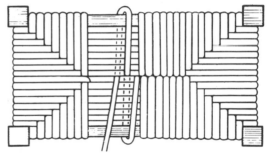

Reef-knot, for joining rushes.

A half completed seat.

Completed rush seat on a ladderback chair.

123

prevents them from slipping. At the same time it strengthens the seat.

When you have finished re-rushing, knot the end of your last strand round one of the rushes on the bottom of the seat, then tuck in the end to give a neat finish.

If the chair frame is not square, but oblong, or wider at the front than the back, the process can be adapted.

If wider at the front than the back, after working once round the seat, instead of wrapping the rush once round the front bar, go round twice on both the left and right-hand side of the bar. In this way the width at the front of the chair will gradually be reduced to that of the back. When this point is reached continue rushing, but only wrapping once round the front bar (see diagram).

SEALS

A seal is a raised wax impression of a design cut into metal or stone. The design is usually a heraldic device peculiar to a person or group. Seals have been used since Roman times as marks of authority, ratification and genuineness. They are also used to fasten letters and documents.

Cleaning wax is a delicate process. Brush it gently with a soft-haired paint-brush. You can also clean seals with a little soft butter, rubbing very lightly with a matchstick covered with cottonwool.

Breaks in wax seals can be mended with a mixture of equal parts of *rosin and *beeswax. Melt them together and apply them while warm to both sides of the fracture. Press together and hold them firm until they cool.

If you want to frame and hang a document with seals attached by ribbon, inlay the whole thing in a card mount, which will support the weight of the seals in case the fabric should be rotten and break.

For breaks in lead seals, see lead.

SILVERPOINT DRAWINGS

Silverpoint is a medium that has been used since the early Renaissance. It consists of coating a sheet of paper with a preparation, which is often coloured buff, blue or pink, and then drawing on it with a fine metal point. The effect is extremely delicate and the lines are very fine and grey. It should not be touched except by an expert restorer because of the sensitivity of the paper.

See frames and mounts.

SOAPSTONE

Soapstone, also called steatite, is a variety of talc, a magnesium silicate. It is a very smooth, extremely soft stone, superficially like marble in appearance, but with a soapy texture, which is greasy to the touch. It will take a smooth polish and is so easily worked that it can be carved with a knife. It is found in a variety of colours, including white, yellow, green, red, a dullish greenish or bluish grey and brown. It is vulnerable to dampness in the atmosphere, and is only suitable for indoor sculpture.

It has been used in most parts of the world since ancient times, especially for more decorative and less permanent carving and sculpture. The Assyrians made cylinder seals out of soapstone, and Egyptians scarabs. The most commonly found objects are the small figure carvings by the Chinese and Japanese. It has also been carved by Europeans, African tribesmen and American Indians.

As soapstone is so soft and easily scratched, it must be treated very carefully. To remove dirt and grease, wipe with a soft rag moistened with *white spirit. This may leave the surface a little dull, in which case polish it lightly with a little silicone polish or *microcrystalline wax. Take care not to remove any painted detail with the solvent or the polish.

Broken pieces should be bonded together with *polyvinyl acetate emulsion. Thoroughly clean surfaces to be stuck together. Then apply a thin layer of adhesive to each. The pieces should be clamped together tightly while the adhesive is setting. Clean away excess adhesive with *acetone.

If any pieces are missing, a filler can be made by mixing fresh *plaster of Paris with melted *paraffin wax or melted *beeswax. Add a little *carnauba wax to make it less brittle. The proportions should be 1 part carnauba wax to 3 parts beeswax. The mixture can be coloured appropriately by adding candle dyes. Alternatively, use *microcrystalline wax coloured with dry pigments.

A missing piece can be modelled with a heated tool, or cast in a mould. The repaired surface should be polished with a little *French chalk.

STONE

Stone of many different varieties has been used for sculpture since the earliest times. Extremely hard stones such as granite and black basalt, are best treated with a greater simplicity than the softer materials such as *marble. This is because of their inherent ruggedness as well as the difficulty of working them.

Limestone, in one or other of its forms, has been the most commonly used material for architectural sculpture in North-West Europe. It can be cut to a fairly sharp edge and is sufficiently easy to work to permit a considerable richness of detail. Softer and coarser stones, such as sandstone and even chalk have sometimes been used, but they do not lend themselves to fine work, so they were often covered with colours to hide the rough surface. Today, when the subtleties of texture are of great interest to modern sculptors, all kinds of materials are employed.

Cleaning

Sculpture and carving in stone may decay from the action of the atmosphere and from fungi if kept outside. Statuary kept inside can be damaged by spilt liquids or candlewax. Both may be affected by sulphur fumes.

Igneous rocks, such as granite and basalt, are extremely hard and almost completely non-porous. If they are covered with grime, smoke and soot, scrub them with stiff brushes, even wire ones, using warm, soapy water. If they have become so badly stained that this is not effective, apply an organic solvent with a brush of 9 parts *carbon tetrachloride and 1 part *benzene emulsified with *Lissopol N. Rinse the stone well afterwards *for about half an hour* to ensure that all traces of the solvent are removed. When dry, apply a protective coating of a 10% solution of *paraffin wax melted to 50°C (122°F) in *white spirit. After about two hours, gently warm the surface of the stone to melt the wax so that is penetrates into all the cracks and porous areas, thus excluding all the moisture and so protecting it from the action of frost.

Sedimentary rocks such as sandstone and limestone are much softer than igneous rocks. Their main problem is surface frailty. The little fragments of grit of which they are composed are cemented together in a matrix

An Italian 18th century stone and marble garden temple with a wrought iron dome.

which leaves the fragments to fall away in powder if disrupted by excess cleaning or other causes, such as urban atmospheric conditions. Stone preservatives are unsatisfactory, and may even intensify deterioration. On the other hand, many sedimentary rocks develop a protective layer or patina which will afford some protection. This should not be disturbed by excess cleaning. Stains from grime and soot can be treated with a prolonged application of fresh running water played over the surface as a fine mist with a hose for up to 48 hours if necessary. Occasionally, during the spraying, loosen the grime with a stiff brush charged with a 5% solution of *ammonia and water. Do not use abrasive powders or any kind of acid on either sandstone or limestone.

Stains from mildew on porous stones can be removed by a mud-pack (*see* marble). Alternatively, they can be removed by the paper pulp method (*see* marble). Either method can be used to remove oil and wax stains, provided that the mud-pack is made of *magnesium silicate powder and *white spirit, rather than water, and that the paper pulp is allowed to dry out and then re-soaked in white spirit before application.

Stone objects with painted inscriptions or decoration should never be wetted until the painted surface has been protected. Coat the painted surface with a 2% solution of *soluble nylon in *ethyl alcohol or *methylated spirit, which will leave a matt surface.

Some objects with painted inscriptions have a layer of plaster under the paint, or have had irregularities in the stone smoothed over with plaster. Such objects cannot be wetted without the plaster coming off, so they should also be treated as above. Plaster casts or small relief medallions are very friable and delicate as well as being highly absorbent. They should never be wetted, and the best way of cleaning them, is to brush with a soft brush charged with dry *plaster of Paris or a mixture of *pumice powder and precipitated chalk in equal parts. Great care should be taken to avoid blunting any sharp relief detail.

Removal of salts

Objects made of sandstone or limestone are often fairly porous and may absorb soluble salts, especially if they have been buried in the ground. These salts will tend to work their way to the surface of the stone, owing to variations in humidity. There they will crystallise, either forming a hard deposit or a loose surface of granulated crystals, causing the whole surface to become fragile and liable to break away. The soluble salts must be removed before such a surface can be consolidated.

Immersion in water is the best way to do this. If the salts have not yet started to crystallise on the surface, the whole object can be completely immersed, taking the necessary precautions if any of the surface is painted or plaster. If the crystals have formed on the surface, they should be dusted off gently with a small brush before immersion. Use a stone or cement basin, but not one made of iron or copper as it may cause staining. Change the water frequently; use ordinary tap water, if it is not too hard, in the early stages of washing, and *distilled water to complete it. It may take many weeks or even months before testing shows that all the salts have been removed. The rate of desalting can be increased if the temperature of the water is raised to about 60°C (140°F). Once the stone is wet, do not let it dry until the salts have all been removed. The growth of algae, which tend to develop especially in warm weather, may be prevented by frequently changing the water and covering the basin so as to exclude the light.

The following test for the presence of salt is recommended. Pour about 10 ml of the washing water into a bottle, and add several drops of dilute *nitric acid. Shake the bottle to mix the solutions. The mixture should be clear when examined in good lighting. Add 5 drops of 2% silver nitrate, mix as before, and allow time for any opalescence to appear, indicating the presence of salt.

The salts can also be extracted by the paper-pulp method. When the surface has become very loose because of the granular flaking nature of the crystals, or when there is painted decoration, consolidation is necessary before applying either the paper pulp or the mud-pack, or immersing the object in water. The purpose of consolidation is to hold the powdery grains together and to prevent damage to the painted surface. Paint the stone with a 2% solution of *soluble nylon in *ethyl alcohol or *methylated spirit. This film of soluble nylon does not prevent the extraction of the salts, although it may slow it up.

Prepare the pulp as for the removal of stains, and apply it so as to cover the whole surface of the object. The water absorbed by the stone will dissolve the soluble salts and at first carry them further in. However, because salts in solution tend to move towards a surface where evaporation is taking place, they will eventually change direction and leave the stone, forming an incrustation in the pulp. The pulp should be left in position for about three weeks, and then replaced with fresh pulp if necessary.

The mud-pack method may be equally, if not more, effective. It should be prepared and applied in the same way as for removing stains.

Consolidation

After the salts have been removed, it is often necessary to strengthen the surface. The best consolidating materials are those that penetrate well into the stone, especially if the object is likely to be exposed to fluctuating temperatures.

One method is to impregnate with wax, providing the stone is completely dry. Pre-heat the surface of the stone to ensure that the wax penetrates right into the pores of the stone. This can be done by placing an electric fire about 3–4 ft from the stone, and allowing the object gradually to warm through. Stir molten white *beeswax at about 85°C (185°F) into petroleum ether at 80°–100°C (175°F–212°F)—beware of naked lights as this is highly inflammable —until the consistency of vaseline is obtained. Apply the wax mixture to the warmed stone. The wax is absorbed into the pores and the inflammable solvent evaporates. After all the solvent has evaporated, re-apply heating, and add further coats of wax until no more is absorbed. Unfortunately, waxing invariably causes a certain dullness and lowering of tone which is particularly noticeable on light-coloured stones.

Repairs
Broken stoneware can be mended with a *synthetic resin. The broken surfaces should be completely clean and free from grease; if necessary swab away any fingermarks with white spirit. Apply the adhesive, clamp the object and support suitably until it has completely set.

With large objects, adhesive alone will not be adequate. Dowelling should be used to give the mend greater strength. Always use stainless steel or brass dowels. Dowels made of iron will rust and stain the stone. They should not be so heavy that their insertion weakens the stone. The ends of the dowel can be notched to give the filler an anchorage, and one side should be flattened or grooved slightly to allow the escape of air which might otherwise be trapped underneath and eventually push the dowel out.

Bore a hole with a power drill in one of the broken surfaces at the appropriate angle, and to a depth of a little more than half the length of the dowel and of a diameter just large enough to admit it. The two holes should be exactly opposite one another, so place a piece of lead or chalk in the dowel hole so that it protrudes slightly. Then place the two pieces carefully together in their eventual position and rotate them slightly so that the correct drilling site is marked on the other piece. Bore your second hole as wide and deep as the first. Try the dowel in the holes to see if the two parts come together without interference, and adjust the dowel if necessary. Mix your filler and fill one of the holes with it before pressing the dowel firmly into position. Clean off excess filler and allow it to dry, supporting it if necessary. When it is completely set, apply the cementing material to the second hole and bring the two pieces together, with a layer of adhesive between them, so that they fit perfectly. (If it is a clean break and the two piecees fit easily together, this can be done in one operation.) When the joint is permanently set, fill in any cracks with filler.

*Plaster of Paris is the most suitable filler for most sculpture, because it is easily applied and removed. When dealing with large amounts of plaster mixes, you can retard its quick setting rate by adding a little adhesive to the plaster. Before applying a plaster filler to stone, moisten the surface a little with water to prevent it absorbing the plaster.

Adhesive mixed with filler and coloured with powder pigments can be used to build up missing pieces. These can either be modelled free-hand, or, if a prototype exists, made with the use of a mould.

TAPESTRIES See **Carpets and Tapestries**

TEXTILES
The weaving of textiles dates back to prehistoric times. Threads can be spun from fibres of animal origin, wool and silk, and of vegetable, cotton, linen and hemp. Wool was probably used first. Hemp and flax originated in Egypt and cotton in India. Silk came to the West in Roman times from China, where it had probably been used since c1200 BC.

Cleaning is the most important process in the conservation of textiles. Remember that it is irreversible, and you can do great damage by not using the correct cleaning methods for the fabrics. Try to keep textiles as clean as possible, as dirt does cause harm.

Begin by vacuuming fabrics. This cannot do any harm and will remove loose dust and dirt. Lay the material flat. Place a square of nylon monofilament over it and vacuum through it. The nylon will hold embroidery or delicate threads in place and prevent straining.

Textiles can be further cleaned by washing

An antique Fachralo Kazak rug from the Caucasus measuring 8 ft. by 6 ft. 3 in.

or dry-cleaning, but if you are in any doubt about the type of fabric, its value, or the age of the piece, get an expert opinion before you start.

Washing is the least harmful method, provided that immersion in water will not harm the textile.

Check that the dyes are fast by damping a section and placing it between sheets of white blotting paper. If no traces of colour appear, the colours are fast. Embroidery should be checked for colour-fastness too. Check there is no hand-painting, which might also run. Colour may sometimes be fixed by treatment with a solution of common salt in water. This depends on the type of dye used, and very careful preliminary tests should be made before immersing the whole fabric.

Check that the material has not been 'finished' to give it a glaze or sheen, as this is likely to have been done with a water-soluble substance and you will not be able to restore it after washing. Watered silk or moiré is produced by running the fabric through patterned rollers, and the effect would be lost through washing.

Washing should only be done in soft water. If the water is hard, use a water softener. Materials should be rinsed in distilled water which precludes the chance of any spots of iron-mould appearing later. The operation is best carried out in shallow baths, such as the trays used to develop photographs. If the object is too large for this, it can be supported in a cradle of perforated polythene or nylon net and washed in the bath. It is important to keep the fabric spread out as flat as possible, and to support its weight when wet. If the fabric is very fragile, it is wise to tack it onto another piece of similar fabric. Soaking for about an hour will probably remove most of the dirt. The water should be changed at least three times during this time.

If the textile is not cleaned sufficiently by soaking, and is still greasy, you will have to use a soap or a detergent. There are three to choose from. *Lissapol N is a neutral detergent which should be used in dilute solution; the fabric must be carefully rinsed afterwards in lukewarm water and then *distilled water. *Spirit soap can be used in a 5% solution with water (or in a 1% solution with white spirit as a dry-cleaning method); it is particularly successful with *carpets and tapes-

tries. *Saponin is very useful for textiles that have to be cleaned *in situ,* such as tapestry upholstery; it is probably the safest method with unstable colours.

Never use very hot water for washing, as it will harden wool and shrink wool and linen. Never rub old textiles, however tough they look. Never use commercial detergents, as they may have harmful bleaches and additives. Remove all excess moisture by pressing the fabric with towelling or white blotting paper. Then lay out to dry on an absorbent backing and pin into shape. Textiles should be left to dry naturally to the right humidity. Direct heat or hot air blowers will make them too dry. If the dyes do bleed, then hot-air blowers can be used to speed up the drying.

Dry-cleaning methods should be employed on fabrics that cannot be washed, i.e., those that are fragile, frayed or with impermanent colour. Textiles can be immersed in *trichloroethane for up to twenty minutes, but first test the dyes. The room should be very well-ventilated and without sources of direct heat around. Another effective method is to spread warm potato flour which can be heated in a double saucepan, on the surface of the textile. It will pick up a certain amount of dirt. Brush it off before it cools.

Treat grease and wax stains as follows: First gently scrape off any excess wax, then place clean blotting paper either side of the material and draw the wax out of the fabric by putting a hot iron over the paper.

It is advisable to line textiles if they are fragile, or if they are to be hung on a wall supporting their own weight. Use a light, strong fabric such as a nylon or Terylene net, longer than the original piece, and stitch with large lock-stitches along the lines of greatest strain. Do not use small stitches on any old fabric, because if the threads are weak, they will cause holes. As machine-made net has more stretch sideways, it is best to use it lengthwise on a hanging to stop the weight stretching the net too much and straining the textile. If the lining is not of synthetic material, it must be pre-shrunk. The backing can be attached to a very fragile textile with a thermoplastic adhesive. This, though, is a job for an expert.

Textiles should always be kept in clean, dry conditions as they are prone to fungal and insect attack. Check for signs of eggs, grubs, cocoons, moths or mould spores at regular intervals. Vegetable fibres are less liable to attack than animal fibres. Do not spray textiles with insecticides; the long-term effects are not known, and they may affect dyes. Stored textiles should not be folded but rolled round a roller (if cardboard, cover with acid-free tissue paper) and surrounded with tissue paper. Polythene is not suitable, as it causes static electricity which attracts dust, and is also liable to rot.

Do not hang textiles in direct light, which weakens many fabrics and fades dyes. This applies not only to sunlight, but also to tungsten and fluorescent light. Do not let iron come into contact with fabric. For example, always use brass tacks for hanging. Iron will rot the material because the iron changes the sulphur dioxide in the air to sulphuric acid. Also remember that the atmosphere of an industrial town will destroy a textile much faster than country air.

See embroidery, carpets and tapestries, lace.

TORTOISESHELL
Tortoiseshell is obtained from the horny plate of certain varieties of turtle. It is

A tortoiseshell George III tea caddy. The panels are bordered with ivory and decorated with piqué in silver.

mottled golden brown in colour and takes a very smooth finish. It is found as an inlay on furniture, and as a veneer, e.g. for mirror-frames, from c1700. It was also used extensively throughout the 18th and 19th centuries for small decorative items such as combs, box-lids, card-cases, and for piqué work.

Tortoiseshell can be cleaned with soap and warm water, provided that you dry it quickly. It can then be polished with *micro-crystalline wax.

If the tortoiseshell is part of an inlay, check the effects of anything you use with the other materials in case you touch them.

Breaks can be repaired with an *epoxy resin.

TUNBRIDGE WARE *see* **Wood.**

UPHOLSTERY *see* **Furniture.**

VELLUM
Vellum is the finest grade of parchment and is made of calf or a harder skin. It should be treated as for *parchment.

For vellum bookbindings, *see* books.

VENEER *see* **Wood.**

VERNIS MARTIN *see* **Lacquer.**

WATCHES
Watches as time-keepers for personal use which could be carried about one's person were first developed as separate articles from clocks in Nuremberg, c1510. Early watches were worn principally as items of jewellery and adornment, with elaborate and ornamental cases and shapes. Cases were drum-shaped, oval, octagonal or in the shape of 'form watches', e.g. crosses, flower buds and *memento mori* (cases made in the shape of a human skull).

As the movement or mechanism of the watch developed and became more important, cases became less exuberant. After 1675 a standard round shape was adopted.

Most watches dating from 1700 can be maintained in reasonable working order, but it is rare to find such an old watch in perfect going condition even if it is mechanically complete.

When considering the restoration of an antique watch, it is important to bear in mind that an over-restored piece loses its value. It is more important to a collector when it is as near to its original state as possible. Any watch that seems to be really valuable should not be touched by the amateur restorer but should be taken to a reputable watch-maker for assessment.

It is not advisable to wear an antique watch, except one made in the 19th century. Jolts and jerks can unbalance the movement, and replacement and repair are more difficult.

A cracked or broken watch glass can be replaced in the right style. This cannot be done by the amateur, as a new watch glass has to be carefully ground into the bezel by a watch-maker.

Watch cases

Remove the movement (*see* watch movements) before beginning to clean or repair a watch case. Follow the correct procedure according to the material.

The vulnerable parts of a watch case are the pendant, the catch and the hinges. The pendant is particularly vulnerable on enamel cases, where it can have been torn away taking part of the enamel with it. The contemporary repair for this was to fit a gold plate, usually engraved, over the damaged area. This is a repair which can still be carried out by a good jeweller.

Hinges are likely to be stiff and clogged with dirt, but it is unusual to find them broken. They should be cleaned and oiled. If the catch of a case will not stay fast, this may be because dust and grease are clogging the case springs or because the springs themselves are either broken or have lost their resilience.

Enamel watch cases. Most 18th century watches have enamel cases. The backs of these cases were manufactured separately and set in gold or gilt metal frames. The metal for the base of the enamel was normally copper, but could be gold. Enamelling techniques widely used for watch cases were *champlevé, cloisonné* and painted enamel such as Blois or Genevan enamels. Many watch cases *c*1790–1820 were decorated with transparent enamel laid over *guilloché* or engine-turned grounds. In the 19th-century, *pinchbeck was sometimes used for watch cases. Clean as for *gold.

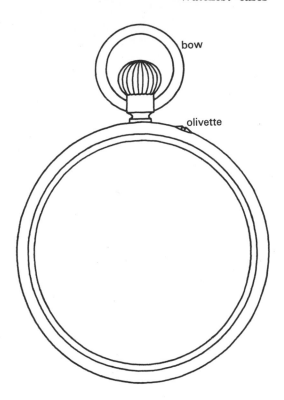

A typical watch case. Front and side views.

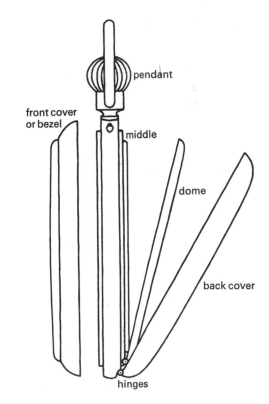

Enamel cases should not be handled too much. Sudden changes in temperature should be avoided as this can shatter the enamel altogether or cause crazing. Watches with enamel cases being displayed or stored should always be placed on a soft surface, e.g. velvet, to prevent them rolling about and getting chipped and scratched.

For cleaning and restoration, *see* enamel.

Metal watch cases. Many metal and metal-work techniques have been popular for the decoration of watch cases. Cases can be made of *gold, *silver, or a gilded base metal such as gilt *copper or *ormolu. It is not a good idea to regild worn gilt base-metal watch cases.

For all cleaning and restoration processes *see* under the appropriate metal.

Techniques used to decorate watch cases are repoussé work, where the metal is embossed and chased, piercing, engraving and filigree work. Wear often obliterates engraving. It is possible to have engraving retouched, provided that the metal has not worn too thin, but this is an expert process not to be attempted by the amateur.

Engine-turned or machine engraved cases, were very popular c1780–1820. They were usually covered with a layer of transparent enamel. They should be treated as *enamel and not metal.

The outside of metal watch cases, when not engraved or engine-turned, can be polished by rubbing them over with a fine cloth which has first been impregnated with an abrasive such as *rottenstone and then with *jeweller's rouge. The cloth should be stretched over a hard surface, such as a board. The final polish is given with the palm of the hand and more jeweller's rouge.

The insides of metal cases can also be polished. This is done with suitably shaped wooden dollies, which are first covered with felt and then with fine doeskin. The dollies are rotated on a lathe. This process, however, is one that cannot be attempted by the amateur.

Pair watch cases. A watch sometimes has a pair case. This consists of an inner case in plain metal with a glass front, and an outer pair case without a glass. This outer case can be decorated with repoussé work, semi-precious stones or enamel. Such cases are usually made in similar metals. However, sometimes the outer case is made of brass, gilt metal, shagreen, horn, tortoiseshell, or covered with leather.

Outer pair cases in leather are often decorated with pinwork, that is, small metal pins set in elaborate patterns on the leather. Care should be taken not to clean pinwork with a metal polish which would destroy the leather. Instead, polish with a chamois leather.

The cases may be lined with a watch paper which should be removed before beginning work on the case.

Watch dials and hands

The design and range of dials has varied enormously. Early watch dials often in gilt metal or silver, elaborately engraved, chased or enamelled for decoration in the centre, with a chapter ring with the numerals engraved or painted on. These dials frequently included smaller dials within dials indicating the date, year, age and phase of the moon, the current sign and degree of the Zodiac. However, most antique watches are 19th-century, with white enamel dials and painted roman or arabic numerals.

Repairing cracked or chipped dials is necessarily limited because enamel cannot be fired again. One method of treating a damaged white enamel watch or clock face is to use 'soft' enamel. Remove the watch glass, carefully rub it into the affected part of the dial, then polish it. However this is only effective for display purposes, because 'soft' enamel does not stand up to knocks and jars.

A quick temporary repair can be effected by using dial wax. This is a soft white wax requiring very little heat to melt it. Melt enough for your purpose, and pour it gently and carefully over the affected area. Allow it to harden. Dial wax is easily removed. It may last if it is protected under a watch glass.

Worn and scratched numerals can be re-painted, but this job is best left to an expert unless you yourself are very skilful at working on a small scale.

The hands on most watches are either blued steel or gold. Hands can be re-cut in style and fitted. Don't try to straighten bent hands yourself. Straightening watch hands is difficult even for an expert.

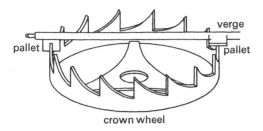

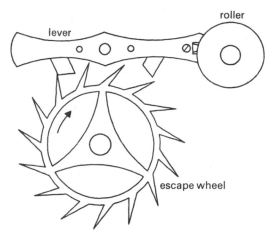

Verge escapement, used in watches until c1800.

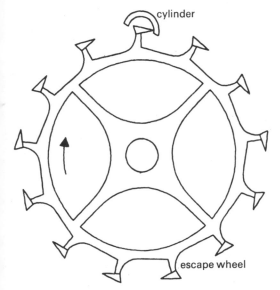

English lever escapement.

Cylinder escapement.

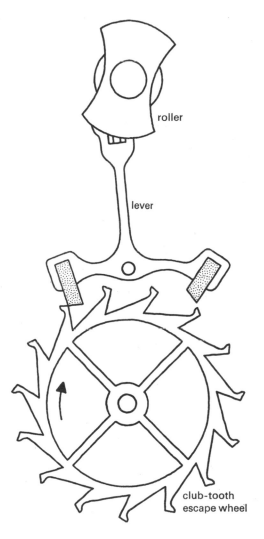

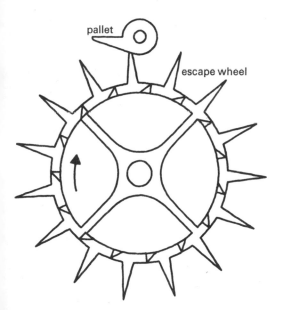

Duplex escapement, from above.

Swiss in-line lever escapement.

133

Watch movements

The mechanism or movement of a watch takes several forms. The most important part is the escapement, which is the device which controls the rate of the unwinding of the train and the movement of the hands, giving the impulse to the watch. The earliest is the verge escapement which remained common throughout the 18th century. Other types at this date were the cylinder and duplex. In the 19th century, the lever escapement was common to most English and continental watches.

No attempt should be made to clean, renovate or restore such mechanisms. These are jobs best left to professional watchmakers, who can replace missing or damaged parts.

Remember, however, that before you start cleaning or restoration work on the watch case, you must remove the movement. Ways of doing this vary, but here are the steps to be taken for most of the principal types.

Pair cases are associated mainly with verge movements. They were discontinued in the 19th century. The outer case is held closed by a catch at the side; the inner case, which also carries the pendant and bow, contains the movement. Both the bezel (the ring holding the glass), and the front plate of the movement, are hinged on a single pin above the figure XII. First lift the lower edge of the bezel by the notch at the figure VI. This will reveal a small steel catch mounted on the front movement plate, which can be depressed to allow the movement to be swung out.

The double bottom case is found on some verge watches, and also on cylinder, duplex and lever ones. It is a modified form of the inner of the pair cases. The back, usually held closed by a button catch on the top of the pendant, opens to show a second layer (hence the name), which is pierced for the winding hole. The movement and the bezel are again hinged to the band of the case, but on separate hinges at figures IX and XII. The back of the movement is protected by a thin brass dust cap which is held in place by a sliding steel strip catch.

Keyless watches. Many keyless movements are housed in cases with two hinged backs to exclude dust. The movement is not hinged, but fixed by two screws on the back plate.

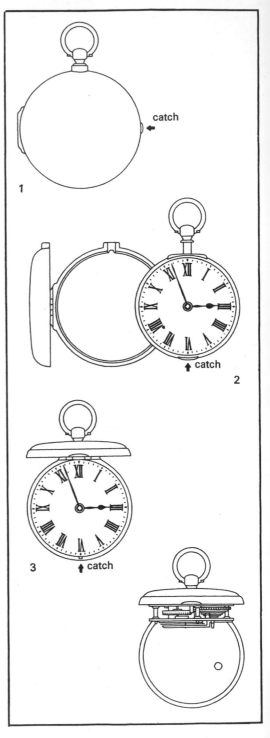

Opening a pair case watch to show movement. (1) Press outer case catch. Remove inner case. (2) Open front of bezel. (3) Press and lift, catch at figure VI to swing out movement.

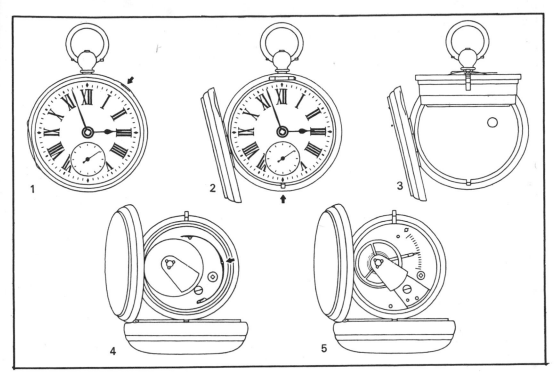

Opening a double bottom case. (1) Open front of bezel. (2) Press and lift catch at figure VI. (3) This reveals dust cap. (4) Turn to show back. (5) Slide dust cap catch.

Below
Opening a keyless watch. (1) Open back at arrow. (2) Open inner cap, or dome, to show movement (3), with its securing screws.

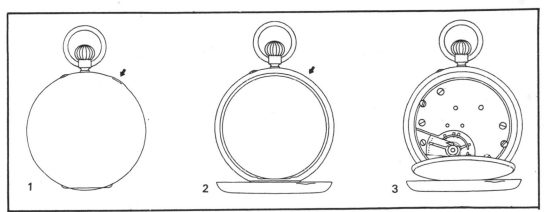

The screw heads are partly cut away, so that they need be unscrewed only about half a turn to release the movement. The bezel and glass must also be removed. Sometimes the winding button must be taken out by partially undoing a small screw in the body of the pendant.

WATERCOLOURS
Watercolour is made by mixing pigment either with gum arabic or tragacanth (to make colour in cakes), or with glycerine and honey (to make colour in tubes). The colour dissolves in water to make coloured washes. The effect is translucent and the paper is visible through the colour. Generally heavy cartridge paper is used to avoid crinkling. Watercolours exist from the 16th century. They reached the height of their popularity during the 18th and early 19th centuries. Subjects tend to be landscapes and to be on a small scale.

Cleaning and restoring watercolours is difficult and really work for an expert. Dry-cleaning methods should only be used with extreme care. This is because colours can be lifted off the surface, for instance, with an eraser. Also watercolour was often used in conjunction with pencil which it is easy to erase.

If cleaned with wet methods, it is obviously likely to dissolve again and run.

Any stains or tear around the edge should be dealt with as described under *paper.

Watercolours fade easily and should not be hung in direct light. Particularly fugitive colours are Indigo, Prussian Blue and Chrome Yellow.

Care should also be taken to frame and mount them properly (see mounts and frames).

Gouache. Gouache is watercolour made opaque with the addition of white. It is also called opaque watercolour, matt water-colour, tempera colour and poster colour. For treatment, see above.

WAX MODELS
Beeswax has been modelled since Egyptian times. The Greeks and Romans modelled funerary masks. Figures and reliefs were popular during the Renaissance, and were often coloured and set with jewels and precious stones. From the mid-18th into the 19th century, wax portrait reliefs were made, also dolls, artificial fruit and flowers.

Lard, flour, whiting and Burgundy pitch were often mixed with wax to harden it and alter the texture. Beeswax was usually amalgamated with vegetable waxes (Japanese, Chinese, Sumatra or *carnauba), or with other animal or mineral waxes, which raised the melting point of the beeswax.

Wax models should preferably be kept under glass domes, or framed and glazed; they should be kept away from direct sunlight and from spotlights.

Cleaning should be carried out with great care because wax is always extremely delicate. First brush of loose dirt with a soft paint-brush. Then, provided that there is no surface colouring, wash with a soft paint-brush. Use either a few drops of detergent in distilled water or *spirit soap and distilled water. For obstinate dirt, the

strongest cleaner is a 3% solution of *ammonia in distilled water.

Repairs should be done with the same wax composition as the object, but with a lower melting point. The colours must be matched too. It is really an expert's job.

Very simple breaks can be mended with an equal mixture of *paraffin wax and *beeswax melted together and applied when warm. The join should be held firm until cool.

WEAPONS AND ARMOUR
The greatest problem for the collector of guns, swords and armour is rust.

It is best to strip down pistols and long-arms completely. Stubborn screws can often be released with penetrating oil and gentle tapping. Always use a screwdriver of the right size, because slips can badly mark the surround. As a last resort, obstinate screws can be drilled out, but it is best to leave this to an expert.

Place all the metal pieces, except silver or brass, in a solution of *paraffin and lubricating oil. Leave for from 2 to 24 hours, according to the amount of rust.

Examine the pieces for *blueing and *gilding which may be damaged by the rust removing methods. Start attacking the rust

A close helmet for the tilt, made in Germany c1570–80.

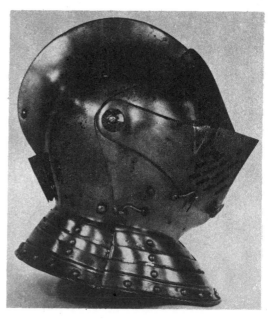

with a wire brush, but don't rub too vigorously. When you have removed most of the surface rust, proceed with a less coarse abrasive such as steel wool, then a fine grade of emery paper, and finally a proprietary metal polish.

If the barrel or other parts have been coated in blueing or gilding, you must decide whether to keep the*patina with the rust, or to remove the rust at the expense of the patina. It is not possible to do both. If you do decide to remove the rust, a patent blueing process can be obtained from a gunsmith, who will also advise you on colour.

If you cannot immerse the objects in paraffin, wipe them regularly with the solution for a few days until the rust disintegrates.

Do not use de-rusting solutions on chain mail, as it will not sustain severe treatment. It is an indication of the delicate nature of chain mail that very few pieces have survived. Clean by dry brushing and finish with a *microcrystalline wax.

Once you have cleaned off all the rust, wash in detergent, rinse, and dry thoroughly.

To protect against rust, polish with a *beeswax or microcrystalline wax polish, or apply a thin film of lacquer which will need to be replaced annually. Check every few months to ensure that there are no traces of rust, for condensation in the air can be enough to start up the corrosion again.

Intricate detail should be cleaned very carefully.

Restoration should be left to an expert. Japanese swords in particular require very special treatment.

WICKERWORK

Chairs woven from osiers (willow) have been popular from very early times. For cleaning and treatment *see* basketwork.

WOOD

Almost all woods have been used in the manufacture of furniture at one time or another. For classification they are divided up into two categories: hardwood and softwood.

Hardwood is the term given to timber from a broad-leaved tree. It is the basic timber for furniture making. Hardwoods

generally take better finishes than softwoods. The principal hardwoods are ash, beech, birch, chestnut, mahogany, oak, rosewood, satinwood, teak and walnut.

Softwood is timber from a needle-leaved tree, and is generally softer than hardwoods. Yew is an exception, being harder than many hardwoods. Softwoods tend to bruise very easily. Some of the main softwoods are Douglas fir, larch, parana pine, pitch pine, Scotch pine, spruce, yellow or white pine and yew. Softwood was often used for the ground of veneered furniture (*see* veneer), painted cupboards and kitchen pieces such as dressers and tables.

In hardwoods, the heartwood is the mature wood. This is what should be used to make furniture. The sapwood is less mature and often much lighter in colour than the heartwood. It is softer and weaker and much more liable to attack from * furniture beetle.

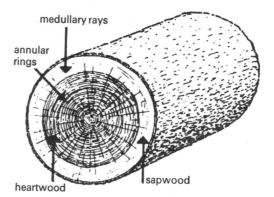

The annular rings in a tree trunk indicate how much a tree has grown in a year. It is these rings that give *grain* to a piece of wood when the wood is sawn as in the diagram.

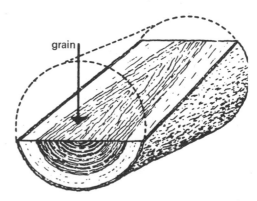

The medullary rays are thin lines radiating out from the centre of the tree trunk. To get the maximum amount of *figure* on a piece of wood, which is particularly marked and attractive in *oak, the log has to be 'quarter sawn'.

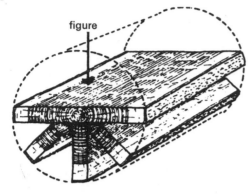

figure

Almost all hardwoods have been used for *marquetry and inlay. However, many so-called 'fancy' woods, which were not suitable for construction purposes, were used for their exciting colour, grain or figuring.

Holly was used during Tudor times for inlaying into oak, and in the late 17th and 18th centuries for general marquetry. A hard, even-grained wood, its very white colour takes dye well, and it was often therefore decoratively coloured.

Olive is a close-grained, greenish wood.

Boxwood is a pale yellow, hard, fine-grained and very even-textured wood much used in *Tunbridge ware.

The most commonly found fruitwoods used in marquetry and inlay were apple, pear, plum and cherry. Cherry was perhaps the finest, identified by its even texture and subtle graining in pale pinks and creams.

Laburnum was often used, especially in the late 17th century, in the form of 'oysters', so named because of the way in which thin slices of veneer cut from across small branches looked like oyster shells.

Amboyna, a highly decorative wood of a yellowish-brown colour with an overall burr pattern, was a favoured marquetry and inlay wood in the 18th and 19th centuries.

Harewood, sycamore or maple dyed a greenish-grey colour, was very popular at the end of the 18th and early 19th centuries.

Bird's-eye maple is a pale yellow, but was often stained or polished to a much warmer colour. It has an all-over pattern of small knots or dots (birds' eyes), and was widely used in the 19th century.

Kingwood was another 'fancy' wood used for inlaying and marquetry. It has black and brown stripes rather similar to rosewood in marking.

Ash

This is a European timber which is creamy white in colour with a grain similar to oak. It is tough and bends well. It is often used for the bow-backs of Windsor chairs. It became popular in the mid-19th century, especially for bedroom furniture.

Beech

Beech is a hardwood found in many parts of Britain and Europe. It is very prolific on the Chiltern Hills around High Wycombe in Buckinghamshire. It was in this area that Windsor chairs were produced in great quantities during the 19th century. All the turned parts of these chairs are of beech.

It is a dense, even-grained timber, usually light cream in colour, though sometimes pinkish when treated with steam. It can usually be recognised by tiny bright flecks set closely together in some parts of the wood. These will show up even when the wood is stained.

Beech was often used for Restoration chairs, when it was polished black. Like birch, it was, and is, also commonly used for the interior rails of cabinets and the frames of upholstered furniture. Its main disadvantage is that it is particularly vulnerable to attack from *furniture beetle.

Birch

Birch grows in Europe and North America. It is rather similar to beech in colour and grain. It was mainly used for upholstered chair frames, as it is a tough wood which will take upholstery tacks without splitting.

Mahogany

True mahoganies, the traditional 'kings' of furniture woods, came from Cuba and Honduras. It is hard to say exactly when mahogany was first worked in Britain, but it was regularly used from 1725. Some few pieces pre-date that by a decade or more.

This early mahogany was called Spanish mahogany, and came, first, from the island of San Domingo and then from Cuba. It was a reddish-brown hardwood, with a fine, even grain and rich figuring. It replaced *walnut as the favourite wood of cabinet-makers, for though not so marked in the grain as walnut, its hard, dense character lent itself to very crisp carving and fine finishes. In the second half of the 18th century, mahogany from Honduras was introduced. With essentially the same qualities as Cuban mahogany, it was lighter in colour and weight, and often had magnificent figuring. It had a tendency to mellow to a golden brown or warm yellow when exposed to strong light over a long period of time.

Today, Cuban mahogany is almost unobtainable and the solid Honduran mahogany, or baywood as it is sometimes called, is extremely costly. Consequently, other so-called 'mahoganies' are used, such as African mahogany, which is softer, often pinkish in colour and with fairly large pores; and Philippine mahogany, which is lighter-coloured and larger-pored than African. Both lack the rich figuring of proper mahogany, and don't take such a fine finish.

These more recent 'mahoganies' were, of course, not used in the true mahogany period, but have often been used subsequently in reproductions and fakes. When it has been polished and antiqued, it takes an expert to distinguish with certainty an African or Philippine mahogany from a Cuban or Honduran one. Occasionally one sees pieces with leg and rails of African wood, and veneers of true mahogany.

To test true mahogany, wet an unpolished part, such as the underside of a table-top, the inside of a carcase, or the back of a drawer. True mahogany will go quite dark, Philippine mahogany will become pale and pinkish, and African mahogany will take on a colour between the two.

Oak

Oak was the main furniture wood used in Britain until about 1660. It is a yellowish, or silvery, large-grained, open-pored wood, tough and hard, and not the easiest wood to work. When cut along the lines of its medullary rays, it can give a very lovely figuring, which is known as wainscot oak.

All parts of furniture were most frequently made of oak before 1660, but after that date it was mostly used for interior parts, drawer linings, etc. This was because walnut superseded oak as the furniture wood of the

cabinetmaker. Oak was used for some years then as the base wood, or ground, of walnut-veneered furniture. Later, however pine took over this role, because it was found that it held glue better. Oak was rarely used for veneers, in spite of the attraction of its radial figuring.

Since oak was used for the oldest furniture now in use, it naturally shows evidence of wear and tear on corners, edges and stretchers. But its strong resistance to *woodworm and rot has enabled it to out-last furniture made at the same time of other woods.

Japanese and American oak are now used in furniture, and when stained, are virtually impossible to tell from English oak. But in the natural state, Japanese oak is lighter than English oak and American is either redder or whiter. Neither grain is as coarse as English oak, and generally less wild in pattern.

Satinwood

Satinwood became popular during the later part of the 18th century and remained so throughout the 19th. A light-coloured wood, sometimes lemony, very often with rich figuring, it takes a very fine finish. It requires even more skill from the cabinet-maker than mahogany, as any blemishes show up plainly. For instance, dark glue lines at a joint are not particularly noticeable in mahogany, but stand out strongly in satin-wood. For this reason rabbit-skin glue—a type of animal glue—or *Scotch glue, with a light-coloured pigment added, was used to mask a joint line. Satinwood was often imitated at the end of the 19th century by staining more ordinary wood, or by using a tinted polish.

Teak

Teak is found principally in India and Burma. It is yellowish-brown when first cut, but darkens considerably with age. The grain is rather coarse and open and the wood feels greasy to the touch because of the natural oil it contains. Antique pieces were brought back from the East. It was not used for furniture in Europe until very recent times.

Walnut

Walnut is a hardwood, and is usually lightish-brown in colour with brown to black markings. The sapwood is cream in colour and prone to attack from woodworm. It is a soft wood to work, and takes a fine polish. Because of these characteristics, it superseded oak as the favoured wood for good furniture from about 1660 until the introduction of mahogany in about 1725. It was invariably used in veneer and inlay form on oak or pine carcases, and it remained relatively scarce, even when most popular, compared with the rough and ready utilitarian pieces which continued to be made of oak. Walnut was sometimes used in solid form for the cabriole and turned legs, and on the backs of the finest pieces, though beech was often stained to imitate it.

Walnut originally came from Persia (now Iran). It was commonly used in furniture of the Italian Renaissance. It was introduced into Britain during the reign of Queen Elizabeth I and extensively planted.

Generally speaking, walnut is a cooler brown and more varied in colour than mahogany, which it otherwise resembles in the size and richness of its figuring and in its easily carved and worked texture.

American, or black, walnut is darker than English or European walnut and ranges from chocolate to purplish-brown. It was used in England in the 18th century, and also became very popular in the second half of the 19th century.

Marquetry and inlay

Marquetry is made from different wood veneers which have been cut out and interlocked to form an elaborate and intricate pattern (see diagram). It is more difficult and complicated to repair than inlay or simple veneer patterns, and, as a general rule, should be left to the expert. Where veneers are laid in simple, geometrical shapes, or in lines of banding set in depressions cut into the solid wood of a piece of furniture, it is called inlay (see diagram).

When a piece of inlay has become loose, take it out of the wood by means of a warm iron laid on a damp cloth (*see* veneer). Clean all dirt and glue from it. Then with a small chisel which fits easily into the groove or shape where the inlay was, clean down the base wood. Glue the inlay back with *Scotch glue or *polyvinyl acetate adhesive. Put a heavy weight on it to ensure that it sets firmly. If required, sand flat and polish.

If the inlay has lifted only slightly, but not enough to allow dirt to get underneath, simply press it down with a moderately warm iron. Then cover it with a thin piece of plywood, place a heavy weight on top and leave until the glue has reset. This may take some time, as inlays are often much thicker than veneers.

If a piece is missing, approach firms specialising in veneer and marquetry supplies. They should be able to provide suitable matching woods, but you may find that you need to stain them to get the exact colour. It must be stressed that only the simplest inlay work can be done by the amateur repairer.

See Tunbridge ware.

Veneer

Veneers are thin sections of timber peeled off a round log, or sawn or sliced from a squared log. Only sawn or sliced veneers are used decoratively on the main structure

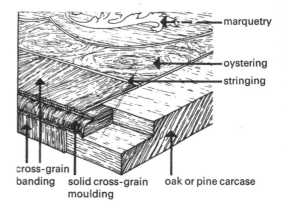

marquetry
oystering
stringing
cross-grain banding
solid cross-grain moulding
oak or pine carcase

Above. *Marquetry.*
Below. *Inlay.*

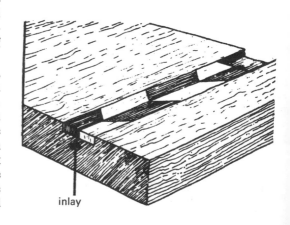

inlay

of the piece of furniture. Veneering was not used in Britain until about 1660, when walnut began to replace oak as the fashionable wood. The fashion grew in the early years of the 18th century and has continued through until today.

Old veneers were invariably thick, sometimes as much as $\frac{1}{8}''$. Modern sliced veneers and paper-backed sheet veneers are much thinner. If you want to replace a piece of old veneer, it is sometimes possible to cannibalise low-grade or unrepairable Victorian pieces, for Victorian veneer was often of excellent quality. *Polyvinyl acetate adhesive is useful for gluing veneer as a supplement to *Scotch glue.

Damage to veneered surfaces ranges from the simplest blemishes, which you can often repair yourself, to major troubles which can be costly and also demand an expert's attention.

Simple problems can be remedied as follows. For blisters, first try sticking down again by applying a medium-hot iron to a cloth placed over the area. Don't use fresh glue.

If this doesn't work, take a razor blade, or a thin, sharp knife such as a scalpel or model-maker's knife, and slit the whole length of the blister. Then slide some Scotch glue underneath the veneer with a knife or slip of veneer. Press the veneer down into place. Cover the area with oiled or waxed paper and cramp down, or put a heavy weight on the top until the glue is set. Wipe away any oozing glue. If you put one or two thicknesses of smooth cloth on the oiled or waxed paper before putting on the weight, the veneer will get extra protection. To get better adhesion, apply pressure with a warm iron to the cloth over the veneer for a minute or so.

If you want to lift or remove damaged old veneer, you will first have to remove all the finish with the appropriate stripper (*see* stripping) or use a scraper. This is because damp cannot penetrate through polish. Moderately heat a soldering iron and place a damp cloth on the veneer to be raised. This will be quite all right for small areas. Apply the iron to the cloth cautiously. The veneer can be gently lifted as the glue melts. For bigger areas, you can use a clothes iron instead, but make sure the area stays damp the whole time. Don't overheat the iron, but gradually increase the heat until the glue starts to melt.

When the veneer is buckled, after removing, damp the buckled area and flatten it between two well-warmed blocks of wood, cramping it together. Leave to dry. Make sure no glue is left on the veneer, otherwise it will adhere to the wooden blocks.

If the veneer is badly crumpled, you run the risk of cracking it if you follow the above method. The better procedure is to dampen the veneer thoroughly for an hour or two before flattening it between the blocks. Add weights to the blocks, gradually increasing the pressure, then finally cramp together.

To replace a chipped piece of veneer on an edge or corner, cut back carefully to a straight working edge, preferably along the grain. If that is not possible, then cut diagonally across the grain. Try to find a matching piece of the same colour, with the grain running in the same direction. Similar grain or figuring is more important than colour, since you can always stain. Then take a thin piece of paper, place it on the part to be mended, and rub it over with a soft lead pencil or piece of heelball to get an outline of the patch on the paper. Next, cut the paper slightly larger than the shape of the pattern, and stick it on to your piece of repair veneer, making sure the grain runs the right way.

Then cut out the shape, with a sharp pointed knife or fine*fretsaw. Cut out your patch as precisely as you can, although it is always better to cut the patch a little larger where it comes over the edge of the piece of furniture for trimming or sanding down. If the patch needs trimming, use a*fine file or *glass-paper wrapped round a suitably shaped block of wood. Keep the paper stuck on until the veneer patch is quite ready to stick in place, as it helps to keep it rigid and helps it not to crack while sanding or filing to fit.

When all is ready, peel off the paper and glue the veneer patch in place. If there is a crack in the patch, leave the paper on and remove after the glue has set, in about 24 hours. Put a piece of oiled or wax paper over the patch, then cramp a piece of well-heated wood over it. Alternatively, use heavy weights.

The important thing is to get the veneer down really tight, without trapping air bubbles underneath. Leave for 24 hours, if the paper pattern is on (as for cracks). Remove the paper and smooth it down exactly to the surface level of the surrounding wood with glass-paper.

Remember it is better to have your veneer patch a little thicker than it need be, so that there is some latitude for sanding.

If a piece of veneer has lifted loose at the edge of a table, chest, etc., it should be repaired like blisters. But before starting, look closely to see if there is any dirt underneath. If so, prise up the veneer until it snaps off. Then scrape the dirt and old glue off both surfaces, and apply fresh Scotch glue to the cleaned wood. Reglue the veneer in position. Gummed paper tape can be stuck on to hold the veneer securely before cramping down.

If you have a clearly defined crack instead of blisters, it is sometimes possible to let in a sliver of wood. It is, however, often hard to get a good match. If you have this problem, try filling with a hard wax of the correct colour instead, which will make the repair less noticeable.

To stain a piece of veneer to another shade, soak it in a colour dye long enough for the dye to penetrate deeply and not be removable by sanding. Remember that the stain always looks darker when wet, so try out on a spare piece of veneer first.

See marquetry.

Tunbridge ware

Tunbridge ware, that is, small boxes, table tops, tea caddies and similar objects decorated with a wood mosaic, was made in and around Tunbridge Wells in Kent. The craft is now dead, but it was at its height in the 18th and early 19th centuries. The inlays made use, altogether, of almost 160 different

Tunbridge ware. A table, c1850, showing a view of the Pantiles, Tunbridge Wells. To give some idea of the complexity of the technique, and the difficulty in restoring it, the border alone contains some 20,000 pieces.

woods, including many 'fancy' ones. Minute squares were cut from thin rectangular strips, or rods, of different-coloured wodds and assembled in a mosaic veneer. This mosaic, which could be arranged in geometrical patterns, or assembled to depict animals, flowers or landscapes, was then glued onto the object.

Be very gentle when you clean a piece of Tunbridge ware, as the mosaic jigsaw can easily be disturbed. First remove the old varnish by rubbing with fine wire wool or scraping gently with a chisel or razor blade. This is preferable to stripping it with a proprietary stripper. If you do use stripper, be sure to wipe the stripper and gooey varnish away thoroughly with *methylated spirit. Next rub down with *flour-paper and apply a good wax polish, either wholly or partly *beeswax. If you want a glazed finish, which will last longer, try brushing on a proprietary *French polish. Brush in one direction only; leave to dry. Second or third coats should be brushed on in the opposite direction from the first coat.

About all an amateur can do to repair a piece of Tunbridge ware is to fill in small gaps in the pattern. A proprietary wood stopper of the appropriate colour is fine for this. Glue back with *Scotch glue whole pieces of mosaic which have come off. Be sure to wipe away any glue which oozes out.

If whole sections of the mosaic are missing, leaving an incomplete pattern or picture, there is little even an expert can do. The craft is dead, and the possibility of getting a new identical replacement mosaic is remote. Rummage round your stock of old veneer pieces to see if you can build up the mosaic. Or make a patch onto which you can draw on the lines of the design with a sharp pencil.

Black spots on wood

These spots look rather like small burn marks. They are caused by water penetrating the finish on the surface and getting into the grain of the wood. Black spots are found on French polished or varnished furniture.

First remove the polish or varnish. Then apply a solution of *oxalic acid crystals in water. The solution should be a 'saturate' one, that is, the crystals should continue to be added to the water until no more will dissolve.

The solution works quickly on softwoods. You may have to allow an hour or so for the solution to penetrate hardwoods, making sure that the surface is kept wet. When you are satisfied that the wood has been well and truly penetrated, wash the remaining solution off thoroughly with *distilled water.

If the surface affected is large, repairs should be left to the expert.

Bleaching

There are two sorts of bleaching. One removes stain which has been applied to the wood; the other removes the natural colour of the wood. The first type of bleaching is what you are most likely to need, and is the simpler of the two processes. The second type of bleaching is used to beautify the wood.

When bleaching, remember that grease, the remains of varnish, or glue on the surface will stop the action of the bleach on the wood. So you must remove these first.

Remember also that the grain of the wood will be raised through the water applied to it, and will need to be smoothed down with fine *glass-paper.

Some woods are more difficult to bleach than others. As a rough guide, you can say that the darker the colour and the denser the grain, the more difficult it is to bleach.

To remove stain, all you need is ordinary domestic bleach. First, remove the finish from the surface as described in *stripping. Then try out the bleach on a part of the furniture which is normally hidden, to see how much you need. Be sure to let the wood dry after applying the test bleach, so that you can see the true final colour. Make tests using diluted and undiluted bleach left on for varying lengths of time: then rinse off with clean water. Now bleach the whole piece, using the strength of bleach and the length of time your testing has shown to be most effective. Rinse off with clean water. Dry thoroughly with a clean cloth. Leave to dry out for at least a couple of days. The piece will then be ready for further work if need be.

To bleach out the natural colour of the wood, use the special two-part solutions that are on the market, then neutralise with *vinegar (unless this is specifically not recommended in the instructions). Follow the instructions to get the degree of bleaching you require, whatever wood you started with, oak, walnut or mahogany.

Bruises

Bruising affects softwoods such as pine much more than hardwoods like maple, mahogany and oak. The treatment consists of applying steam to the bruise by means of a damp cloth and hot iron.

If you have a small bruise on a piece of plain, unfinished wood, a spot of warm water will often be enough to remove the depression.

For larger bruises, press an iron down on a damp cloth which you have placed over the place. When you think that the steam has penetrated into the wood, turn the heat down, but leave the iron where it is. When the cloth dries out, re-wet it to the same degree of dampness. Continue to do this until the bruise has gone, then rub down any raised grain with fine *glass-paper.

It must be stressed that these methods are only suitable for unfinished wood.

You must use other methods for finished surfaces, however, because damp cannot penetrate the finish. You have two choices. Either strip the finish off, then proceed as for the bare wood described above; or can patch the bruise with shellac stick or coloured *beeswax. The latter method calls for considerable skill, and is best left to an expert.

Burn marks

The treatment of burns on wood depends upon the depth of the burn.

You will be able to rub down a very shallow burn mark with *flour-paper, very fine steel wool, or a safety razor blade. Then, in order to match the affected area with the surrounding surface, mix some artists' oil colour of the appropriate shade and smooth it in gently with your fingertip. Wait until the colour has completely hardened, then re-polish the area with a matching *French polish.

Another, but more drastic method, is to strip off the whole of the polished surface (*see* Stripping). Then re-stain the top. When the stain has thoroughly dried, seal it with a coat of French polish (*see* Finishes). The next step is to cover the blackness of the burn marks with some artists' oil colour mixed to match the wood. Again, the best

implement for applying the paint is your fingertip. The advantage of this method is that the French polish allows you to work on the area until you are completely satisfied that the mark has become unnoticeable (or virtually so).

If the burn has charred the wood, first clean away all the charred part with steel wool or a fine, sharp knife. Melt some coloured beeswax and fill the depression with it, taking care not to get any wax on the surrounding surface. Finally re-polish with French polish of the correct colour.

You could use *epoxy resin mixed with powder colour, for a tougher filling. This is much harder than the wax filling, and therefore less easy to rub down to a smooth and level surface.

Cracks

Cracks in panels, running along the grain, are common in old furniture. Remove the panel if possible. Repair by putting glue into the crack and using cramps to draw the two edges together (*see* Cramping). Another method, if you cannot remove the panel, is to cut a tapering strip of wood, or, if the crack is narrow, use a piece of matching veneer. To get the wood strip or veneer to fit really tight, you may have to prise open the end of the crack with a knife or thin chisel. Glue the new piece into the crack. When the sliver is in place, and when the glue has set, smooth it down flush and take great care not to scratch or damage the adjoining surfaces.

Make sure that the wood of the panel on each side of the crack is in line. To test, take a thin piece of wood with a straight edge and cut a notch in the middle to bridge the filling piece. Lay it against the two parts of the panel. Any unevenness will show itself clearly.

Stain as required, and re-polish until the new wood blends in with the old.

An alternative to gluing is to use coloured *beeswax. The treatment is the same for the deeper sort of *scratches, except that you may have to melt the wax into the wider end of the crack. To do this, take a pointed metal rod, heat it just enough to melt the wax. Hold it over the crack, and press the coloured beeswax against it so that the wax runs into the crevice.

Afterwards, level carefully with a chisel

or razor blade, and finish with a fine glass-paper if necessary.

See marquetry and inlay and veneer for other techniques in treating cracks.

Cramping

Cramps (called clamps in the USA) are used for holding pieces of wood together while the glue is hardening. They can easily be bought. The most widely used is probably the G-cramp (known as a C-clamp in the USA). Spring clips are good for cramping small items. You can cut up some old up-holstery coil springs into C shapes, which make effective cramps for light or intricate jobs.

A clothes line, or other length of soft but strong cord, can be extremely useful. It is, in fact, the best sort of cramp to use where no other ordinary cramp will fit, such as around chair or table frames. Twist the rope tightly round the frame with a short stick inserted between a double length, like a tourniquet.

Never screw a cramp direct to the piece of wood being glued together. Always put a wooden block, and a layer of cloth for delicate surfaces, between the cramp and the surface to avoid bruising. This block also serves to spread the pressure of the cramp and make it more effective over a wider area.

Since you should always avoid nails and screws as far as possible, cramps are essential for holding glued pieces firmly together while the glue hardens.

Remember always to protect corners and edges with thick rags or a piece of plywood, to avoid chafing or damaging them with the cramps. Self-adhesive tape can be very useful for holding in place a small moulding or a cock bead. When gluing long or wide pieces together, use at least two cramps and long blocks of wood to ensure even pressure along the whole of the glue line.

Never use a spanner to tighten G-cramps, as the increased pressure may twist the frame of the cramp. Screw up tightly by hand. Make sure you wipe away any glue that oozes out. Otherwise, you may find that the pad gets stuck to the wood, giving a good chance of damaging the finish.

Dowelling

Hardwood dowels of various diameters can

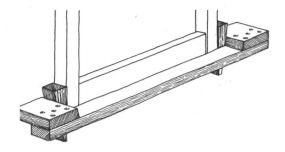

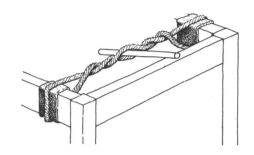

Two types of improvised cramp. Above: *securing a glued frame with wedges.* Below: *a tourniquet cramp.*

be bought at hardware stores. The most widely used are ones of $\frac{1}{4}''$ and $\frac{3}{8}''$ diameter. They provide a good, simple way of strengthening existing joints, and of effecting various other repairs to old furniture.

Where dowels have broken at the hole, they can be pulled, tapped or drilled out and replaced by new ones. You can also use dowels for plugging screw holes which have become too big. Bore a new hole of the correct size in the dowel to take the new screw.

New dowels should always fit tightly, but take care they aren't so large that they split the wood. If the dowel does not already have a fine channel or spiral cut into it, cut one down one side of the dowel with a tenon saw. This will allow air and glue otherwise trapped beneath it to escape, and the dowel to be driven right home.

True matching holes are important. So use precise measurements when drilling dowel holes, to ensure that the dowel fits absolutely right, or that it protrudes out of the hole to the exact length. If you don't, a dowel that is too long will not allow the joint to come completely together. A dowel that is too short in the hole will reduce the strength of the joint. When fitting new dowels always make sure that the old dowel hole is quite free from glue and bits of dowel.

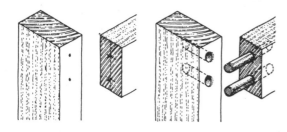

To make a dowel joint, first draw a line down the centre of the end of the rail, then mark on this the position of the centre for each dowel. Now cut $\frac{3}{8}''$ off the pointed end of two fine nails and gently tap the cut-off ends into the centre mark until about $\frac{1}{8}''$ of the points projects. Place the end of the rail onto the other piece of wood and press down, thus giving the position for the other two holes. Now bore all four holes and very slightly countersink them afterwards. Cut the dowels a fraction shorter than the total depth of the two holes and slightly round off the ends. Then glue and drive home the two dowels into the one of the members, and wipe off surplus glue. Next, insert the dowel ends into the holes of the other members and glue and cramp together until set. Hot *Scotch glue is best, and sets hard in about 24 hours.

Dry rot

Dry rot is caused by a fungus that makes wood dry and powdery; it attacks wood that has been kept in damp conditions. By the time a reddish-brown growth is apparent, the condition is serious, and any affected wood should if possible be burnt. Dry rot is often found in the legs and feet of old furniture which has stood on damp floors. The condition should be treated with a *fungicide such as Cuprinol. The infected wood can then be consolidated with hot *paraffin wax, or the rotten wood scraped away and replaced by *plastic wood

Finishes

Although the word 'polishing' is widely used, the term 'finishing' should be used for the applying of a protective and/or decorative surface to either wood which has not received any previous treatment, or which has been stripped and needs to be treated.

Wax and oil were the first finishes to be used. The oak and walnut furniture of the later part of the 17th century was often oil-varnished. Early mahogany pieces of the first decades of the 18th century were oil polished, usually with linseed oil, but later, oil-varnish was used. French polish was introduced round about 1820 and quickly became very widely used. Cellulose lacquers are of even more recent date.

In theory it should be possible to establish the date of a piece of furniture by its finish alone. But in practice this is an unreliable guide, since pieces may have been re-finished at a later date; in fact many 18th century pieces of furniture were French polished during the 19th century. Traces of the original finish can often be found in hidden corners or on the back of furniture.

Beeswax

This is the oldest finish and used almost exclusively for early oak furniture, although we know, from traces which are sometimes still visible, that decorative painting was also used. Beeswax absorbs dirt, and this accounts for the very black colour of old oak furniture. Waxing is however a simple and easy finishing method, giving a good, hard-wearing protective surface.

It is usually best to make one's own polish (see beeswax), although proprietary brands can be bought.

Apply the polish with a cloth. For carving, mouldings or panelling use a fairly stiff brush. Leave for about 24 hours before polishing with a coarse cloth. Repeat this process until a good even finish has been built up. Reduce the amount of wax applied at each successive coat but increase the time spent in really hard polishing.

Before waxing soft woods, such as *pine, it is advisable to give them a sealer coat of either *French polish, or *polyurethane lacquer slightly thinned with turps. This hardens the wood, helping to reduce bruising, and prevents darkening. Apply the sealer with a brush, or cloth pad, working it well into the wood, and making sure no runs or pools are left on the surface. When dry apply a second coat and allow this one to dry completely before rubbing down with fine steel wool (00 or 000 grade). *Always rub with the grain, never across it.* The wood is now ready for waxing.

Wax can be used over any other finish, but no other finish should be applied over wax. However, you should note that waxing heavily or or too frequently over French polish will tend in time to obscure the grain of the wood. This can be removed by a mixture of equal parts of *turpentine, *vinegar and raw *linseed oil, and a quarter of a part of *methylated spirit shaken together in a bottle and applied with a cloth pad. If the old wax proves stubborn to remove from a wax finished piece of furniture, soak a pad of 1 or 0 grade steel wool with turps substitute, then rub hard, working along the grain, until all the wax is removed. Finally, clean off with a turps-soaked rag, and wipe dry with a clean cloth.

Linseed oil
Using *linseed oil takes time to build up a good finish but it gives a highly protective surface which is especially useful for table tops. The surface is water-resistant, unaffected by hot plates, and improves with age, especially if maintained by applying a light coat of oil every few months and giving plenty of hard polishing with a soft cloth.

Too much oiling over the years can make the surface appear rather dull and sticky. This can be removed with a cloth pad soaked in *turpentine, after which the surface should be well dried with a clean cloth. A fresh coat of linseed oil can now be applied.

A linseed oil finish should only be used for hardwoods such as oak, mahogany and teak (although for teak it is better to use one of the special teak oils, which are readily available and give a finish much more quickly). Apply the finish to the surface with a lint free cloth, rubbing vigorously all the time. Never flood the surface with oil, but work it into the wood with a cloth. Continue this treatment daily for some 3 to 4 weeks, and a really tough surface will build up.

Oil varnishes
One of the problems in applying *oil varnishes is 'bloom', caused by moisture being trapped below the surface of the varnish as it dries. Dust is another problem during varnishing, due to the length of time it takes to dry completely. For the best results, always try to varnish early in the day in a room free from draughts and dust. Use a varnish brush (this has rather softer bristles than a paint brush). Dip the brush carefully into the varnish, then lay it on to the wood with a series of even up-and-down strokes. Follow up by brushing across the surface, then finally with all the strokes going upwards only.

The first coat of varnish should be thinned with turpentine substitute (about 3 tablespoons to a pint of varnish). Subsequent coats should be applied at full strength—three coats are required to give a reasonable finish. Between coats rub down with a rag dipped in linseed oil and fine *pumice powder. Make sure that the surface is completely dry and clear of all pumice powder before applying the next coat.

Spirit varnishes
These are very quick drying compared with oil varnishes and easier to apply. Use a soft, camel-hair brush for applying spirit varnish, taking care that each coat is very thinly applied, working the brush in the direction of the grain of the wood. In a warm room the varnish will usually dry in a few hours. It should then be rubbed down with either 000 grade steel wool or *flour paper. This is of great importance, because spirit varnish does not level itself out to the same extent that oil varnish does. Before varnishing, seal the wood with *French polish. This will stop it being absorbed unevenly and reduce the amount of rubbing down required between coats.

French polishing
This requires considerable practice and skill before a really professional finish can be achieved on large surfaces. It is therefore recommended, as with other finishes, that you learn the art on spare pieces of wood first. The basic principles for French polishing are given below and should give good results on small simple pieces of furniture. With valuable pieces or large areas such as table tops it is best to leave them for the professional polisher to cope with.

To start, sand the wood, and stain if required (see sanding, staining), then brush on two coats of *French polish. If the grain needs filling, rub in *plaster of Paris which has been tinted with powder colour to match the wood, using a damp pad of cloth. When the plaster is dry, rub a thin film of raw *linseed oil all over the surface, and rub down with very fine *glass-paper. Finally wipe the wood completely clean with a dry, soft cloth. The wood is now ready for polishing.

For doing the actual polishing a fad and a rubber are used. The fad is a pad of un-bleached wadding which can be bought either from your polish supplier or a draper's. To make the fad, soak a 9 inch square of wadding in polish and leave until dry, then soften with methylated spirit, then fold it together until you have a triangle with about 4 inch sides. Take care to see that any raw edges of the wadding are tucked inside the fad. Dip the fad into a bowl of polish, then press it down on to a piece of card or wood to give it a flat sur-face. Now, working backwards and forwards in the direction of the grain, cover the whole area, following up with small circular movements of the fad over the surface. Finally, return to giving backwards and for-wards movements. Continue until the fad is beginning to dry out, but not sticking to the work, then recharge with polish and repeat the process three or four times. A further three or four coats are now given, adding a touch of raw linseed oil to the face of the fad to stop any chance of sticking. Always allow a few minutes' drying time between each coat.

For the next and final stages a rubber is used. This is made by folding a piece of wadding as for a fad and covering this with a piece of clean linen or cotton cloth. Press the rubber down on to a flat surface with the fingers and thumb, holding the twisted ends of the covering cloth in the palm of the hand. Still holding the rubber in the same way and using a gentle pressure, work with a circular motion all over the surface. Next, change to working in large figure-of-eight movements taking in the whole width of the area, then finish with long straight backwards and forwards strokes. Touches of raw linseed oil should be put on to the rubber, so that it slides with a slight feel of gripping and is not slipping. Only practice will tell you exactly how the rubber should feel on the surface. After leaving for at least

8 hours, the oil is removed by using either a mixture of one part polish and one part methylated spirit on the rubber, or a piece of soft cloth lightly damped with methyl-ated spirit.

Never overcharge the fad or rubber with polish, it should only ooze out slowly as pressure is applied. Make sure that all edges and corners are worked over as meticulously as the centre of the area.

Polyurethane lacquer
This gives probably the hardest of all finishes to wood and is highly resistant to heat, water and spirits. Use interior grade lacquer for furniture, such as pine dressers.

*Polyurethane lacquer is particularly use-ful for softwoods such as pine, for it hardens up the wood, so reducing the likelihood of bruising. In the case of softwoods, the lacquer should be thinned with turps sub-stitute for the first coat, so that it soaks well into the wood. Prepare the raw wood by damping with water to raise the grain, let it dry, then rub down with fine glass-paper.

Lay the lacquer on with a fully charged paint brush, working in the direction of the grain, taking care not to allow runs of lacquer to remain lying on the surface. When the lacquer has hardened, rub down with fine glass-paper on a cork block. Two further coats should be given, rubbing down with glass-paper between each. A pleasant satin finish can be given by finally rubbing down with 00 or 000 grade steel wool charged with *beeswax polish. Rub down with the grain, not across it. Finish off by polishing with a fairly coarse cloth, allowing air to get to the surface as you rub.

Although the general principles are the same for all polyurethane lacquers, it is important to read each manufacturer's instructions carefully before using.

Care and polishing of furniture
Under this heading fall the various ways in which to preserve and maintain furniture finishes in good condition. A good general rule for all types of finish is always to brush or flick off all dust and grit, making sure that the duster or cloth which is to be used for polishing is also free of anything which might mark or scratch the finish.

For furniture with a wax finish, use a

good wax polish sparingly but give plenty of hard rubbing with a soft, open weave cloth. Allowing air to get at the surface being polished is of particular importance with wax finished furniture. Use a soft shoe brush for polishing carved decoration. Too great a use of wax can give a sticky appearance to furniture as well as fill in finely carved details.

A linseed oil finish only requires very occasional rubbing with a cloth lightly damped with oil, once the surface has been achieved. Plenty of rubbing and burnishing with a soft cloth is the best everyday treatment.

Oil varnished surfaces respond to light, occasional waxing with a soft or liquid wax polish, but, generally, polishing with a soft cloth is enough. If the piece of furniture has received too much wax in the past, it will have combined with dust and dirt to obscure the figure and grain of the wood. Carefully clean off this excess of wax with turpentine substitute on a soft cloth, then lightly wax and polish. Rubbing with a cloth damped with raw linseed oil is a good way of considerably improving a poor varnish finish.

A French polish finish as well as modern finishes such as cellulose, polyurethane and polyester (catalyst) lacquers do not require to be fed with wax or oil polishes. They need only a daily wipe with a soft, dry, lint-free cloth. Occasional careful rubbing with a good proprietary cleaning and polishing emulsion will remove surface dirt and smears. Afterwards, polish with a soft, dry cloth.

A well-tried treatment for French polished surfaces which have become ·dulled with wax and dirt is an emulsion of *paraffin and soapy water. Dip a soft cloth into the emulsion, wring out, and gently rub away the wax and dirt. When all has been removed, dry off with a clean cloth, finally polishing with a furniture cream to remove any smears.

With veneered furniture always keep an eye on any pieces of veneer which have become unstuck and refix as soon as possible. It is all too easy when dusting or polishing to break off loose veneer through the cloth catching under it. Something which you have to decide for yourself is how highly polished a piece of furniture should be. But it is worth remembering that a soft, mellow sheen can often bring out the beauty of wood better than a bright, dazzling shine.

Furniture beetle

All objects made from wood should be regularly and carefully checked for the tell-tale small round holes made by the furniture beetle. The holes, about $\frac{1}{16}''$ in diameter, are where the mature beetle has eaten its way out of the wood, but they are only the end of a long, continuous hole which the beatle in its larval stage (woodworm) has bored in its two-year search for food. New flight holes usually appear from April to June. The female beetle, which is about $\frac{1}{4}''$ in length, lays her eggs in cracks and crevices in the wood; as soon as the eggs hatch, the larvae start to bore through the wood. Small amounts of fine wood dust are a sign of fresh flight holes. Severe attack by woodworm can reduce a chair leg or a desk foot to a thin shell riddled with holes, so that a replacement may have to be made (*see* Furniture). Alternatively it may be possible to fill and strengthen the worm-eaten parts with a *synthetic resin glue. Infestations of woodworm can be treated with *fumigation (the most effective method), or by spraying, brushing, or injecting a suitable insecticide, e.g. Rentokil, Cuprinol (England); Decays-Not, Xylamon (U.S.A.). Injecting the insecticide hole by hole is a slow method, but more effective than brushing or spraying, especially when the infection is not too serious. The three best preventive measures against woodworm are:

1. Check any piece of furniture before bringing it into your house.
2. Make sure when moving house that the floorboards in the new house are not infected.
3. Clean all dirt and dust from your furniture, filling any cracks and crevices with wax polish. If the crack is too wide pack it with thin pieces of wood, or an *acrylic resin.

Heat marks

These usually appear as white rings, the outline of hot plates or cups left standing on a polished surface. (Proprietary ring removers are available.) They are generally superficial, that is, they do not usually penetrate the finish. Nevertheless they are often quite hard to remove, and you may have to repeat the treatment several times. Irregular marks, caused by spilling, say hot water, on a polished surface may be similarly treated.

First, warm a soft cloth. Then mix equal quantities of *linseed oil and *turpentine. Put some on the warm cloth, and rub it on the affected area. Camphorated oil can also be used instead of the linseed oil.

Allow the oil to remain for a time before finally removing it with a rag impregnated with *vinegar.

You may have to resort to rubbing along the direction of the grain with very fine steel wool in order to remove very stubborn marks. But take great care not to destroy the polished surface. Finish off with a good wax furniture polish.

There is a third method, which should be employed with great care. Apply *methylated spirit very sparingly to a warm, soft cotton pad. Allow time for it to be absorbed, then rub with a quick, light strike along the mark. Make sure that the surface is not actually wetted. This method slightly softens French polish, so if you apply the methylated spirit carelessly, or too liberally, you will find yourself with the task of repolishing a much larger area than the original mark.

Humidity

Change in the moisture content of wood is the most ruthless destroyer of furniture. Wood naturally and inevitably gives up its innate moisture in an atmosphere drier than that to which it was seasoned, and shrinks as it does so. Similarly, in damp conditions, wood absorbs moisture from the surrounding air, and swells. Movement in wood due to changes in humidity only takes place across the grain.

*Cracks and splits in solid wood and veneers are the warning signs. In many very early pieces of oak furniture, such as chests, no allowance was made for this natural tendency to react to the humidity in the atmosphere. Later, the framed and panel method of construction was evolved in which, in chests, for example, the panels fit loosely into grooves in the frame without glue, and may shrink or swell within them. Today, shrinkage tends to be more common than swelling because old furniture reacts to the lower humidity of modern centrally heated homes.

Ideally, keep any valuable pieces in a room regulated by a humidity control unit. A small container of water can help in raising the humidity, but professional advice should be sought where valuable antiques are involved. It is sensible never to store pieces in a damp cellar or outhouse where high humidity will make wood swell and glue soften, causing loose joints and veneer to lift. Don't stand old furniture close to radiators, storage heaters or open fires. The damage does not become apparent overnight, but even over a short period of a month or so, cracks can appear.

Ink stains

Assuming that the ink is not of a special indelible type, use a solution of *oxalic acid crystals. Stir a quarter of a teaspoonful into ¼ pint of warm water. Make sure the crystals have completely dissolved, then apply the mixture with a small pad or brush. If the stain proves stubborn and resists this treatment, try an ordinary, domestic bleach. Paint it undiluted over the stain only, with a fine brush, and wash off with water immediately the mark has disappeared.

Alternatively, use a weak solution of *nitric acid, and, again, be sure to wash it off as soon as the stain has vanished. One possible disadvantage of using nitric acid is that it can sometimes turn the mark white, instead of making it disappear. If this happens, try rubbing over the mark with *linseed or *camphorated oil.

If the stain is a big one, you may find yourself faced with the much bigger task of repolishing the whole surface after cleaning off the stain. If the piece is at all valuable, it is advisable to leave it to an expert.

Mildew

Mildew is a tiny parasitic fungus that appears in the form of mould on objects which have been kept in damp, dark conditions. It can be treated with *fungicides or by *fumigation.

Sanding

When sanding wood the cardinal rules are: never use coarse glass-paper for fine work, and always rub in the same direction as the grain.

Most people use glass-paper by holding it in the palm of the hand. However, to ensure an even finish on a flat surface, use the glass-paper wrapped round a cork block. These are cheap to buy and well worth getting. For shaped work and mouldings, the professional method is to cut a block of wood to match the curve to be dealt with, and place a layer of cloth between the block and the glass-paper.

Glass-paper can be made more flexible by pulling the piece, paper side down, across the edge of a bench or table.

When sanding, apply a firm pressure and keep the block moving in a straight line with the direction of the grain. Remember, a newly-sanded surface is easily bruised and discoloured. Start with coarse glass-paper, follow with medium, and finish with fine. Never use worn, coarse glass-paper for final finishing: even though it may feel smooth, it can cause deep scratches on the wood. When you have finished, brush away loose dirt and grit from the surface.

Veneers, being very thin, call for great care when sanding. For delicate work such as this, rub two sheets of glass-paper together to reduce the bite. Corners are particularly vulnerable to a heavy hand.

Any blemishes you encounter, or splits or small knots, can be filled with *plastic wood which comes in a range of colours. Just press it into the hole or crevice, let it dry, and then sand flat.

Scratches

The treatment of scratches depends on how deep they are, that is, whether they have penetrated the raw wood below the finish or not, and also on the type of polish used.

There is an appropriate method of treatment for slight, medium and deep scratches. But it must be stressed that it is a mistake to damage a fine, old patina just to remove a few scratches. This is a question of individual taste, and will depend on the balance between the basic excellence of the piece and the extent to which it is marred by scratches. But remember that the cure can often cause more damage than the affliction, for on antique furniture a few marks from years of usage are part of the character.

A few slight scratches on French polish, which do not penetrate the polish, may be treated as follows. Dip a piece of *flour-paper or very fine steel wool (preferably 000 grade) in *linseed oil, and gently ease down

each scratch. You can restore any colour which is taken off by giving a touch or two of *French polish with a fine camel-hair brush to the area. You can darken it by adding a little spirit aniline dye to get a good match.

If there are many scratches over the whole surface, it may be necessary to re-polish completely. Or you could rub down the surface with fine steel wool, then wax polish it (see wax finish). This is a simpler method than French polishing, and quite effective.

Shoe polish of the solid wax variety is often a simple and effective way of losing small scratches and marks.

When the scratch is really shallow and merely shows up as a white slit, all you have to do is colour it. A simple trick, apart from brushing in shoe polish finely, is to rub the white exposed face of a brazil nut kernel along the mark. The nut exudes its oil and makes the mark less apparent.

When the scratches are medium-deep, apply French polish with a finely pointed camel-hair brush along the mark. It is best to use a shade of polish slightly darker than the original one. The polish tends to build up slightly above the sides of the scratch. To correct this, wait until the polish is thoroughly hard, then take a piece of flour-paper just touched with linseed oil, and very gently level the surface. You can also use a mixture of very fine *pumice powder and linseed oil on a small pad. The important thing is that the polish should be completely hard before you do this, so wait till at least the following day.

If the scratches are deeper, the most effective treatment is to use *beeswax. Melt the beeswax and mix it with dry powder colour of the matching shade, which ideally should be slightly darker than the surrounding surface. Let the mixture cool, then with your finger rub it into the scratch until it is filled. Let the wax cool completely.

Finish off by rubbing lightly along the grain with flour-paper to make the whole area level. You can use a cotton pad instead of flour-paper, provided that you rub it really vigorously. Follow with a rub of matching French polish.

Spirit marks

Whisky, gin and other spirits can soften and

even remove French polish, unless they are wiped off instantly with a clean rag. If the polish has tangibly softened, which can happen within seconds, wait until the polish has hardened again before rubbing or re-polishing it.

Repolish with the appropriately coloured *French polish and a small brush until the surface level of the original is matched. Allow time for the polish to dry hard between coats. Then leave for at least two days.

The next step is to rub down gently with *flour-paper or very fine 000-grade steel wool dipped in *linseed oil. Finally, rub over with a cloth pad until you have achieved the right degree of shine.

For small marks, try rubbing with a mixture of linseed or *camphorated oil and *turpentine on a warm rag.

Staining

Staining is the obvious way to alter the appearance of wood. But it has another advantage, the right stain can emphasise and highlight the natural qualities of the grain and figuring of wood.

Softwoods, particularly pine and poplar, take stain very easily, but hardwoods can also be stained. The main problem is getting the right colour. If you are unable to buy the exact colour you want, try blending two or more stains. If the result is still not quite right, you can edge nearer to the required tint by adding or thinning in a judicious way.

As for all finishes, bleaches and stains, it is wise to try it out first on a part normally hidden from view, or on an odd bit of wood. It is much better to have too much stain mixed, than to have to keep mixing up more while seeking the right colour match.

It is best for the first coat of stain to be on the light side, because subsequent coats will darken and intensify the colour.

The type of finish will also influence the final colour, usually making it richer and stronger.

If you have stained the wood too dark, apply some domestic bleach rinse with clean water, dry well with a clean cloth, and leave for a day.

End grain will soak up more stain and become darker than the rest of the wood. Put on less stain at this point, or, use a more dilute solution.

After staining, leave the piece to dry for a whole day. Whatever finish you are thinking of applying, the stained wood must have two coats of French polish first.

There are several types of stain on the market: aniline dyes, colours ground in oil, oil based stains, sealer stains, spirit stains and water stains.

Aniline dyes tend to be strong colours, so proceed carefully. They come in a wide range of colours and shades. They are made for dissolving in water, oil or *methylated spirit. Careful mixing and testing is required in order to achieve the colour you want.

Colours ground in oil can be bought to tint oil-based varnish. They can also be used for staining, but you will have to thin them down with *turpentine.

Oil-base stains can be dissolved in white spirit or turpentine. They are similar to spirit-based stains, but have the advantage of drying more slowly. Apply with a cloth or wadding pad. For large areas, use a brush. They must be primed with two coats of *French polish before varnishing or polishing.

Sealer stains have the constituency of varnish. They penetrate and seal the wood, but keep the grain visible. Just brush on, leave for ten minutes, then wipe off any excess from the surface. When dry, rub the surface down with steel wool. It is then ready for further work.

Spirit stains are bought in powder form and mixed with methylated spirit. Because they dry very quickly, take care to avoid a patchy look, as the edges can easily dry out before the next strip of stain is brushed or rubbed on. This problem makes it unwise to use spirit stains on large areas.

Water-base stains are cheap and easy to use, but raise the grain more than oil or spirit stains. However, they may safely be used with any kind of finish. Damp the wood, allow it to dry, then rub it down with fine *glass-paper before staining. This way you avoid rubbing through the stain, which you would otherwise have to do.

*Bichromate of potash crystals are good for staining mahogany. Add only enough water to make a concentrated solution, and then dilute as required. Though the resultant liquid is a bright orange colour, it stains mahogany a warm brown. A more concentrated mixture will give it a cold looking brown. Used at full strength it turns the wood almost black. Thus you have scope to adjust the shade. The darkening takes place as the wood dries out, not immediately the stain has been applied.

Vandyke crystals dissolved in water provide the basic stain for oak. Ammonia, generally used for stripping wood, will darken oak and mahogany. Permanganate of potash is a good stain for pine and oak, though it tends to fade more rapidly than the others.

If you intend to do a lot of staining, or re-staining, it is worth remembering that all you really need is a basic palette of five stains from the wide range available. These will give you all the colours and shades you require.

Stripping

It is better not to tamper with the surface of antique pieces unless it is really in a hopeless condition. Even then, it is usually better to put it in the hands of an expert. Ignore minor blemishes, such as cracks, dents and burns, for attempting to repair them carries the risk of making the damage worse.

You have a much freer hand to strip off existing finishes when dealing with blemishes on pieces which do not come under the heading of 'antiques'. You also have a wide choice of decorative finishes which will probably improve the appearance. However, a good example of an antique is a Victorian painted and grained over pine chest-of-drawers, which will make a fine-looking piece when stripped and waxed. But you can come across some pieces which cannot properly be called antiques, but which have a patina fine enough to be worth preserving.

Whatever you are stripping, use a non-caustic proprietary paint or varnish stripper. They are the easiest and safest to apply, and you do not have to neutralise the wood afterwards. Furthermore, they are kind to your hands. Follow carefully the directions given on the container. The main difference between the various brands is that some have to be left on longer than others.

After the paint has been softened, clean off with 1, 0 or 00 steel wool, a paint scraper or a piece of hard wood with a square edge. Wash down with warm water to which a little soap has been added. Then wash again with warm water, to which you have added a little distilled *vinegar. The grain of the wood will have been raised slightly by the stripper and water, so, when the wood is completely dry, smooth it down with fine *glass-paper in the direction of the grain.

There are other strippers you can use. *Ammonia, for instance, is excellent for cutting into the old milk-base paints commonly found as the original first coat on some antiques. Wear gloves when using ammonia, and work either out-of-doors or in a well-ventilated room to minimise the unpleasant fumes. Pour some straight from the bottle on to medium-grade steel wool, rub the wood for 5—10 minutes, then rinse off the dissolved paint with warm water and a rag. Leave to dry completely, then rub down the raised grain. The piece is now ready to stain, if required, and can be re-finished with wax, polyurethane varnish or any other finish (see finishing).

Ammonia turns some woods, especially oak, dark. You can, in fact, use it as a stripper-and-stainer in one, though proper stains are to be preferred. To remove its darkening effect, give the wood a final wipe with ordinary domestic bleach or *oxalic acid crystals dissolved in water. A steel scraper must be used with great care because of its sharp corners but it can speed up the removal of paint or varnish from large, flat areas.

If you want to use a power sander, choose an orbital sander. A disc sander can leave deep, semi-circular depressions in the wood which are very difficult to remove. An *orbital sander must be used with care but it will save time on large, flat surfaces. Even so, corners and details must be cleaned off with wire wool or scrapers. Use medium glass-paper to start with, and fine glass-paper to finish.

*Methylated spirit is the solvent for French polish, which it dissolves very quickly. But it has no effect on varnish.

Paint and varnish removers come in liquid and paste form, with many brands available. Liquid paint remover tends to be rather more messy than the paste variety, and less easy to use on vertical surfaces and turned members.

*Caustic soda is a very powerful stripper, favoured by professional craftsmen but calling for great care. You need warm conditions, rubber gloves, and overalls or old clothes. It is best to work out-of-doors, or in a well-ventilated shed. Add ¼ lb of caustic soda to 2 pints of water in a bucket. If you pour the water onto the dry soda, the mixture spits violently and could burn your skin if you are bending low over the bucket. Soak the wood thoroughly using a mop to apply the soda solution, When the paint has dissolved, sluice the furniture with several buckets of water. Then wipe dry, giving a final swab down with vinegar to neutralise. If there is any stubborn paint in odd corners, use a stiff brush, knife or scraper to ease it off. Like ammonia, caustic soda tends to darken wood, but it can be bleached back with domestic bleach or an *oxalic acid solution. You can skip a stage here by missing out the vinegar rub and using bleach instead. Caustic soda is very volatile, and you must take care to remove it all. The slightest bit of caustic soda left on a piece can spoil any finish it comes into contact with.

Remember that drenching furniture with chemicals and water can cause wood to split, joints to swell and glue to soften. So do not over-wet the piece, and be sure to take the necessary step of drying it as soon as possible and as thoroughly as possible. Then leave the piece in a warm, ventilated place, but not close to direct heat.

Using nails and screws

Avoid using nails and screws when making repairs to furniture as far as you possibly can. The exceptions to this general rule are: (a) if the piece was originally made with screws, then screws can be used, (b) if *inner* members need strengthening, and (c) in the case of some mouldings, it is better to use veneer (very fine) pins in addition to adhesive when re-fixing them.

Removing old nails and screws. Always take great care when you do this, as you can easily split or bruise the wood. You can use *pincers or *pliers to pull a nail out, but exercise care and protect the surface with a smooth piece of plywood to avoid bruising. The expert would probably use a hollow drill to remove a nail. The drill is placed over the nail end and the wood is then bored out. The resultant hole is plugged with a matching piece of wood fixed with adhesive.

Driving in nails. Always make sure the face of the nailhead is smooth and clear from dirt. This can be done by rubbing it on to a piece of *glass-paper. Use a *nail punch to drive in the last bit of the nail down to slightly below the surface of the wood, and fill the hole with *plastic wood or coloured *beeswax. Trying to knock a nail flush with the surface will only result in bruising the wood.

Fitting screws. There are several points to be borne in mind when using screws. Always make two different-sized holes. The clearance hole in the piece of wood being attached should be slightly larger than the diameter of the screw, and countersunk at the top to take the head of the screw. The hole in the other piece of wood should be smaller than the diameter of the screw so that the thread bites securely into the wood. When screwing into softwood, make a rather smaller hole than you would on hardwood. It is a good idea to lightly lubricate screws before use, making them easier to drive in, and preventing rusting.

Try always to use a *screwdriver, the blade of which is the same length and width as the slot in the screw. If you do this there is less chance of the screwdriver slipping and burring the screwhead, or, more seriously, scoring the wood.

Woodworm
See furniture beetle.

Appendix I

Materials

ABRASIVES
Abrasives are used to remove rust, tarnish, corrosion and scratches from metalwork, and to clean up and tidy the surface of *wood before it is given a finish.

Abrasives are available in a variety of forms, and you should make sure you always use the correct grade for a particular job. Advice on which is the best abrasive to use is given under the appropriate material.

Abrasives suitable for metalwork include corundum, crocus powder, emery, jeweller's rouge, pumice powder, rottenstone, Tripoli powder, steel wool, swansdown cloth, and whiting.

Abrasives for wood include flour paper, garnet paper, glass-paper, steel wool, and wet and dry paper.

Abrasives used for polishing glass are putty powder and zinconium oxide.

ACETIC ACID
The acid constituent of vinegar: can be used in this form as a stain remover. An effective solvent for organic substances and used to restore fabric colours damaged by an alkali such as caustic soda. Used in a 10% solution to clean lead objects and to remove stains from prints. Should be kept away from copper, on which it reacts, and not allowed to touch the skin as it is liable to burn. It can be purchased as acetic acid from a chemist, or, in a dilute form, as distilled or 'white' vinegar in any supermarket.

ACETONE
A colourless, volatile liquid derived from petroleum. It is a powerful solvent for paint, lacquer, pitch, cellulose cements, waxes and varnish, and is particularly useful for stripping paint and varnish which resists other solvents. It should be applied with care, as it acts very quickly; its action can be slowed down by diluting with turpentine substitute, or stopped by applying kerosene.

It is highly inflammable, and should be stored carefully and never used near a naked flame. Care should be taken not to inhale the fumes, which can be dangerous.

ACIDS
Acids form a class of substances that are compounded of hydrogen and another element or elements. They are neutralised by, and neutralise, alkalis.

While the corrosive properties of acids renders them invaluable for cleaning objects, particularly metal ones, they are potentially very dangerous. Acids used for cleaning and restoring should be kept in glass bottles, with ground glass stoppers, in one place, away from other substances, and obviously well out of the reach of children. Acid containers should be clearly marked and acid should *never* be transferred into other containers, such as old lemonade bottles, in which they could be mistaken for something else, or into plastic containers which they would corrode causing leakage and spillage which could result in accidental burning.

The cardinal rule when using acids in dilute solutions is *always add acid to water*, NEVER *water to acid*.

See acetic acid, aqua regia, citric acid, hydrochloric acid, nitric acid, oxalic acid, sulphuric acid, where precautionary methods are clearly set out.

ACRYLIC RESIN
Acrylic resin is clear and colourless, with a treacle-like consistency. Proprietary brands include Pliantex, marketed for halting leather disintegration, and the polymethyl methylacrate, Technovit 4004A. The latter, which is available both as a powder and as a liquid, sets in about twenty minutes at room temperature. It can be used as a filler for *glass and *ceramics, for strengthening bronze objects, or as an adhesive. In a 5% solution in *acetone, it serves to seal the ink before bleaching manuscripts (*see* ink drawings and manuscripts).

Other polymethylacrylate resins are Plexigum, and Tensol 7.

ADHESIVES
Modern adhesives are so strong and efficient that stuck joins have tended to supersede older methods of repairing such as dowelling and riveting. Most modern adhesives will stick a wide variety of materials, but some are more suitable than others for particular jobs.

Certain basic rules apply whatever material you are repairing or type of adhesive you use.

Follow the instructions on the container to the letter.

Always use fresh glue. Read the container to find out its shelf life, i.e. how soon it loses its power when exposed to air.

In general, temperatures above 20°C (68°F) provide the best conditions for the strongest bond, though certain adhesives, such as urea formaldehydes, are not affected by temperature.

Surfaces to be joined must always be clean. Always scrape off any old glue or paint, clean away any dirt and remove every speck of dust.

Glues and adhesives should be applied as evenly as possible over all contact surfaces.

*Scotch glue must be applied hot, but all other glues and adhesives can be applied cold.

For better adhesion, smooth surfaces should be roughened before using.

Always wipe away at once any adhesive which oozes out. It is much more difficult to get rid of it once it has hardened.

Adhesives are not interchangeable, so make sure you always use the same type on both surfaces.

See acrylic resin, casein glue, cellulose adhesives, contact adhesives, epoxy resin adhesives, flour paste, gold size, natural latex adhesives, polyvinyl acetate emulsion, urea formaldehyde adhesives.

ALCOHOL

There are various grades of alcohol: ethyl alcohol (or ethanol), the type used in beers, wines and spirits, is absolutely pure and very expensive; methyl alcohol (or methanol) is used in methylated spirits; isopropyl alcohol is a cheap substitute which can be used whenever alcohol is recommended in this book.

Alcohol is an effective solvent for fats and oils, paints and varnishes, resinous cements and *shellac. It is also useful as a rapid drying agent; it absorbs water and evaporates quickly. Use it for drying fragile objects, or recently washed paint-brushes.

ALKALI

The term alkali is applied to the soluble hydroxide of the group of metals comprising sodium and potassium (and also lithium, rubidium, and caesium). Alkalis neutralise acids by forming salts with them. They are highly soluble in water. Some alkalis, notably caustic soda, are highly corrosive and potentially harmful; care should be taken when dealing with these.

See ammonia, borax, caustic soda, sodium perborate, sodium bicarbonate.

AMMONIA

Ammonia is a gaseous compound of nitrogen and hydrogen. It is usually used for household purposes as a 10% solution in water, and can be bought in this form as Scrubb's Cloudy Ammonia.

Ammonia is a mild alkali and is useful for removing grease and dirt—particularly from glass and porcelain—acid and blood stains, and some kinds of tarnish on silver. It should not be used on bronze, however, as it attacks the metal. It also removes lichens and mosses from stonework, and a weak solution will remove spirit varnish from prints. It also makes a good varnish and paint stripper, and is very good for cutting into the old milk-base paints often found on antiques, though it tends to stain some woods (see Wood: stripping).

Ammonia is a powerful irritant and gives off strong unpleasant fumes; when using it, wear rubber gloves, and work in a well-ventilated room. A bottle of ammonia should be kept in a cool place, and never left in sunlight.

AMMONIUM ACETATE

Available as crystals or as a colourless 50% solution in water, ammonium acetate is a safe non-toxic preparation with a slight smell of ammonia. It can be purchased in small quantities from any laboratory chemical suppliers.

AMYL ACETATE (or banana oil)

Amyl acetate is a colourless liquid which has an unmistakeable smell of pear drops. It dissolves celluloid completely, so it is an ideal solvent for cellulose paints and lacquers, which are often difficult to remove. It can also be used to clean stains from fabrics.

It is highly inflammable, and because of the unpleasant fumes should not be used in a confined space.

AQUA FORTIS

An alternative commonplace name for *nitric acid.

AQUA REGIA
This is a mixture of three parts *hydrochloric acid to one part *nitric acid and is used in testing the caratage of gold. No common mineral acid will dissolve gold, but aqua regia will. As the ingredients for this are two of the most dangerous acids, it should be handled with extreme caution.

See acids.

BARBOLA PASTE
A putty-like filler which sets hard; extremely useful for building up small pieces when remodelling ceramics, such as flowers and leaves. After use, make sure that the lid is replaced carefully, as it dries out easily.

BEESWAX
The wax made by bees when building a honeycomb. It is available as fine grade white wax or in a natural, yellowish-brown colour, and is used as the basis of various furniture and floor polishes.

You can make your own furniture polish by mixing 3 parts of beeswax and 9 parts of real *turpentine. Melt the beeswax (melting point 65°C (149°F)) in a double saucepan or in a tin standing in a saucepan of water, and then stir in the turps. *Never* try heating over a naked flame as turps is inflammable. *Carnauba wax can be added to give a harder finish. For a dark polish use natural beeswax, or, if you want a lighter finish, use bleached beeswax. *Paraffin wax can be added: it is cheaper and will lighten the colour, but reduces the hardness of the polish. Enough turpentine is required so that the wax is of the consistency of a stiff paste when cold. Keep the polish in a tightly closed tin. Apply it with a soft rag (*see* Wood: finishing).

The polish is also useful for disguising old woodworm holes, and can be used as a protective coating for alabaster and marble, bronze, iron and steel, and leather.

BENZENE
Benzene (benzine), a volatile, colourless liquid obtained from the distillation of coal-tar, dissolves fats and oils, resins, phosphorus, sulphur, rubber and iodine, and is very useful for cleaning fabrics. It is highly inflammable and gives off a toxic vapour, so don't use it near a naked flame or in a confined space. It is available from chemists, and is also sold under the name Benzol.

BICARBONATE OF SODA
See sodium bicarbonate.

BICHROMATE OF POTASH
Obtainable as crystals, this is used in solution with water for staining wood (*see* Wood: staining). The degree of dilution is judged according to the hue required.

BLEACHING AGENTS
Bleaching is whitening by exposure to a chemical process. Ordinary domestic bleach, such as Parazone, can be used for bleaching wood. However, for more delicate operations, as in the treatment if *paper and *prints, other, more refined bleaches are used. (*See* Chloramine T, chlorine dioxide, citric acid, sodium perborate, hydrogen peroxide, sodium hypochlorite.) When using any bleaching agent, always do so in moderation, as over-use can irreversibly weaken an object.

As with acids and alkalis, great care should be taken in the storage of bleaching agents, ensuring that they are clearly labelled and safely out of the reach of children. Bleaches should always be stored in the containers in which they are purchased and *never* transferred to alternate containers in which they could be mistaken for another, less harmful, substance.

BORAX
Borax, known chemically as sodium pyroborate, is available in the form of crystals. A mild alkali which will remove acid stains, its main use in antique restoring is as a flux for hard soldering, or as an additive to strengthen plaster casts.

BRITISH MUSEUM LEATHER DRESSING
An excellent preparation for cleaning and preserving leather. It can be bought ready made, or prepared as follows. Dissolve $\frac{1}{2}$ oz white beeswax in 11 fluid oz hexane (no heat required). Add 7 oz anhydrous lanolin, mix well, and then add 1 fluid oz cedarwood oil. As hexane is highly inflammable, don't make up or use the dressing near a naked flame. It should be applied sparingly, and rubbed into the leather; 2 days later the surface may be polished with a soft cloth. (A similar preparation is available under the name Pliantine.)

BRONZE POWDER

Bronze powders, mixed with *amyl acetate, provide a substitute for lustre glazes when retouching ceramics. They are obtainable in a variety of colours.

Contact between bronze powders and sulphur fumes, or acids, must be avoided, as this causes oxidisation and consequent discolouration.

CALCINED MAGNESIUM

This is a powder derived from burning magnesium carbonate. When mixed with *benzene it can be used as a paste to brighten dull glass.

CAMPHORATED OIL

A preserving oil consisting of 5% camphor dissolved in olive oil, used in this book as an alternative to *linseed oil when removing *heat marks, *ink stains and *spirit marks from *wood. It is available from chemists as liniment of camphor.

CARBON TETRACHLORIDE

Carbon tetrachloride is a volatile, colourless liquid that smells rather like chloroform, from which it is derived. It is an excellent solvent for grease and oils, and is widely used as a cleaning fluid. It has the advantage of being non-flammable, but *don't* use it near heat or a naked flame as a dangerous vapour may be formed. *Don't* smoke while using it, and always work in a well-ventilated room. Carbon tetrachloride can affect some colours, so always make a spot test first when cleaning fabrics. It is the basis of many dry cleaning fluids, but can also be bought from a chemist under its own name.

CARNAUBA WAX

A very hard type of wax obtained from the Brazilian palm. It is added to wax polishes to make them harder.

CASEIN GLUE

This comes in powder form and is mixed with water. It hardens below 20°C (68°F). It is useful for woodwork and moderately resistant to damp, but joints must be cramped. (*See* Wood: cramping.) Good brands are Casco Casein Glue and Sondal. (*See* adhesives.)

CAUSTIC SODA

This is a powerful, poisonous, highly corrosive alkali known chemically as sodium hydroxide. It can be used as a 5% solution in water for removing organic stains, tea stains, and for cleaning brass and stripping paint, but it should not be used on anything porous. In preparing solutions of caustic soda, considerable heat is produced which may cause a glass vessel to crack or break. Therefore, when making up such solutions do so slowly, adding the solid to the water in a porcelain dish or metal vessel standing in a sink. Great care should be taken to avoid splashing. Caustic soda should always be kept in a safe place and used with care. Protect hands, clothing and furniture. Any burns should be neutralised at once with vinegar or lemon juice.

CELLULOID VARNISH

see polyurethane lacquer.

CELLULOSE ADHESIVES

These are quick drying and moderately waterproof and heatproof general *adhesives. They are readily obtainable as Sellobond Clear, Joy Stivin, and Durofix (known as DUCO Cement in the USA).

CELLULOSE FILLERS

A form of water-soluble cellulose with a calcium sulphate aggregate. Cellulose fillers are particularly good for repairing porous materials, e.g. terracotta, earthenware, and stoneware. They neither shrink nor expand, and once set, are largely insoluble in water. Mix with water to a firm, dough-like consistency. It remains workable for at least half an hour. An excellent commercial brand is Polyfilla.

CITRIC ACID

This is a weak acid that gives lime and lemon juice their sourness. It can be used as a 10% solution in water to bleach stains from paper, and as a 5% solution to remove green corrosion from silver. A solution of 1 part citric acid to 2 parts concentrated solution of *borax in 10 parts *distilled water makes an effective bleach for ink stains. Citric acid can be used to treat alkali burns in an emergency.

CHLORAMINE T
This is a mild *bleaching agent available from chemists in the form of a fine white powder. It is particularly suitable for bleaching paper and prints because, once applied, its bleaching properties are soon lost and nothing corrosive remains on the paper. The powder should be dissolved in water (preferably distilled) immediately before use, and made up as a 2% solution. The solution can also be used to remove fungoid stains from marble. Chloramine T should always be stored in a well-stoppered bottle.

CHLORIDE DIOXIDE
An oxidising bleach, this is the safest *bleaching agent to use when treating paper, as there is little chance of its weakening the fibres.

To prepare the bleaching solution, 20gm of technical grade sodium chloride is dissolved in three litres of water to which 75ml of 40% formaldehyde (*formalin) is added. The solution turns yellow owing to the formation of chloride dioxide.

CHLOROFORM
A volatile liquid, not inflammable at ordinary temperatures, chloroform should not be used in a confined space because its fumes are dangerous. It is a useful solvent for *beeswax.

CONTACT ADHESIVES
These *adhesives are convenient for joining together flat surfaces quickly. However, they are not suitable for joints such as mortice and tenon, as once the two surfaces touch they cannot be adjusted. Another disadvantage is that the glue line is rather thick, but it is very strong for flat surfaces. To apply, coat both surfaces, leave to become tacky, and then press the surfaces firmly together. Good brands are Bostik 3 and Evostik Impact 528.

CORUNDUM
This is a mineral consisting of alumina (i.e. aluminium oxide). It occurs as an ingredient in certain abrasive papers, e.g. aloxide paper, but is not itself purchasable as an abrasive powder. Aloxide paper can be purchased as Carborundum.

CROCUS POWDER
The coarsest grade in the range of 'red-stuff' abrasive powders. 'Red-stuff' is an iron oxide derived from iron sulphate. It gets its name from its colour—in manufacture the ferrous oxide is burnt (more than *jeweller's rouge) until it becomes a purple powder. It is particularly useful for removing scratches from metalwork.

DENTAL PLASTER
This is a high grade of *plaster of Paris used as a filler for fine work when repairing ceramics. It can be obtained under the name Paribal.

DISTILLED WATER
Distilled water is free from the impurities found in ordinary tap-water, which often contains varying amounts of calcium sulphate, calcium bicarbonate, magnesium and chlorine. These make water hard, reducing the effectiveness of soap, and corroding metalwork. Always use distilled water when washing valuable or fragile objects; it is particularly important to use it for the final rinse. Buy your distilled water from a chemist, not from a garage.

EMERY
Emery is a naturally occurring mixture of *corundum, magnetite and other minerals. It is mined, crushed, and then graded. It is used as an abrasive and is available in the form of powder, blocks, wheels, or as emery-cloth or emery-paper. The finest grades are called flour emery (and the finest of these, minute emeries). It can also be purchased in the form of automobile valve grinding paste.

EPOXY PUTTY
This is the strongest and most suitable filler used in the repair of *ceramics, particularly the more opaque porcelains (for translucent porcelain, *acrylic resin is preferable).

You make the putty by mixing an *epoxy resin adhesive with enough *titanium dioxide pigment to obtain a dense white colour. You then add enough *kaolin to make a stiff putty. For small cracks or chips, epoxy resin mixed with titanium dioxide powder alone is sufficient. If a coloured filler is required, mix in powder pigments until you have the exact shade.

Epoxy tends to stick to everything, so fingers and modelling tools should be dusted with kaolin or *French chalk. The fact that it sticks to itself allows further layers to be added after the first layer has set. This filler needs a certain amount of support until it has set, and for modelling, it needs a firm foundation. It sets slowly, allowing plenty of time for modelling, unless accelerated by heat. An hour of cold setting should always be allowed first, as immediate heat causes it to soften and sag. When dry it has a clean, unpitted surface, and provides an excellent medium for over-painting.

EPOXY RESIN ADHESIVES
Epoxy resin adhesives can be used for joining metals, glass and ceramics. They should not be used on earthenware, terracotta or stoneware, however, as they are easily drawn into these porous materials and may cause discolouration under the glaze. Much modern china tends to be rather porous, and if you use an epoxy resin you should wait until it has become tacky—about an hour after being mixed. Epoxy resins give an exceptionally strong bond and are highly resistant to heat and water. Cramping or supporting is needed until the adhesive has set, which normally takes about 12 hours, developing maximum strength within a week. The process can be speeded up by exposing the adhesive to gentle heat.

Epoxy resins are also useful *fillers. They come in two-part packs, containing resin and hardener, and once mixed should be used within an hour. However, the mixture can be stored for a few days in the freezer compartment of a refrigerator. The best-known make is Araldite. *See* epoxy putty.

ETHER
Ether is a volatile, colourless liquid which can be used as a cleaning agent and is a very powerful solvent for paints and varnishes. It needs to be used with the greatest care as it is highly inflammable and explosive, and in most cases it is best to use a safer substance, e.g. *acetone.

ETHANOL
See alcohol.

FILLERS
These are used in the repair of ceramics, glass, wood, and, on rare occasions, metalwork.

For fillers used for ceramics, *see* acrylic resin, barbola paste, cellulose fillers, epoxy putty, resorcinol-formaldehyde resin.

For glass, *see* acrylic resin.

Wood fillers, *see* plastic wood.

FLOUR PAPER
Flour paper is the name given to the finest grade of glass-paper, used as an abrasive for wood. *See* glass-paper.

FLOUR PASTE
Flour paste is the best adhesive for sticking paper because it is free from any ingredient that could harm or stain. You can make it yourself quite easily. Use $4\frac{1}{2}$ oz of plain, white, wheat flour to just over 1 pt of water. Mix the flour to a smooth paste with a little water and then boil the rest of the water and stir it into the paste. Thicken the mixture by heating it in a double saucepan. When you use it, it will probably need to be thinned down with a little more water. The paste will keep for several days in a cool place, and if you want it to last for a week, stir in half a teaspoon of *formalin.

FLUX
Fluxes are used in soft soldering to prevent the metal becoming oxidised under heat, thus assisting the solder to adhere to the metal.

They are obtainable in two varieties: the first contains chlorides (most commonly, *zinc chloride). While these act very effectively as fluxes, they are difficult to remove completely from the metal afterwards, causing corrosion.

The second variety is based on resins or fats, and whilst being less efficient, do not corrode the metal. (*See* Metalwork: soldering.)

FORMALIN
Formalin is a 40% solution of formaldehyde in water and can be bought from chemists. It is a powerful antiseptic and preservative, and is often used as a fungicide to combat the growth of mould on paper, prints and paintings. It should not, however, be used for parchment or vellum.

FRENCH CHALK
French chalk is powdered soapstone, available from chemists as a white powder. It is a useful grease absorbent, and can be

sprinkled on to stained fabrics, rubbed into the stain and then brushed off to remove the stain. Alternatively, it can be mixed with a cleaning fluid such as *carbon tetrachloride to make a cleaning paste. French chalk can also be used as a mild abrasive for polishing.

FRENCH POLISH
Known as Shellac in the USA, French polish is the most widely-known *spirit varnish. It is produced by dissolving shellac (the resin of the lac tree) in *methylated spirit. It is usually made up by professional polishers for their own use, but can be obtained commercially. There are three types of French polish:

White polish. Made from bleached shellac, this gives a milky, semi-transparent finish. It gives a fairly delicate finish and should only be used when on objects which will not be touched a great deal, or for marquetry. The transparent version of white polish is a light golden, straw colour.

Pure button polish. This gives the hardest finish and is used for golden-coloured woods, e.g. oak (N.B. this finish tends to reduce the clarity of the grain).

Dark garnet polish. This is best used for warm, dark-coloured woods such as walnut or mahogany.

There are transparent versions available of both button and garnet polish.

For guidance on the techniques of French polishing, see Wood: finishes.

French polish can also be used on some occasions as a varnish for leather objects, see leather.

FUMIGATION
Fumigation is a useful process for destroying harmful fungi and insects.

The object in question should be enclosed in an airtight box with about ¼ oz of an insecticide or fungicide such as *paradichlorobenzene or *thymol. An electric bulb underneath the container will melt the chemical and release the vapour. Leave the article inside for about 6 hours.

See paper, parchment.

FUNGICIDE
Damp, dark, warm conditions encourage the growth of fungi such as mildew (which attacks anything that feeds it, such as glue, leather and paper), or the fungus that causes *dry rot.

Fungi often leave obstinate stains which can be removed with a solution of household bleach, *Chloromine T or permanganate of potash (½ teaspoon to 1 pint of water). After removal, fungi should be prevented from reappearing by treating the object with a solution of a fungicide such as *orthophenylphenol or *thymol.

GARNET PAPER
This is a sand-coated abrasive paper used to sand wood. It is longer lasting and more flexible than *glass-paper. However, it is fairly uncommon and not easy to obtain.

GASOLENE
See petrol.

GLASS-PAPER
Glass-paper is the name given to abrasive papers, often wrongly called sand-paper. The papers are coated with granules of glass or silicone-carbide, and range from coarse to fine, graded from 3 down to 00, the finest grade being known as *flour paper.

GLYCERINE
Glycerine, a by-product of soap, is a clear, odourless liquid available from chemists. It is a useful solvent because it dissolves most water-soluble substances and also metallic oxides. If you use it to remove stains, be sure to wash it off thoroughly with water, as it cannot later be removed by grease solvents. Glycerine can also be used as a lubricant, and to help remove glass stoppers which get stuck.

GOLD LEAF
Gold leaf consists of a thin piece of gold approximately 1/200,000th of an inch thick. It can be bought from art shops in books of 25 sheets interleaved with a thin tissue which is put on with the gold leaf but removed once it is in position. It is available in several shades and grades. It needs to be handled with great care because it is so fragile. It is applied using *gold size.

GOLD SIZE
This is used as the adhesive for *gold leaf. It

It is a weak glue specially adapted for the purpose, made from boiled *linseed oil and ochre.

It is obtainable in two forms, one to dry in 2–4 hours, the other in 8–12.

GRANULAR CLEANER

A friable rubber substitute useful for cleaning suede, buff and any leather with an abraded surface. It can be bought either in a granulated form or in a solid block similar to india rubber. The solid form can be crumbled using a kitchen grater. Rub the granules well into the leather surface with your fingers, and then brush out using a stiff brush. The type of granular cleaner most suitable for this purpose is sold as Whitbro 821.

GRAPHITE

A form of carbon, also known as black lead and plumbago. As a fine powder it is a useful lubricant for situations in which vegetable or mineral oils might attract dust.

HYDROCHLORIC ACID

This is a strong and dangerous acid sold commercially as 'spirits of salts'. It can dissolve gold and platinum, and when mixed with a third as much *nitric acid forms *aqua regia, which is used to test gold between 9 and 18 carats.

Great care should be taken when opening a bottle of hydrochloric acid, as the fumes which are immediately given off can cause eye damage.

See acids.

HYDROGEN PEROXIDE

Hydrogen peroxide is a clear, colourless liquid which is used for bleaching. It is available from chemists in three strengths—100 vols, 20 vols and 10 vols. The vols refer to the amount of oxygen produced by 1 volume of solution, and the most commonly used strength is 20 vols. Peroxide is sold in dark glass bottles and needs to be kept in a cool, dark place.

See bleaching agents.

HYDROLISED SILICA

Silicon dioxide mixed with hydrofluoric acid, hydrolised silica is used as a matting agent, e.g. when retouching ceramics. It is added to the paint to create a matt finish. It is commercially available as TK 800.

JEWELLER'S ROUGE

Jeweller's rouge is an abrasive red powder obtained from iron oxide. It is used for polishing and removing scratches from metalwork, and can either be used dry or made into a paste with *methylated spirit or water.

KAOLIN

Kaolin is hydrated aluminium silicate, formed by the weathering of granite and volcanic rocks. It is obtainable from chemists in the form of a white powder.

Kaolin is used in the manufacture of fine porcelain, and is a constituent of gesso, watercolours, and some paints and pigments. It can be mixed with an *epoxy resin adhesive and *titanium dioxide to form a useful filler for repairing ceramics. (*See* epoxy putty.)

LINSEED OIL

A light, vegetable oil obtained from the crushed seeds of flax, linseed oil can be purchased either raw or boiled. It has many uses in the treatment of wood and is the principal ingredient in *oil varnishes, and as a finish in its own right.

To make a linseed oil finish, mix together 8 parts of raw linseed oil with one part of *turpentine. This finish should only be used on hardwoods (*see* Wood), and produces a particularly tough surface after several applications. For the method of applying this finish, and maintaining it, *see* Wood: finishes.

LISSAPOL N

A liquid detergent, used as a non-ionic wetting agent. It is used for washing paper after bleaching, when cleaning textiles, or on any other occasion when an ordinary mild household detergent is not appropriate. Use in a dilute solution, as specified by the manufacturers. Other similar liquid detergents are Igepal and CA Extra.

MAGNESIUM SILICATE

Magnesium silicate, also known as soapstone, soap-rock, talc, or steatite, is an extremely soft stone which is easily worked. When ground to a powder it is sold as *French chalk.

Attapulgite and Sepiolite are two naturally occurring magnesium silicates which are obtainable as dry powders. When mixed with *distilled water, they are used as a 'mud pack' for cleaning marble and ceramics.

METHYL ALCOHOL
This is the commonplace name for *methylated spirit in the USA and is also an alternative name for methanol (wood *alcohol).

METHYLATED SPIRIT
Methylated spirit is composed mainly of *ethyl alcohol and contains wood spirit (methyl alcohol), fusel oil, paraffin oil as well as a violet aniline dye to discourage anyone from drinking it. Methylated spirit is also known as *methyl alcohol in the USA.

It is a useful solvent for removing *French polish and wax stains, and is used for cleaning bone, ivory, porcelain, pottery, jewellery and mirrors among other things.

Methylated spirit should be stored carefully, as it is inflammable.

METHYLENE CHLORIDE
A clear, colourless volatile liquid, related to *chloroform, which dissolves *epoxy resin adhesive. It gives off dangerous fumes, and should not be used in a confined space.

MICROCRYSTALLINE WAX
Microcrystalline wax is used in the form of a wax polish. It is used to remove surface dirt and to give a protective finish to a wide range of materials such as leather, various metals, marble, and stone. A good brand is sold under the trade name Cosmolloid 80 H.

To stabilise painted or varnished surfaces, use a microcrystalline wax compound with a polythene wax. Such a preparation is sold under the trade name Renaissance Wax.

NAPTHALENE
A crystalline hydrocarbon obtained by the fractional distillation of coal-tar. It has a strong, but not unpleasant odour and is extremely volatile. It is manufactured commercially in various forms, being widely used as an insecticide, and is most commonly available as moth-balls.

NATURAL LATEX ADHESIVES
These are particularly useful for sticking fabrics as they do not mark the materials being stuck. They are not at all suitable as adhesives for wood. Brands widely available are Copydex, Jiffytex, and Bindina.
See adhesives.

NITRIC ACID
Nitric acid is a strong, colourless, fuming acid also known as aqua fortis. It is used as a 5% solution to clean gilt and gilding, coins and medals, wine stains from decanters and ink stains on wood. It is also used to test metals (*see* gold, platinum, and silver) and is one of the constituents of *aqua regia.

Nitric acid should be used with great care as it can cause dangerous burns. If you get any on your skin, it must be washed off at once in running water.
See acids.

NYLON, SOLUBLE
See soluble nylon.

OIL VARNISHES
Oil varnishes are made from resins dissolved in *linseed oil and a small quantity of *turpentine. A good varnish of this variety is made from copal, a hard, translucent, sweetly-smelling resin obtained from several tropical trees. When purchasing this varnish, you should ask for copal. For the method of applying oil varnishes and how to clean and maintain them, *see* Wood: finishes.

ORTHOPHENYLPHENOL
Orthophenylphenol is less volatile and more potent than *thymol and is the basis of the proprietary fungicides Topane and Dowicide. These can be dissolved in alcohol or water to make a 2% solution used for protecting leather, paper, pictures, textiles and watercolours against fungus.

OXALIC ACID
Oxalic acid is a weak but poisonous acid which is sold in the form of white crystals. Its uses are mainly as a stain remover, and it will remove ink, rust and iron mould stains from fabrics, black spots and ink stains from wood, iron stains from leather and ink stains from paper. It should be rinsed away thoroughly; it will produce bright stains on wood if not completely removed A weak solution will also remove small amounts of corrosion from copper.

Like all acids, it can burn, so protect hands, clothing and furniture when using it.
See acids.

PARADICHLOROBENZENE
Paradichlorobenzene is available from

chemists in the form of white crystals. It has similar properties to naphthalene, and can be used as a protection against silver-fish, clothes-moth and furniture beetle, for the vapour is highly poisonous to insect life of all kinds. It works best in a closely confined space without ventilation.

PARAFFIN
Paraffin, also known as kerosene, is obtained from crude petroleum. It is a useful solvent for oil and grease, will soften rust so that it can be easily removed, and may further be employed as an insecticide.

PARAFFIN WAX
Paraffin wax is a white wax distilled mainly from petroleum. It is not affected by acids or alkalis, but it can be dissolved by *petrol or *benzene and melts at approximately 60°C (140°F). It is used to strengthen objects such as bone, ivory, gesso, wood, when they are in a fragile condition, as a polish for plaster casts, in making moulds for repairing ceramics, and in darkening woods.

(*See* Wood: finishing).

PETROL (GASOLENE)
Petrol is distilled from petroleum or rock oil and is a solvent for grease, bitumen and mineral pitch. It must be used with care, as it explodes easily, and should *never* be used near any form of naked light. Even sparks from an electric switch could be enough to explode it if a sufficient vapour had been formed.

It can be used to remove grease stains from paper, alabaster and marble. Never use it to clean silk, however, as the electricity produced by rubbing the surface could cause an explosion. Unless you are planning to clean a large area, it is safest to buy petrol in the form of lighter fuel.

PLASTER OF PARIS
Plaster of Paris is a calcined gypsum, a fine powder which forms a hard, porous mass when mixed with water. It takes 5–15 minutes to set and is useful for making moulds, but it is not strong enough to be used as a filler. The addition of 10% borax to the mixing water will make it harder.

See dental plaster.

PLASTIC WOOD
Wood in a putty form useful for filling small holes in woodwork, and for remodelling broken parts of carving and mouldings. When hard it can be treated as wood. It is available in a range of colours and can be purchased as Plastic Wood, Super Wood. Another form of plastic wood, superior in that it will retain any staining applied to the surrounding wood, is obtainable as Brummer Stopping.

POLYETHYLENE GLYCOL WAX
Polyethylene glycols are synthetic materials which have the physical properties of wax, but are freely soluble in water. They are available in several grades, the most useful being: 4000—a hard, white solid with a melting point of 54°; 1500—a blend in equal parts of the solid wax 1540 and the liquid polyethylene glycol 300, widely used in the treatment of leather objects; 6000—a particularly hard wax.

POLYMETHYLACRYLATE RESIN
See acrylic resin.

POLYURETHANE LACQUER
A clear lacquer, giving an extremely hard finish; polyurethane lacquer is resistant to heat, water, spirits and abrasion. It can be obtained either pre-mixed or in a two-pack variety of lacquer and catalyst (hardener). This latter gives the hardest finish. When making up the two-pack variety, always follow the manufacturer's instructions closely, as the proportions required vary from one make to another.

For use on wood buy an interior grade lacquer (*see* Wood: finishes). Polyurethane lacquer is also used on *bamboo, *brass (*see* Metalwork) etc. as a protective finish once cleaning and restoring is complete.

POLYVINYL ACETATE (PVA)
This is a synthetic resin. When dissolved in ethyl alcohol (20 grammes of PVA to 100 ml. of alcohol), it forms a varnish used for re-varnishing painting. A good adhesive for ceramics and wood is made as *polyvinyl acetate emulsion.

POLYVINYL ACETATE EMULSION

An *adhesive which is very good for gluing wood and particularly suitable when mending porous ceramics. It has a strong bonding action, but is not resistant to water. It is colourless when dry. Good brands are Unibond, Dufix, and Bostik Bond PVA adhesive.

POTASSIUM CYANIDE

The only use of potassium cyanide to the restorer is as a 5% solution in water for cleaning badly tarnished silver. It is, however, a dangerous poison and great care should be taken when handling it.

POTASSIUM LACTATE

Potassium lactate is available as a 50% solution and is used to protect vegetable-tanned leather from the effects of sulphur dioxide. It will not stop chemical decay once it has started, but offers useful protection.

The solution should be diluted in the proportion of 1 part to 9, and sprayed or sponged on. This dilute solution can be kept for a short while in a stoppered bottle with the addition of a little *chloroform, but it is better to mix a fresh amount each time.

PUMICE POWDER

Pumice powder (or powdered pumice) is ground volcanic rock. It is used as a fine abrasive for polishing, and is friable, i.e. the powder breaks itself down into finer granules in the course of abrasion. The customary grade to start with is 120. The finest grade available is 240.

PUTTY POWDER

Putty powder is a crude form of tin oxide. It is used as a fine abrasive for polishing, and is particularly effective on glass. However, it is regarded as somewhat old-fashioned and *zinconium oxide is now widely used in its place.

PYRIDINE

Pyridine is a colourless liquid with an unpleasant smell. It is a useful solvent and can be mixed with water. Use the refined grade which can be bought from a chemist. Pyridine is inflammable and extremely dangerous to inhale.

RESORCINAL-FORMALDEHYDE RESIN

This is used as a filler for repairing unglazed ceramics. It is cold-setting and resistant to boiling water once set. A good proprietary brand is Aerodux 185.

ROSIN (or Colophony)

Rosin is the solid residue left after the distillation of oil of turpentine from crude turpentine. It is used as a *flux in soldering. and for the repair of wax seals.

See Metalwork: soldering, seals.

ROTTENSTONE

This is decomposed siliceous limestone that has lost most of its chalky matter. An abrasive used for polishing metals, it is particularly appropriate for polishing enamel, e.g. *cloisonné*. Although it is still easily found in the Peak District, it is otherwise practically unobtainable commercially. *Tripoli powder has become the customary replacement.

RUST REMOVERS

There are several commercial preparations available for the removal of rust. Good brands are Jenolite, Ferroclene, ACP Deoxidine. Follow manufacturer's instructions to the letter.

Some rust removers, e.g. Ferroclene, have the added advantage of also being rust inhibitors, i.e. they leave a protective film on the surface of the metal after treatment.

SAND-PAPER

A frequently employed misnomer for glass-paper.

See glass-paper.

SAPONIN

Saponin is derived from the soapwort plant and can be obtained as a white powder which is mixed to a froth with water. It is ideal for washing delicate fabrics because its action is neutral and it forms emulsions with resinous and oily substances very easily.

SCOTCH GLUE

Scotch glue is the best-known animal glue and is the traditional adhesive for furniture. It was universally used until the development of modern adhesives.

It is strong, hardens within 6 hours, and requires cramping. It does not resist damp or heat. It comes in cake, jelly, granule and powder form, and needs to be soaked overnight before heating in a container such as a jam jar stood in a saucepan. Heat from cold, but never boil. When it runs off the spoon in a continuous stream, it is ready. A recommended variety is Croid, which comes in jelly form in a tin, and can be heated in the tin. Croid Universal and LePage Liquid Glue can be used cold.

See adhesives.

SHELLAC
See French polish.

SILICA GEL
Silica gel is a drying agent available from chemists in pellet form. It will not stain, or otherwise affect, any material. The pellets, or granules, are tinted with cobaltous salts, which are deep blue when dry, but turn pink when moisture is absorbed. Silica gel can be re-used indefinitely simply by heating it in a moderate oven (266°F).

SODIUM BICARBONATE
Commonly known as bicarbonate of soda. A mild alkali useful for removing acid stains.

SODIUM HYDROXIDE
See caustic soda.

SODIUM HYPOCHLORITE
An oxidising bleach, Sodium hypochlorite is also known as Eau de Javelle or chlorinated soda. It has a very strong bleaching action. It can be purchased from chemists marked '10% w/v available chlorine'.

See bleaching agents.

SOLUBLE NYLON
Soluble nylon is obtained by treating nylon 66 with formaldehyde. In restoration and conservation work, use grade DV 55, available as a white powder under the trade name Calaton CB. It is made up into a 2% or 5% solution by pouring the powder into a solvent such as *methylated or *surgical spirit and warming gently in a double saucepan while stirring often. It sets to a gel when cold, and should be warmed to about 40°C (104°F) to apply. The solution should be kept tightly stoppered. Soluble nylon is used to consolidate fragile or flaking surfaces of bone, ceramics, ivory, stone and textiles.

SOLVENTS
Solvents, as the word suggests, are used to dissolve, and are useful in cleaning to reduce the substance you are trying to remove to a condition where it may be wiped or rinsed away.

All the most important solvents used in cleaning and restoring antiques have a separate entry. Details of the particular substances each dissolves are given, and the most suitable solvent is mentioned in all cleaning and restoring processes.

> *See*: acetic acid, acetone, alcohol, amyl acetate, benzene, benzine, carbon tetrachloride, chloroform, ether, glycerine, methylated spirit, petrol, pyridine, trichloroethane, turpentine, white spirit.

SPELTER SOLDER
Spelter solder is an alloy of 50–53% copper, with zinc. It has a relatively low melting point and is useful for brazing copper, brass and iron when hard-soldering. The higher the amount of zinc present, the lower the melting point. Some spelters contain small amounts of lead or tin, but these weaken the alloy and should be avoided. Nickel and silicon are spelters for soldering cast iron and steel.

SPIRIT SOAP
Spirit soap is a form of soap that dissolves in an organic solvent such as *white spirit or *trichloroethane and increases the solvent's effectiveness. It is available under the trade name Vulpex, and should be used as a 1% solution. It is particularly useful for cleaning textiles.

SPIRIT VARNISHES
Spirit varnishes are produced by dissolving brittle gums or resins in *methylated spirit, and have the advantage of being quicker drying and easier to apply than *oil varnishes. The best known spirit varnish is *French polish. For how to apply a spirit varnish, clean and maintain it, *see* Wood: finishes.

SULPHURIC ACID
Sulphuric acid is a very dangerous, colourless, oily liquid which is also known as vitriol. Its only use (in this book) is as the basis of a pickle bath in which metals are quenched after being annealed (see annealing). Sulphuric acid can cause serious burns, so it should always be handled with the greatest care, and any splashes should be washed off at once in running water.

It is important to remember, when diluting the acid with water, to add it to the water: never add water to it.

SURGICAL SPIRIT
A form of alcohol very similar to *methylated spirit, lacking its violet colour and with the addition of castor oil, diethyl phthalate and wintergreen to make it non-potable. It is sold in chemists for most general purposes.

SWANSDOWN CLOTH
A raised calico with mild abrasive properties. It is used for the final glossing of silver and gold.

SYNTHETIC RESINS
A large group of man-made plastics modified from chemicals and naturally occurring materials in order to provide them with characteristics most suitable for their intended use. Synthetic resins fall into two categories: thermoplastic and thermosetting resins. Thermoplastics are softened by heat, and may then be pressure-moulded to any shape required. When set or cured, they can still be re-melted and re-formed if necessary (see vinyl moulding material). Thermosetting resins generally require the addition of a catalyst: they provide the basis of a wide range of *adhesives, gap-filling compounds, lacquers and varnishes. However, they must be carefully selected in order to match the conditions under which they will be used, as different products possess different tolerances of heat, cold, damp etc. There are cold-setting and hot-setting varieties: once cured, they cannot be re-melted although in some cases they can be dissolved. See acrylic resin, epoxy putty, polyethylene glycol wax, polyvinyl acetate, resorcinal-formaldehyde resin.

THYMOL
Thymol is an antiseptic of the phenol group and is made by distilling oil of thyme. It dissolves in alcohol or ether, and is a useful fungicide because it is safe to use for delicate articles. It vaporises at a fairly low temperature and can be used for *fumigation. A 10% solution in alcohol can be used to make impregnated paper (see paper).

TITANIUM DIOXIDE
Titanium dioxide is available as an iron-grey powder. It is used as an ingredient of *epoxy putty.

TRICHLOROETHANE
A stain-remover which can be used to clean leather and textiles. It is available under a brand name such as Genklene, and should always be used in a well-ventilated room. Don't smoke while you are using it.

TRIPOLI POWDER
Tripoli powder is a fossilised aluvial deposit which includes amorphous silica and iron oxide. Though deriving its name from where it was initially found, Tripoli powder now mostly comes from Arkansas, USA. An abrasive, it is used for polishing metals, and is gradually replacing *rottenstone for this. It is a friable powder, i.e. its granules break down into finer ones during use, and thus can go one being used throughout the course of the polishing.

TURPENTINE
Turpentine is a volatile oil obtained from the gum of the pine tree. It is an excellent solvent for paint, enamel, varnish, resins and waxes, but in most cases a turpentine substitute such as *white spirit, which is much cheaper, is just as effective. The quality of turpentine can be tested by dropping a spot on clean blotting paper. If it evaporates without leaving a mark, it is good quality. Turpentine should be kept in the dark, as it tends to thicken and discolour if exposed to sunlight.

UREA FORMALDEHYDE ADHESIVES
These adhesives are most useful for treating loose-fitting wood joints, especially where there is a gap to be filled. They resist moisture better than animal, casein and PVA adhesives. Setting begins at once, and

cramping is needed (*see* Wood: cramping). Good brands are Aerolite 306, Aerolite Red Pack and Cascamite.

VINEGAR
Dilute *acetic acid, which should be purchased as distilled or 'white' vinegar. It can be used as a stain remover whenever acetic acid is mentioned.

VINYL MOULDING MATERIAL
A retrievable thermoplastic synthetic resin with a low melting point of 180°–200° which cools to give a true, flexible, re-usable mould. The advantages of this material lie in the wide variety of sizes it can cover and range of materials with which it is compatible. Bought in solid chunks, you melt it by heating in an aluminium saucepan on an ordinary gas or electric stove, placing an asbestos mat between the ring and the saucepan to ensure an even heat. Certain precautions should be taken when handling this material. Follow the manufacturer's instructions to the letter. Avoid breathing the fumes given off when the material is melting (overheating aggravates the fumes), working in a well-ventilated room. Once molten, vinyl moulding material is highly inflammable. In case of fire, use dry sand or flour to extinguish the flames, *never* water. Vinyl moulding material is sold under the trade name Vinamold.

VITRIOL
See acids, sulphuric acid.

WET AND DRY PAPER
A resin-bonded silicon carbide paper which is sold graded according to abrasiveness. Its name derives from the fact that it can be used dry, or moistened with water. When dry it is used like *glass-paper; when wet, for smoothing off paintwork on metal or wood between coats. The paper lasts a long time when used wet, provided it is kept merely damp: it should not run with water.

WHITE SPIRIT
White spirit is distilled from petroleum and is often sold as a turpentine substitute. It is a safe and useful solvent for removing grease, oil paint, enamel and varnish. It should be stored and used with care, as it is inflammable. *See* turpentine.

WHITING
Whiting is made from chalk (calcium carbonate) which has been ground with water It can be used as a pigment, hence its name. It can also be used as a metal polish, less for its mildly abrasive qualities, than for its alkaline character, which renders it useful for removing any remaining traces of acid which may have been used on the metal. It is also good for wiping off grease and finger-marks.

YELLOW SOAP
A coarse soap, less refined and therefore more alkaline than soft soap (i.e. toilet soap). It is only suitable for coarse washing, but is useful when cleaning *brushes. A good brand is sold under the trade name Sunlight Soap.

ZINC CHLORIDE
One of the commonest *fluxes used in *soft soldering. It is dissolved in *hydrochloric acid until bubbles of hydrogen are no longer given off; the flux is then ready for use. This is a highly corrosive substance and great care should be taken when using it. When you have finished using it as a flux, it should be rinsed off immediately with plenty of warm water.

ZINCONIUM OXIDE
A white, abrasive powder useful for polishing glass. Commonly used today as a replacement for *putty powder.

Appendix II

Tools

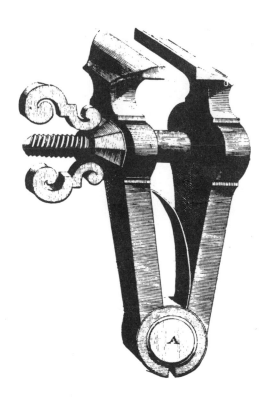

BRUSHES

Cleaning and care of brushes

Cleaning brushes immediately after use prolongs their life. Rinse all but wire brushes in a *solvent, then clean them with warm water and *yellow soap. Never leave a brush in a jar standing on its hairs, as this will weaken and distort them. Brushes clogged up with hardened oil paint or varnish can be cleaned with *acetone, or a proprietary cleaner such as Polyclens. Wire brushes should be knocked out after use in order to dislodge loose particles of rust, paint, etc.

Artists' brushes

These can be bought from an artists' supplier. Oil painting brushes are made either of hog's bristle, or softer red sable hair. The best-quality watercolour brushes are also made of red sable, and are obtainable in a wide range of sizes. The softest brushes are known as camel-hair brushes—in fact, they are made of cow's hair.

Artists' brushes should be used for all delicate work. The type required for a particular job—watercolour brush, camel-hair brush, etc.—are specified in the entry concerned.

Glass fibre brushes

Brushes with 'hairs' made from glass fibre are impervious to acidic corrosion, and consequently should always be used to apply acid when necessary. Bristles of any other material will be irreparably damaged by all corrosive substances.

See acids, alkalis, bleaching agents, solvents.

Wire brushes

Wire brushes, i.e. with bristles made of steel, iron, or brass wire are widely available. No other kind of brush is suitable for cleaning metalwork (*except* gold or silver). *See* metalwork (under the appropriate metal), musical boxes.

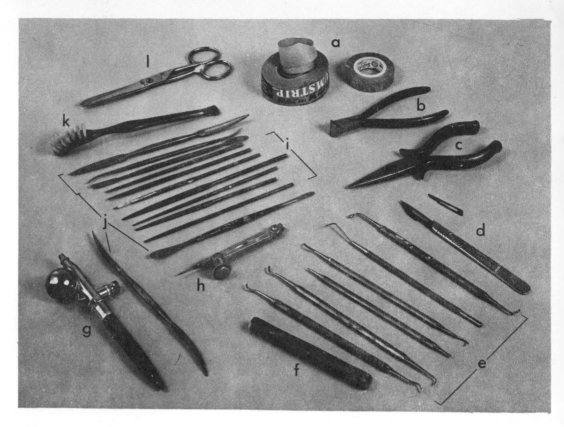

CERAMICS TOOLS

The illustration shows a selection of the tools you are most likely to need when cleaning, repairing, and restoring ceramics.

a   brown gummed paper, and self-adhesive tape. Used for taping breaks once they have been glued (see Ceramics: simple breaks; multiple breaks).

b   wire cutters. For cutting wire when dowelling (see Ceramics: dowelling).

c   snipe or long-nosed pliers. Used for bending wire dowels etc. (see Ceramics: dowelling).

d   scalpel knife. Obtainable from artists' suppliers with boxes of blades. Useful for scraping away surfaces before applying adhesive, removing rivets, and any fine cutting work.

e   dentists' tools. Available from any dental supplier. Used for all kinds of fine work, particularly good for picking old glue out of cracks.

f   sharpening stone.

g   air brush. Used for applying paint in a fine vapour. Obtainable from any good graphic design shop. After use a little *acetone should be sprayed through it

to keep it clean (see Ceramics: retouching).

h   pair of compasses.

i   needle files. Widely available from most hardware stores, useful for smoothing down modelling work, etc.

j   rifflers or riffler files. Engraving tools used when modelling. Obtainable, as with needle files, from good hardware stores.

k   toothbrush. An old toothbrush is an invaluable aid for cleaning ceramics.

l   scissors.

SOLDERING IRONS

There are two main types of soldering irons suitable for *soft soldering. The best for amateur use is the electric soldering iron—the other is heated on a gas-fired tinman's stove, or with a blowtorch.

The heads or 'bits' of soldering irons are made of copper, which as it is an excellent heat conductor. They vary in size and weight according to the type of work being undertaken, the heavier ones retaining their heat longer.

WOODWORKING TOOLS

Restoring antique furniture requires caution and finesse, as has been pointed out. Because of the value of the piece and the delicacy of the repairs, many problems will have to be taken to the expert, who has the knowledge, skill and range of tools necessary. However, with a small workshop, the amateur can do quite a lot and the following tools will allow the amateur a very wide scope.

Hand tools

Bench vice

A vice is essential if you want to undertake very much joint-cutting, shaping, or similar work requiring the wood to be held rigid. Ideally, a woodworking vice should be a permanently fixed accessory to the woodworking bench. If you do not have a bench, use a detachable vice on a table. Make sure, however, that you fit a detachable vice above a table leg, in order to transmit the force of any work done to the floor.

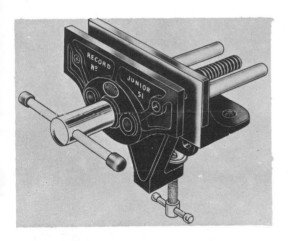

Bits (or drills)

The detachable steel tools, including drills, countersinks, which fit into the adjustable jaws of a *wheelbrace, *hand or *swing brace, or *power drill, are always referred to as bits. There are two types, the round-ended, which can be fitted to a wheelbrace or power drill; and the square-ended, which only fit into a swing brace.

Round-ended bits. There are three sorts used in woodwork, all of which are graded with respect to the different gauges of screws for which they are intended.

Twist bit. The standard metalwork bit which is, however, just as frequently used in woodwork. They can be purchased singly, or in sets of graded sizes, for both wheelbraces and power drills.

Auger bit. A woodworking tool bit with a projecting centre spur at the point, which allows the drill hole to be centred.

Countersink bit. Has a steel shank terminating in a conical bit, available in angles of 90°, 65°, 60°, 45°. Its function is to cut a conical depression at the top of an existing drill hole so that the head of the screw can be sunk slightly below the surface of the wood.

Square-ended bits. These drills have a square end to fit the chuck of a swing brace and are not interchangeable with bits for hand or power drills. The most useful are:

Countersink bit. This has a working end similar to the countersink bit described above.

Centre bit. This is most commonly used with a brace for making large, shallow holes, ½–2in across, and is available in corresponding sizes.

Screwdriver bit. A bit terminating in a screwdriver blade. The considerable leverage exerted by a swing brace deals speedily with large screws.

Jennings bit. This type has a double spiral cutter for keeping the hole straight while drilling.

Solid centre bit. For fast work, but the single spiral is slightly less accurate than the Jennings bit.

Bradawl

A tool, having either a square or tapered point, with which to make starting holes for screws smaller than gauge 6. Bradawls should be twisted into the wood by hand, as they are difficult to get out if driven with a hammer. Screws always follow the holes made by a bradawl, so it is important to keep the hole straight.

Cabinet scraper

A flat steel rectangle with a cutting edge, used to give an extremely smooth finish to hardwoods, preparatory to polishing. Before it can be used, the edge must be prepared as follows: using a file and oilstone, rub the bottom edge of the scraper absolutely flat and square; then, holding the scraper flat on the edge of the workbench, so that the edge projects about $\frac{1}{4}$in, turn up a burr on both sides with a piece of hard steel, such as a *bradawl or the rounded side of a gouge. You will need to press hard, with a downward motion, until the burrs stand at right angles to the scraper, forming the cutting edge of the tool.

The scraper is held in both hands, and

pushed forward and downward in a series of firm strokes. The action shaves, rather than scrapes, thin slices from the wood surface; its advantage over *glass-paper is that the grain is left free of wood dust. It is also less likely to rough up the surface of wild-grained wood.

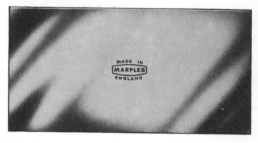

Chisels

Chisels are fine-edged tools for precise paring and cutting out operations. They should be used with, or across the grain, but *never* against it, as the blade will tend to follow the grain down into the wood and cause it to split. The three main types are as follows:

Bevel-edge chisels. For general paring work.

Firmer chisels. These have blades of rectangular cross-section, and are used for heavier general purpose work than bevel-edge chisels. They range in blade size from $\frac{1}{8}$in to 2in, the most useful being $\frac{1}{4}$in, $\frac{1}{2}$in and 1in.

Mortice chisels. Designed to be used with a mallet, these are the strongest chisels of all. The $\frac{3}{8}$in and $\frac{1}{2}$in sizes should suit most of the jobs you will face.

Cork sanding block

A cheap and invaluable accessory for sanding. Always wrap the glass-paper around a block, as this will ensure that the paper presses evenly upon the wood, giving it a smooth, uniform finish. It is difficult to press evenly using the hand alone.

Cramps

There are two main types of cramp (clamp in the USA) the use of which is described in this book.

G-cramp (C-clamp in the USA). This is an indispensable tool for holding wood steady for operations such as sawing and drilling, or for clamping together pieces of wood when they have been glued (*see* Furniture: cramping). Two G-cramps, an 8in and a 4in, serve as the basic kit. They should always be tightened with the fingers, *never* with a spanner.

Sash cramp (Joiner's clamp in the USA). This is useful for large work, e.g. when you are working on a chair frame. The cramp consists of two adjustable shoes mounted on a large bar; one of them slides along the bar, and can be fixed with a pin inserted through the bar in one of the holes provided. The other tightens up in the manner of a vice. 4-foot cramps are the most useful to buy, although it is possible to purchase the shoes separately and fix them to a home-made hardwood bar. Sash cramps with wooden bars always bend upwards in use. This can be prevented by fitting spacers between the bar and the work, but it is better to use two sets of cramps, one on each side of the work, while the glue is setting.

Files

It is useful to have at least one file on hand for smoothing ragged edges, rounding corners, etc. A 10 inch model, with fine cut blade, should be sufficient. It should be used two-handed with a firm forward *motion*; any rocking of the stroke will produce a curved, rather than a flat surface.

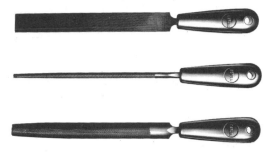

Files are generally made in flat, round, and half-round patterns.

Hacksaw

A metal-cutting saw consisting of a flexible or brittle steel blade held under tension in a rigid frame. The teeth of the blade are set pointing forward, so that it cuts on the forward stroke only. Blades are commonly of three main sizes, 8in, 10in, or 12in, of which the 10in is the most suitable for general work. In woodwork a hacksaw is useful for cutting nails and screws that cannot be removed in any other way. This often happens when dismantling a joint. On no account should a woodsaw be used for this purpose.

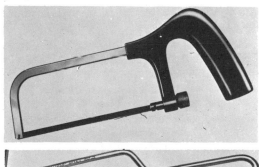

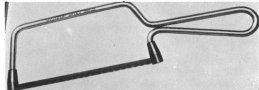

The junior hacksaw, with a 6in. blade, is a useful addition for tight corners.

Hammers

The three types of hammer that you are most likely to need are: a medium weight cross-pein hammer, a soft headed hammer and an upholsterer's or pin hammer.

Cross-pein hammer. The Warrington design, weighing about 11 oz, is best for most general work. The striking face should be kept free from grease, and should be sanded before use with a very fine glass-paper. If this is done, the hammer is less likely to slip off the nail head.

Soft-headed hammer. A hammer made with a rubber or nylon head, which will not leave marks. It is useful for knocking apart joints, and general dismantling jobs. If you do not possess one of these, an ordinary hammer with the head muffled in rags will serve.

Upholsterer's hammer. A light hammer for driving in upholstery tacks and gimp pins. It is interchangeable with the pin hammer, the lightest weight cross-pein hammer, used on pins that a heavier hammer would bend.

Marking gauge

The marking gauge is used for marking out lines parallel to an edge, a task which occurs particularly frequently when making joints. The adjustable head is set at the required distance from the fixed pin, screwed tight, and drawn along the edge. The pin will then scratch a line parallel to the edge.

Mitre box

A right-angled wooden frame, with pre-cut, diagonal guide slots, for cutting mitre joints. The work is held in the mitre box and cut by a tenon or dovetail saw, working through the guide slots.

Nail punch

A pointed metal tool about 4in long used for driving nails or pins below the surface of the wood (*see* Furniture: using nails and screws). The point sizes vary from $\frac{1}{16}$in to $\frac{3}{16}$in across, the point itself being ground hollow in order to rest centrally upon the nail head. Always use a size slightly *smaller* than that of the nail.

Oilstone

A sharpening stone for fine edge tools, such as chisels and plane blades, made in three grades of grit: coarse, medium and fine. Medium is the coarsest stone needed for home use, the fine stone being used to give the final cutting edge to the tool. A convenient size of stone for the workshop is 8in by 2in. It should be kept in a hardwood box, away from dust and grit, and should never be used without first lubricating with oil or white spirit.

Planes

The job of the plane is to reduce wood to exact dimensions, leaving it smooth, flat and ready for finishing. The longer the plane, the flatter it cuts a surface, since a short plane tends to 'ride' the bump. The depth of the plane's cut can be adjusted by turning the knob which controls how far the blade protrudes from its slot, or in traditional types by removing the securing wedge and resetting the blade.

The three basic sorts of metal planes are the jointer plane (22–24in long), the jack plane (14–15in long), and the smoothing plane (8–10in). The best plane for all-round use is undoubtedly the jack plane. Of the many small special purpose planes, the block plane (width of blade $1\frac{3}{8}$–$1\frac{5}{8}$in) is the most commonly used for fine work, and smoothing the grain at the end of a piece of wood (end grain). Before starting work, always make sure that the blade is properly adjusted and newly-sharpened. You should check, too, that the blade protrudes evenly from its slot, by looking down the sole of the plane; if the blade is correctly adjusted, it will appear parallel with it. In use, the sole of the plane should be lubricated with candlegrease.

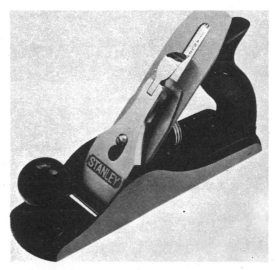
Smoothing plane.

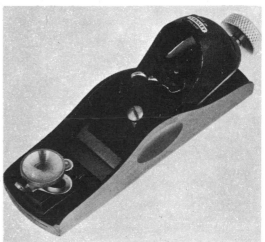
Block plane.

Pincers

Pincers are used for extracting nails that are firmly embedded. The fine claw on the end of one handle slips under well-driven nail heads and lifts them sufficiently for the pincer jaws to grip. When using pincer jaws, it is best to make a series of short, sharp pulls, as removing a nail in one pull will leave a bad hole. Care must be taken not to bruise the surrounding wood when a levering action is used.

18in. jointer plane.

Rasps

Rasps are steel tools for shaping wood, of circular or semi-circular section. They are available in a variety of lengths and grades of coarseness; although they are usually sold without handles, interchangeable wooden handles are readily available. They should be used two-handed, with a similar motion to that of filing. It is necessary to finish with a file and glass-paper wood that has been shaped in this way.

Saws

The basic woodworking tool. The variety of types indicates its importance for a wide range of tasks. Saws can be divided into three major categories:

Large handsaws are used for roughly cutting lengths of timber to size. Of these the panel saw is the best for cabinet work.

Back saws are shorter saws for cutting joints and other fine work, e.g. tenon and dovetail saws.

Special-purpose saws are used for cutting curves and complicated shapes. They include coping saws, bow saws and padsaws.

Almost every type of saw has the teeth bent out from the blade, alternate teeth projecting in opposite directions. This is called the 'set', and allows the saw to cut more easily, without getting clogged. Accurate set is as important as sharpness.

Panel saw. A large all-round handsaw, 20–24in long, 10 teeth to the inch. In use, it is important to use the whole length of the blade, applying light pressure on the downward stroke only; the index finger should point along the blade to increase control. Always make the cut to the waste side of the line you are working to, otherwise the required length will be fractionally undersize. In all sawing operations the wood should be firmly secured, large pieces on trestles, small pieces in a vice.

Tenon saw (Backsaw in the USA). Has a blade 12–14in long, held in a brass or steel stiffener for extra rigidity and strength. It is used in nearly all joint-cutting work.

Dovetail saw. A smaller (8–10in) version of the tenon saw, with the same rigid-backed construction. It is used for fine cutting, such as the angled dovetail joint.

Coping saw. The best general saw for cutting curves and holes. It consists of a D-shaped steel frame holding a narrow blade. The blades are of standard size, and are discarded after use. It is important to specify woodworking blades when buying them, since these can be adjusted to cut at various angles; metalworking blades are non-adjustable. The coping saw can cut into the wood only as far as the distance between the blade and the top of the frame.

Bow saw. Is similar to, and performs much the same function as the coping saw. However, its heavier, coarser blade can cut faster, and tackle stouter timber. Blades are replaceable, and secured by tapering retaining pins.

Padsaw or Keyhole saw. This consists of a tapering blade projecting from a wooden or metal handle, to which it is clamped. It is used for cutting holes which are too far from the edge of the wood to be accessible to a bow or coping saw.

It is a rather laborious tool to use, as it

cuts slowly and is difficult to keep straight, a problem which increases with the length of the blade.

Care of saws. To prevent rusting, saw blades should be wiped over with light oil when out of use. If your saw has become rusty, it should be cleaned with steel wool dipped in white spirit, and oiled as instructed. Do not, however, saw with oil on the blade as this will mark the wood; if you wish to lubricate a saw during use, you should rub the blade over with a candle.

Between jobs, always hang saws upright by their handles, if left lying on their sides the teeth may become damaged.

Screwdrivers

The general bench screwdriver is known as a cabinet screwdriver, but a ratchet screwdriver allows you to work without changing grip. Before putting in any screw you should make a starting hole, a *bradawl can be used for screws below gauge 6, and the appropriate drill for larger gauges. Always choose a screwdriver whose blade fits as exactly as possible into the slot on the screw head. Too wide a blade may damage the surrounding wood, while too narrow a tip can burr the screw head.

Above: a cabinet screwdriver.

Below: a ratchet screwdriver.

Spokeshave

The spokeshave is a transverse plane for cutting and smoothing wood surfaces, giving a fine finish which needs no further cleaning up. It must always be used with the grain. Wooden and metal types are available—the wooden spokeshave can be used for planing both concave and convex surfaces, while of the two varieties of metal spokeshave, the flat-bladed is used for convex, flat, and gentle concave work, and the convex-bladed type for cutting sharply concave curves.

Surform

A tool with a base made up of a regular pattern of rasp-like cutting edges, useful for shaping and smoothing jobs preparatory to accurate finishing. They are available in a number of designs, including file and plane-like forms.

Swing brace

The swing brace is used for boring holes, which it does with speed and accuracy, being able to make larger holes than a power drill. The radius of the circle traversed by the grip is known as the brace's 'sweep'. The wider the sweep, the more power, but too wide a sweep will render the tool difficult to use in confined spaces. A 10in. sweep is a good compromise. Further space-saving advantages may be gained from using a ratchet brace, which does not need to describe a full sweep.

Try-square

The try-square is an essential tool for marking out and correcting right-angles. It has a metal blade at right angles to the stock, which should be of metal or plastic, as a wooden one may swell or contract, and give an untrue right-angle. Adjustable squares, giving other angles as well as right-angles, are also available.

Wheelbrace

The conventional hand-drill is known as a wheelbrace. It can take any drill bit with a shank size of $\frac{1}{4}$in and below. It has main and side handles, a turning handle and a vertically maintained main drive wheel, transferring the drive to the central shaft through two horizontal cogs. The cover for the adjustable jaws that secure the drill bit is known as the chuck. (*See* bits.)

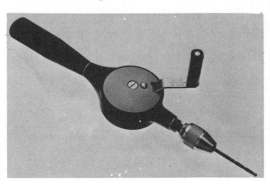

Electric drill with wood working accessories – twist drill bits, wood augers and a wood countersink.

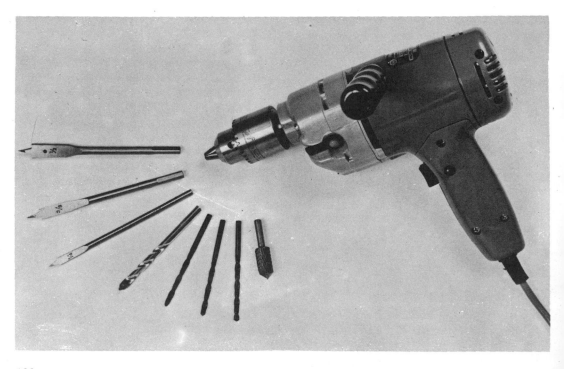

POWER TOOLS
Electric drill

An electric drill can drive a range of attachments, which can be bought when the need arises, and is thus a most useful investment. Drills are usually graded according to their chuck capacity. The chuck is the piece of the drill that grips the *bits (or drills), and its capacity is the maximum diameter of bit shank which can be secured in the chuck—usually $\frac{1}{4}$in. or $\frac{5}{16}$in. Apart from the single speed electric drill, two speed and variable speed power units are available: these are more flexible than the single speed type, but are naturally more expensive. On the other hand, the cost of a single speed drill plus a speed reducing gear is higher than for a variable speed drill.

Using an electric drill. Always use an electric drill with the cable hitched over your shoulder, out of the way. Always drill at right angles to the surface—it is possible to buy jigs to help ensure that you do so.

With a variable speed drill it is important to use the right speed setting for the job, otherwise you are in danger of overloading it, which can burn out the motor. A sure sign of overloading is a drop in speed while the drill is in use, heard as a drop in the pitch of the motor. To avoid possible damage and reduce overheating, remove the tool from the work and run it briefly at full revs before using it again.

Care of electric drills. Examine the carbon brushes in the motor occasionally. Replace unevenly worn brushes, and clean others with turps substitute. Periodically, open the gearbox, clean out the old grease, and repack with the lubricant that the manufacturer recommends.

Circular saw

This is a useful attachment to have, although it doesn't perform quite as well as a circular saw with its own integrated power unit. The depth of cut available with the circular saw is determined by the blade's diameter. Since the largest attachment blade is 6in in diameter, the maximum depth of cut available will be $1\frac{7}{8}$in. There are several types of saw blade, the most versatile being the combination rip and cross-cut, which will cut thin or thick hardwoods and soft-

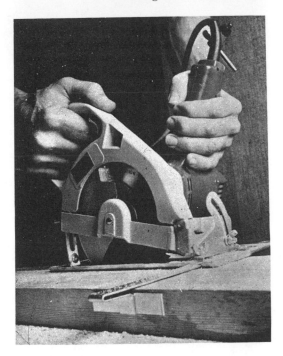

woods, with or across the grain. It will also cut plywood and hardboard.

Orbital sander

This can be obtained either as a separate power tool, or as an attachment for a power drill. It has a flat cushioned pad over which is fixed glass-paper of the appropriate grade, which is bought in specially prepared packs. It is used for finishing work only, and is not suitable for removing large quantities of material; however, it is perfectly useful for work on antiques. Disc sanders can cause too much damage to be used for such work. Even orbital sanders can leave tiny circular marks, and cannot match the standards of careful hand-finishing.

Bibliography

Art Restoration, Francis Kelly (David & Charles, Newton Abbot, Devon, 1971).

Bookbinding and the Care of Books, Douglas Cockerell (Pitman, London, 1953).

The Care of Antiques, J. F. Mills (Arlington Books, London, 1965).

China Making and Restoration, C. S. M. Parsons and F. H. Curl (Faber & Faber, London, 1963).

China Repairs and Restoration, Rena Cross (W. Foulsham, Slough, 1972).

The Cleaning of Paintings, Helmut Ruhemann (Faber & Faber, London, 1968).

The Conservation of Antiquities and Works of Art, H. J. Plenderleith (Oxford University Press, 1962).

Dictionary of Wax Modellers, E. J. Pyke (Oxford University Press, 1973).

Embroidery & Lace, Ernest Lefeburé (H. Grevel & Co., 1899).

English Barometers, N. Goodison (Cassell & Co., London, 1969).

Guide to the Collection of Carpets (Victoria & Albert Museum, 1931).

A Guide to the Conservation and Restoration of Objects Made Wholly or Partly in Leather, John Waterer (G. Bell, London, 1972).

History of Engraving and Etching, Arthur M. Hind, (Dover, London, 1963).

How to Repair and Dress Old Dolls, Audrey Johnson (G. Bell, London, 1967).

How to Restore China and Bric-A-Brac, Paul St. Gallen and Arthur Jackson (Bailey Bros. & Swinfen Ltd., 1953).

Ivory, Geoffrey Wills (Arco Books, London, 1968).

Mending and Restoring China, Thomas Pond, (Garnstone Press, London, 1970).

Metal Techniques for Craftsmen: a basic manual for craftsmen on the methods of forming and decorating metals, Oppi Untracht (Robert Hale, London, 1968).

Metalworking for Schools, Colleges and Home Craftsmen, Oscar Almeida (Mills & Boon, London, 1967).

Musical Boxes, John E. T. Clark (Fountain Press, London, 1948).

Notes on the Technique of Painting, Hilaire Hiler (Faber & Faber, London, 1934).

Papier Mâché in Great Britain and America, Jane Toller (G. Bell, London, 1962).

The Preservation of Leather Bindings, H. J. Plenderleith (British Museum, London, 1970).

Processes of Graphic Reproduction in Printing, Harold Curwen (Faber & Faber, London, 1947).

Refurbishing Antiques, Rosemary Ratcliffe (Pelham Books, London, 1971).

Repairing Antique Clocks, Eric P. Smith (David & Charles, Newton Abbot, 1973).

Restoring Junk, Suzanne Beedell (Macdonald, London, 1970).

The Story of Watches, T. P. Camerer Cuss (MacGibbon & Kee, London, 1952).

Watch & Clockmakers' Handbook: Dictionary and Guide, F. J. Britten (Spon, London, 1884, 15th edition 1955).

ACKNOWLEDGEMENTS

The editors would like to express their gratitude to the following people, firms and organisations for their help in compiling this book:

Anchor Chemical Co. Ltd., Manchester.
Bethnal Green Museum, London.
Black & Decker Ltd., Maidstone, Kent.
N. Bloom & Sons Ltd., London.
BP Chemicals International Ltd.,
Technical Research Laboratories, Barry,
Glamorgan, Wales.
Christie, Manson & Woods, London.
City Museum & Art Gallery, Birmingham.
The Cooper-Bridgeman Library, London.
Crowther's of Syon Lodge, Isleworth,
Middlesex.
Delomosne & Son, London.
Gedge & Co. (Clerkenwell) Ltd., London.
Angelo Hornak Esq.
T. A. Hutchinson Ltd., London.
W. King Esq.
Negretti & Zambra Ltd., Aylesbury,
Buckinghamshire.
James Neill & Co., Sheffield.
Sotheby's Belgravia, London.
Spear & Jackson (Tools) Ltd., Sheffield.
Stanley-Bridges Ltd., Sheffield.
Charles Stewart Esq.
Victoria & Albert Museum, Conservation
Department, London.
Vinatex Corporation, Havant, Hampshire.